What Shall We Do?

What Shall We Do?

Eschatology and Ethics in Luke–Acts

Joseph M. Lear

PICKWICK *Publications* · Eugene, Oregon

WHAT SHALL WE DO?
Eschatology and Ethics in Luke–Acts

Pickwick Publications
An Imprint of Wipf and Stock Publishers
199 W. 8th Ave., Suite 3
Eugene, OR 97401

www.wipfandstock.com

PAPERBACK ISBN: 978-1-5326-1820-8
HARDCOVER ISBN: 978-1-4982-4357-5
EBOOK ISBN: 978-1-4982-4356-8

Cataloguing-in-Publication data:

Names: Lear, Joseph M.

Title: What shall we do? : eschatology and ethics in Luke–Acts / Joseph M. Lear

Description: Eugene, OR: Pickwick Publications, 2018 | Includes bibliographical references.

Identifiers: ISBN 978-1-5326-1820-8 (paperback) | ISBN 978-1-4982-4357-5 (hardcover) | ISBN 978-1-4982-4356-8 (ebook).

Subjects: LCSH: Bible. Luke—Criticism, interpretation, etc. | Bible. Acts—Criticism, interpretation, etc. | Eschatology | Bible. New Testament—Ethics | Ethics in the Bible.

Classification: BS2589 L42 2018 (print) | BS2589 (ebook).

Manufactured in the U.S.A.   03/15/18

For Holly Lear—
my breadwinner, prayer partner,
and merry-maker

Contents

Abbreviations | ix

1. Introduction | 1
2. John the Baptist and Jesus: Opening Proclamations | 28
3. Received and Rejected in Luke: The Way to Jerusalem | 68
4. Sharing in the Last Days: The Jerusalem Church | 101
5. Received and Rejected in Acts: Hospitable Gentiles | 140
6. Conclusion | 177

Bibliography | 183

Abbreviations

Ancient Sources

Abbreviations for ancient sources from *The SBL Handbook for Ancient Near Eastern, Biblical, and Early Christian Studies* (Hendrickson, 1999). All translations of ancient texts are my own unless otherwise noted.

1QM	*War Scroll*
Abraham	Philo, *On the Life of Abraham*
Ant.	Josephus, *Jewish Antiquities*
CD	*Damascus Document*
Jub.	*Jubilees*
J.W.	Josephus, *Jewish War*
T. Benj	*Testament of Benjamin*
T. Levi	*Testament of Levi*
T. Naph	*Testament of Naphtali*

Modern Works

AB	Anchor Bible
ABD	*Anchor Bible Dictionary.* Edited by David Noel Freedman. 6 vols. New York: Doubleday, 1992

BDAG	Walter Bauer, Fredrick W. Danker, W. F. Arndt, and F. W. Gingrich, eds. *A Greek-English Lexicon of the New Testament and Other Early Christian Literature*, 3rd ed., Chicago: University of Chicago Press, 2000
BZNW	Beihefte zur Zeitschrift für die neutestamentliche Wissenschaft
JBL	*Journal of Biblical Literature*
JSNTSup	Journal for the Study of the New Testament Supplements
NovT	*Novum Testamentum*
NovTSup	Novum Testamentum Supplements
SBLDS	Society of Biblical Literature Dissertation Series
SNTSMS	Society for New Testament Studies Monograph Series
TDNT	*Theological Dictionary of the New Testament*. Edited by Gerhard Kittel and Gerhard Friedrich. Translated by Geoffrey W. Bromiley. 10 vols. Grand Rapids: Eerdmans, 1964–1976
WUNT	Wissenschaftliche Untersuchungen zum Neuen Testament

1

Introduction

Justification for this Study

Ministry begins in Luke's Gospel with John the Baptist. He is the voice in the wilderness from Isa 40 (Luke 3:4–6) proclaiming that the "way of the Lord" (τὴν ὁδὸν κυρίου) must be prepared.[1] "Crooked" (τὰ σκολιὰ) paths must and will be made straight so that all flesh will be able to see the salvation of God (τὸ σωτήριον τοῦ θεοῦ, 3:5–6). When the crowds come to hear and be baptized, John asks them who told them to flee the "wrath that is about to be" (τῆς μελλούσης ὀργῆς, 3:7). John the Baptist's eschatological proclamation is not unique to Luke. All of the canonical Gospels identify John the Baptist as the voice of Isa 40.[2] Matthew moreover puts verbatim the same eschatological announcement about the coming wrath on John the Baptist's lips (Matt 3:7).[3] But what follows immediately upon eschatological proclamation in Luke is unique among the Gospel writers. Luke says that the crowds respond with a question, "what shall we do?" (τί οὖν ποιήσωμεν; 3:10). John the Baptist answers with a short series of ethical exhortations:

1. All biblical quotations are my own translations.

2. Mark 1:3; Matt 3:3; John 1:23.

3. τίς ὑπέδειξεν ὑμῖν φυγεῖν ἀπὸ τῆς μελλούσης ὀργῆς; (Matt 3:7); cf. τίς ὑπέδειξεν ὑμῖν φυγεῖν ἀπὸ τῆς μελλούσης ὀργῆς; (Luke 3:7). I am not assuming in this study that Luke used Matthew [see Goulder, *Luke: A New Paradigm* and Goodacre, *Goulder and the Gospels*]. Where the question of source arises I address both possibilities of Matthew and Q. I make no assumptions about sources first because the debate about sources has by no means come to a conclusion. Scholarly responsibility, therefore, necessitates openness to various possibilities concerning sources. Secondly, I make no assumptions about sources because it is unnecessary for the exegetical process in this work. The exegesis of the passages addressed in this study does not rise or fall on the question of Luke's litearary (and perhaps oral) sources.

people should share their food and clothing with those who have none; tax collectors and soldiers should cease corruption (3:11–14). The coming wrath, evidently, necessitates sharing possessions.

Acts begins on a similar note. The Holy Spirit is poured out, which occasions another appeal to the Prophets. Peter announces through the prophet Joel that the outpouring means that it is the last days (ταῖς ἐσχάταις ἡμέραις, Acts 2:17).[4] After Peter explains that the last days are here because of Jesus' resurrection, Luke says that the Pentecost crowd responds to Peter's announcement with the same question with which the crowd responded to John the Baptist: "what shall we do?" (τί ποιήσωμεν, 2:37). Peter tells everyone to be baptized (2:38). But Luke then adds that Peter continued to urge the crowd to be saved (σώθητε) from the present "crooked generation" (τῆς γενεᾶς τῆς σκολιᾶς). Peter's words concerning salvation and crookedness recall the Isa 40 quotation about John the Baptist in Luke 3. The first summary statement of Acts immediately follows the conclusion of Peter's sermon: a new community is formed around shared possessions (2:42–47). The last days, evidently, occasion the sharing of possessions.[5]

The present investigation was prompted by my observation that the anonymous author we know as Luke[6] brings together the announcement of eschatological fulfillment with an emphasis on the sharing of possessions near the beginning of both of his books (the shorthand "eschatology" and "ethics," respectively, will be used to refer to these two matters throughout this study).[7] Because eschatology and ethics have an apparent relationship

4. This phrase does not appear in Rahlf's version of the LXX Joel and there are some manuscripts of Acts that omit it. On this matter, see p. 115.

5. One of the goals of this study, and particularly in Chs. 4 and 5 (which focus on Acts), is to push back against the suggestion that eschatology "is not a prominent topic in Acts" [Pervo, *Acts*, 25]. Luke, it seems to me, does not have to raise eschatological subjects explicitly in every instance in order to have a "concern about the subject,"(Pervo, 25). Pervo's claim that Luke is unconcerned about the subject is a modification of a dominant view about eschatology in Acts. Haenchen, *Acts of the Apostles*, says that the lack of eschatological material in Acts is evidence of a theological concern on Luke's part. Luke was writing, says Haenchen, to account for the delay of the parousia (94–98). Thus, while Pervo and Haenchen agree that there is a lack of eschatological material, Haenchen concludes from this not that Luke had little concern for the subject, but that eschatology was one of the major motivating factors for writing Acts.

6. I make no assumptions about the identity of the author of Luke–Acts.

7. The day of Lord (i.e., "the final judgment") is the central belief of any Judean or Christian eschatology, which is why I have chosen it as my definition for this study (cf. "the central foci of [early Christian eschatological] beliefs are the judgment of sinners and the salvation of the righteous," ABD, 2:594). Within Luke's narrative, there are tensions between imminence and delay, arrival and expectation. Bock, *God's Promise Program,* suggests that Luke has a realized eschatology, 389–405. This may be true in general sense, but to reduce Luke's eschatology to a term he himself does not use

near the beginning of both of Luke's books, it seemed important to investigate whether this relationship shows up elsewhere and, if so, what that might mean for the study of this major New Testament text.[8]

Aims of this Study

As I will demonstrate in the coming chapters, not only do eschatology and ethics continue to appear at key moments in Luke's two volumes,[9]

violates the particularity of his narrative. This study therefore rejects the use of systematic terminology in an attempt to attend to the nuance Luke's narrative has, which no terminology can hope to sum up (cf. p. 25 below). Ethics has been defined as the sharing of possessions because, as the survey of scholarship below demonstrates (p. 5 below), scholars almost unanimously agree that to investigate Luke's ethics is to investiagate what he has to say about possessions. There are, of course, other ethical issues Luke addresses (e.g., marriage [Luke 16:18]), but Luke's substantive ethical contributions all revolve around the matters of possesssions (on Luke 16:18, see p. 86 below). Even what he has to say about politics focuses on possessions (cf. Acts 16:16–40; 19:23–41).

8. The question of soteriology naturally arises in a discussion of eschatology and ethics. The question "what shall we do?" is a soteriological one, for it is to ask "what shall we do to be saved on the day of judgment?" Soteriology is touched on throughout this work, but is not a major focus of the study. Similarly to my approach to Lukan eschatology, systematic categories are resisted to describe what "Lukan soteriology" is, which is why no soteriological and/or eschatological framework is laid out at the beginning of this study. Rather, exegesis has been put at the forefront in an attempt to let Luke's narrative tell the story of eschatology and ethics within the story of salvation of Judeans and Gentiles. Luke's stories of repentance may at times appear Pelagian (see e.g., p. 53 below), and at other times sacramental (see e.g., p. 148 below). But no term can sum up Luke's soteriology, for his narrative at once says much more and much less than systematic terminology (especially anachronistic ones) can say (again, see p. 25 below).

9. I am unconvinced by Parsons and Pervo's thesis that Acts should be seen as a sequel to Luke as opposed to a second volume of a planned two-volume work. See Parsons and Pervo, *Rethinking the Unity*. See also Gregory, *Reception of Luke*, and Gregory and Rowe, *Rethinking the Unity*. It appears to me that Acts was conceived as a second volume to a double work from the beginning. Given that Luke was using Mark as a source, we can notice that the dietary laws, for example, are not revoked in the earthly lifetime of Jesus as they are in Mark (Mark7:19). Rather, they are revoked in the life of the early church when Peter receives a vision just before his encounter with Cornelius (Acts 10). It might be suggested that Luke had another reason for excluding Mark's account of Jesus declaring all food clean, but the fact remains that Luke informs the reader from the beginning that the nations will be included in the people of God (see Luke 2:32) and yet leaves the major hurdle of the dietary laws unaddressed until the book of Acts. It seems likely that Luke left the abolition of dietary laws until Acts precisely because of his commitment to a properly ordered narrative, as he claims his narrative is in the prologue to his Gospel (Luke 1:1–4). A similar case can be made for the delaying of the growing conflict with the Judeans and their leaders until the book of Acts.

but where eschatological proclamation and shared possessions do appear, those passages often, like the beginning of Acts, recall John the Baptist's preaching. So the first aim of this study is simply to demonstrate this linkage of eschatology and ethics throughout Luke's two volumes and thereby to show that sharing possessions in the last days appears to be one of Luke's major theological concerns.

But there is also a second aim. While demonstrating that eschatology and ethics are both central to Luke's theology, I shall at the same time ask "why?" Why does Luke think that an ethic of shared possessions is necessary in the last days? I resist a singular, systematic answer to this question. Luke wrote a narrative because a narrative—as opposed to any other category of literature—was the best way to say what he wanted say, and narratives as a genre resist tidy summarization.[10] But there is nevertheless one recurring matter that appears to be part of the connective tissue throughout the passages addressed in this study.

That matter, in sum, is the identification of God's people. When John the Baptist exhorts the crowd to share food and clothing, the injunction comes on the cusp of his telling them not to say to themselves that they have Abraham as a father (Luke 3:8). In Luke 16, Jesus tells his audience to make friends with unrighteous mammon (16:9). At the beginning of Acts, it is a community of people that is formed around shared possessions (Acts 2:42–47). And, finally, it is in part through sharing possessions that the Gentiles demonstrate their inclusion in the people of God (e.g., Acts 10:2). As I shall demonstrate, these diverse passages seem to indicate that the identification of the people of God is sometimes called into question, sometimes suggested, and sometimes confirmed all around the matter of possessions. Moreover, the identification of people of God appears from the outset of Luke's narrative to be an eschatological question. In the opening scene we are told that John the Baptist will prepare a people for the Lord (ἑτοιμάσαι κυρίῳ λαὸν κατεσκευασμένον, 1:17). When he begins his public ministry, he tells the crowds to prepare in order that they might escape the coming wrath.

Before I turn to exegesis, a few more remarks are in order. First, I give a short survey of Lukan studies to show where I hope to make a contribution with this inquiry. Second, I make some remarks about my interpretive method.

---

10. For more, see Method section (p. 16) below.

Survey of Scholarship

Scholars have consistently recognized the importance of eschatology in early Christian ethics. There is an easily observable relationship throughout the NT. In 1 Cor 7, for example, Paul suggests that the unmarried should stay as they are because of "the present distress" (διὰ τὴν ἐνεστῶσαν ἀνάγκην, 7:26) and because "the time is drawing close" (ὁ καιρὸς συνεσταλμένος ἐστίν, 7:29). Elsewhere in Rom 13, Paul says that his audience should observe the time, "that the hour has come" for them to rise from sleep (εἰδότες τὸν καιρόν, ὅτι ὥρα ἤδη ὑμᾶς ἐξ ὕπνου ἐγερθῆναι, 13:11), and that they should therefore (οὖν, 13:12) "walk properly" (εὐσχημόνως περιπατήσωμεν), not in orgies, drunkenness, sexual immorality, sensuality, strife, and jealousy (13:13). Passages such as these are what lead Richard Hays to suggest that "Paul's moral vision is intelligible only when his apocalyptic perspective is kept clearly in mind."[11] Similarly, Richard Burridge says about Jesus' ethics that it "like all his teaching is to be understood in light of the *eschaton*."[12] The centrality of eschatology in early Christian ethical reflection is why both Hays and Burridge in their comprehensive studies on NT ethics consider each NT author's eschatology before considering his ethics.[13]

Scholars recognize the importance of eschatology for early Christian ethics, yet there is to my knowledge no monograph addressing eschatology and ethics in Luke–Acts. One motivation for this study is therefore simply that such an investigation might add to our understanding both of Lukan writings and to their relationship to other early Christian documents. But this study is also occasioned by scholars' acknowledgment of the importance of Luke's eschatological outlook for his ethical concerns. This acknowledgement is what I shall presently detail. Scholarly recognition of eschatology and ethics in Luke–Acts is a complicated story, for eschatology and ethics have both individually been matters of debate.

Debates about Luke's eschatology and debates about his ethics will be identified in the following short survey. But scholars have typically addressed either only eschatology or ethics in Luke–Acts, though they acknowledge the importance of one for the other. Because eschatology and ethics have typically only been discussed separately, that is how I proceed

11. Hays, *Moral Vision*, 19.

12. Burridge, *Imitating Jesus*, 46, cf. 40–45.

13. This is clear from the table of contents in both Hays and Burridge; see Hays, vii–x; Burridge, vii–xiii. Numerous other scholars have also noted the eschatological context of early Christian ethics, see e.g., Sanders, *Ethics in the New Testament*; Wilder, *Eschatology and Ethics*; Verhey, *Great Reversal*; Schrage, *Ethics of the New Testament*; Matera, *New Testament Ethics*.

in this review. I look first at scholars' discussion of Lukan eschatology and their acknowledgment of its relatedness to Lukan ethics. Thereafter, I look at scholars' discussion of Lukan ethics and their acknowledgment of its relatedness to Lukan eschatology.

Scholars on Lukan Eschatology (and Ethics)

Hans Conzelmann's 1953 publication on Lukan theology is seminal in the field.[14] His account of Lukan eschatology not only received much attention in the years following, but also set the terms of the debate.[15] He claims that history necessitated that early Christians revisit their expectations of an imminent eschaton. Jesus had not come back when the earliest Christian communities thought he would. Paul said in 1 Cor 15:51 that "we will not all sleep." The first generation of Christians evidently thought that some of them would still be alive when Christ returned. But the first generation of Christians had come and gone. Luke's generation, Conzelmann suggests, had to deal with the problem of delay. 2 Peter had his own response. He simply reasserted imminence in the face of disappointment.[16] But Luke had a different answer; he found a "new departure," which, Conzelmann claims, was his "great achievement."[17] In the face of delay, rather than denying it Luke embraced it, deliberately eliminating from his theology any hope for an imminent return of Christ.[18] Luke accomplished his great theological achievement by integrating his theology into his sources, schematizing history into three stages. Jesus' words in Luke 16:16, Conzelmann says, signify this division. "The Law and the Prophets were until John," Jesus says, and "from then the kingdom of God is proclaimed as good news" (Luke 16:16). John the Baptist closed the first period and Jesus' ministry formed the second.[19] The third is the indefinite, long-term period of the church.

The first passage Conzelmann turns to in order to demonstrate Luke's new departure in Christian eschatology is John the Baptist's preaching (Luke 3:1ff). There he notices that Luke adds a series of ethical exhortations that are

14. The English translation was published in 1960. Conzelmann, *Theology*.

15. It is important to note, however, that though Conzelmann is often the name associated with the following understanding of Lukan eschatology, Paul Vielhauer had a very similar analysis before him. See P. Vielhauer "On the 'Paulinism' of Acts," in Keck and Martyn, *Studies in Luke–Acts*, 33–50. Vielhauer's article was originally published in German in 1951.

16. See 2 Pet 3:1–13.

17. Conzelmann, *Theology*, 13.

18. Ibid., 95–96.

19. Ibid., 16–17, 95–96.

not in his sources (Luke 3:10–14; cf. Mark *ad loc*). This new material, according to Conzelmann, indicates that the Lukan John the Baptist is no longer proclaiming an "eschatological call to repentance," as he was (presumably) in Mark. Rather, he preaches "timeless ethical exhortation."[20] Ethics, in other words, replaces imminent eschatology. Conzelmann does not ignore John the Baptist's words about the coming wrath (Luke 3:7). Indeed, he admits that John threatens judgment. But he nevertheless suggests that "the threat of judgment is now independent of the time when the judgment will take place." The Lukan "John does not declare that judgment is near."[21]

Conzelmann has little else to say about Lukan ethics in his monograph. But what he does say is that by inserting ethical exhortations into John the Baptist's preaching, Luke "creates a pattern of preaching which can be seen in other passages as well . . . John's preaching as a whole provides the basis for the preaching of the 'Gospel', of 'the kingdom of God'."[22] Conzelmann's analysis of John the Baptist's preaching, in other words, implies that Luke's eschatology occasions his ethics.

Conzelmann's work received some initial criticism.[23] Nevertheless, whatever disputes scholars had with Conzelmann's account, scholars through the 1970s generally seemed to be convinced that, at the very least, Conzelmann was correct to see that Luke makes a shift in Christian eschatology.[24] Joseph Fitzmyer is representative. In the introduction of

20. Ibid., 102.

21. Ibid., 102.

22. Ibid., 102.

23. According to H. J. Cadbury, Conzelmann's overall argument rests on "subtle, partial, or selective considerations." See Cadbury, "Review," 304–5; Paul Minear, "Luke's use of the Birth Stories," in Keck and Martyn, *Studies in Luke–Acts*, suggests that Conzelmann's analysis would not have been able to hold had he not excluded Luke's infancy narrative from his analysis. In addition, Minear says, Luke 16:16 is not able to bear the interpretive weight Conzelmann wants to place on it, 111–30.

24. Robert Maddox noted in his 1982 publication that Conzelmann's account of Lukan eschatology "has become the 'classical' theory of eschatological doctrine intended by Luke." (100–102). For those whose analyses were similar to Conzelmann's, see e.g., Haenchen, *Acts*, 94–98, 143; Käsemann, *Essays*, 28–29; Kaestli, *L'Eschatologie*, 60–62. For those who disagreed with Conzelmann, see e.g., Ellis, *Eschatology in Luke*; and Maddox, *Purpose*, 100–157.

The far-reaching impact of Conzelmann's analysis of Lukan eschatology can be seen in the analyses of NT ethicists and theologians in the last 10–20 years. R. Hays, *Moral Vision*, suggests that Luke pushes "the day of judgment into an indefinite future . . . [and] in effect creates an infinitely expanding historical "middle" in which the role of the church is paramount," 131. Speaking of a "middle" recalls the German title of Conzelmann's work (*Die Mitte der Zeit*). Burridge, *Imitating Jesus*, while stating that "eschtology reinforces the ethical implications of [Luke's] portrait of Jesus' mission" (249) nevertheless acknowledges the element of delay in Luke's Gospel and substantially

his respected 1981 commentary on Luke, Fitzmyer says that, though he thinks "some modifications ... are necessary," the tripartite division of Lukan salvation-history presented by Conzelmann is correct.[25] By way of modification, he says that while Luke "obviously coped with the delay of the parousia, which puzzled the early Christians," he nevertheless has not "completely abandoned" the belief in "an early expectation of the end-time" as Conzelmann had suggested.[26] Fitzmyer thus insists that a more nuanced account of Lukan eschatology is necessary than Conzelmann allowed. But, again, Fitzmyer agrees most fundamentally with Conzelmann that a shift in eschatological expectation takes place in Lukan thought. The change that Fitzmyer sees is one of emphasis: Luke wishes "to shift the emphasis in many of Jesus' sayings from the *eschaton* to the *sēmeron* to show that they are still valid guides for conduct in his generation." This shift, he says, directs Christians to see Jesus' conduct "as an inspiration and guide for Christian life." Thus, he concludes, Luke has "dulled the eschatological edge of some of the sayings of Jesus to make them a hortatory device for everyday Christian living."[27] Similarly to Conzelmann, then, Fitzmyer concludes that Lukan eschatology occasions ethics.

Within a few years of the completion of Fitzmyer's commentary on Luke's Gospel, John T. Carroll's monograph on Lukan eschatology was published.[28] His study, he reports, was occasioned in part by the "prevailing

---

engages Conzelmann's ideas, 246–50. Schnelle, *Theology*, also argues that Luke removed eschatological expectation from his theology. He points to the ascension as evidence that "*the architecture of the final events*" have been completely "*remodeled*," for "*there is only a minimal connection between sudden and catastrophic apocalyptic events and an expectation of the parousia understood in continuity with the ascension.*" He moreover thinks the readjustment of eschatological expectation in Luke makes "*provision for carrying out the divine plan of the saving acts of God in history,*" 517–19.

25. One of the modifications Fitzmyer thinks is necessary to admit is that the threefold division is not "fully explicit in Luke." Luke 16:16, on Fitzmyer's reading, only speaks of two periods of history, Israel's and Jesus', Fitzmyer, *Luke*, 1:18.

26. Fitzmyer, *Luke*, 1:234. Fitzmyer says this in view of passages like the sending of the Seventy, where Jesus counsels his emissaries to announce that the kingdom of God has drawn near (Luke 10:11). Before Fitzmyer, S. G. Wilson had come to a similar conclusion that in Luke one finds "two apparently contradictory strands of teaching, both of which he asserts with equal firmness." The two strands are (1) a clear move away from imminent expectation and (2) a clear maintaining of imminent eschatological expectation, Wilson, *Gentiles*, 82; cf. 59–87. Fitzmyer believes that these two strands are reconcilable. Wilson believes that at most one could suggest a pastoral context in which Luke thought it was necessary to assert both strands which are both used to achieve "practical" aims, 85.

27. Fitzmyer, *Luke*, 1:234.

28. Carroll, *Response*.

confusion" about the nature of Lukan eschatology.[29] As others said, Carroll claims there is evidence of a shift in Lukan eschatology from his early Christian predecessors. But despite a shift toward delay, Carroll also sees evidence of hope for an imminent end. Carroll's observations, in other words, are not far from Fitzmyer's, though Carroll wishes to lay more stress on imminent expectation than Fitzmyer would allow. In order to reconcile evidence for delay with that for early expectation, Carroll offered a thesis different from Fitzmyer's: he claimed that Luke added to and adjusted his source material in order to recognize and account for delay (in e.g., Luke 17:20–21),[30] but at the same time maintains an expectation of an imminent parousia to his own audience.[31] Carroll thus makes distinction between the literary and social setting of Luke's writings. Conzelmann was correct, he says, to the extent that he recognized delay in Luke's handling of his sources.[32] But Luke nevertheless wanted to maintain imminent hope in his current social setting. Indeed, Carroll claims that Luke had to adjust his sources in order to maintain credibility about the hope of an imminent end. He had to demonstrate that "delay and duration" were the "orders of the day" throughout the narrative.[33] Doing that, he could claim that Jesus and the apostles had foreseen delay and that his audience should now therefore believe in an imminent end. On his account, "delay does not oppose but undergirds expectation of an imminent End in Luke's own situation."[34]

Carroll concludes his monograph by claiming that the reason Luke proclaimed an imminent end is because of a practical problem in his community. Complacency had taken root, and he needed to motivate his audience to action. For Carroll, in other words, Luke's ethics occasions his eschatology.[35] He claims that "only because Luke continues to expect

---

29. Carroll, *Response*, 2.

30. Ibid., 88, 123–8.

31. Ibid., 165–7. Carroll's conclusions look very similar to those in Richard Hiers's "Problem," 145–55. He claims that Luke expected the end to come after the Gentile mission, which was "completed, or about to be—if not by Paul, by others" and that after that, there "remained only for the Kingdom of God . . . to come," 155. Delay in Luke's writings is thus accounted for by Luke's Jesus knowing that "many years would pass and much would have to happen before the Parousia would occur," 152.

32. Carroll, *Response*, 166.

33. Carroll, *Response*, 166–7.

34. Carroll, *Response*, 166–7.

35. This is not to say that Carroll thinks that Luke was dishonest in proclaiming an imminent end. Luke did not invent his eschatology simply for the sake of his ethics.

a sudden return of Jesus (and soon!) does his appeal for an alert, faithful manner of living have motivating force."[36]

In his 2005 revised edition of *Luke the Theologian*, François Bovon claims that scholars have been fatigued by the question of Lukan eschatology. Luke, he says, is now considered to be "less original concerning eschatology than first thought."[37] And this is, according to Bovon, a good development for, "according to the evangelist, this question should not preoccupy us."[38] Now, he says, scholars have more appropriately focused on, among other things, "the moral life of the community."[39]

Nevertheless, questions about Lukan eschatology have not completely disappeared,[40] though they often come in a different guise.[41] Outi Lehtipuu's monograph, for example, explores Luke's theology of the afterlife.[42] She does not shy away from venturing an analysis of Lukan eschatology (or lack thereof) as a whole: "eschatological teaching and its coherence is not of primary interest to Luke or the key for understanding the purpose of his writing but it serves other, more practical aims."[43] Luke's practical aims, she goes on, are "paraenetic" ones.[44] Similarly to Carroll, then, Lehtipuu suggests that Lukan ethics occasions his eschatology.[45]

Whether scholars who have written on Lukan eschatology suggest that in general eschatology occasions ethics in Luke's works or that ethics

36. Carroll, *Response*, 167. Carroll here explicitly disagrees with Fitzmyer's claim that Luke "dulled the edge of eschatology to make of it a paraentic device," 166–7.

37. Bovon, *Luke the Theologian*, 55.

38. Bovon, *Luke the Theologian*, 55. And, he adds, "the exegetes of our century have hardly followed these instructions!"

39. Bovon, *Luke the Theologian*, 12.

40. See e.g., Haacker, "Der Geist," 325–45. Haacker suggests that Conzelmann's understanding of the Spirit as a substitute for the eschaton has been the most influential view of Lukan eschatology in the last fifty years. He challenges this view by suggesting that the coming of the Spirit can actually be seen in Luke's writings as an eschatological event. Cf. also Marshall, "Political and Eschatological Language in Luke" in Bartholomew, Green, and Thiselton, *Reading Luke*, 157–177; and Nielsen, *Lukan Eschatology*.

41. See e.g., Salmeier, *Restoring the Kingdom*; Horton, *Death & Resurrection*. There has also been much work done on the restoration of Israel in Luke and Acts, all of which are in part analyzing Lukan eschatology. See e.g., Bauckham, "Restoration," 435–88; Pao, *Acts*; Lyons, "Paul," 345–59.

42. See also Rindge, *Parable*.

43. Lehtipuu, *Afterlife*, 237.

44. Lehtipuu, *Afterlife*, 241, 264.

45. A major difference between Lehtipuu and Carroll, however, is the coherence of Lukan eschatology. Carroll, unlike Lehtipuu, thinks that there is a carefully thought out and consistent eschatology in Luke's two works.

occasions eschatology, there is a general agreement that the two are related. Moreover, the scholars considered here generally agree that eschatology and ethics are central to Lukan thought. For Conzelmann, John the Baptist's preaching is the pattern throughout Luke's works. For Fitzmyer, Luke's shift from *eschaton* to the *sēmeron* can be seen from Jesus' first public announcement in Nazareth (Luke 4:21).[46] For Carroll, Luke's community had become lax and needed eschatological motivation for action. This study intends to affirm, at the very least, the shared assumption of these scholars that there is a link between eschatology and ethics.

Scholars on Lukan Ethics (and Eschatology)

The nature of Lukan ethics, like Lukan eschatology, has been a matter of perennial debate. The discussion at least since the 1960s has centered on whether Luke has a consistent ethics. Why does Luke on the one hand require complete divesture of one's possessions to be a follower of Jesus, but on the other does not require it of all people? Jesus says to the crowd before him that they are not able to be his disciples unless they renounce all their possessions (Luke 14:33). Yet Zacchaeus gives only half of his possessions to the poor and Jesus declares him a "son of Abraham" (19:8–9). In what follows, I briefly consider some of the ways in which scholars have answered this question. While eschatology does not feature in many of these studies, scholars in recent decades have recognized that eschatological expectation does seem to be linked in some way to Luke's ethics. Yet even where eschatology's influence is recognized, it is never addressed in a substantial way.

Hans-Joachim Degenhardt's 1965 study not only set the terms of debate about Lukan ethics by bringing the issue of consistency to the forefront, but also influenced the way in which studies attempted to resolve the problem.[47] There is no contradiction in Luke's ethics, he suggests, if one has a proper appreciation for the diversity Luke's audience. Luke had at least two groups of people in mind. There were on the one hand "disciples" (μαθηταί), who correspond to office holders in the church in Luke's own day who were required to give all, and on the other hand there was another general group of "people" (λαός) who did not have the same demands

---

46. Cf. Fitzmyer, *Luke*, 1:533–534.

47. Though there was, of course, an interest in Luke's material on possessions and wealth well before Degenhardt. See e.g., Henry Joel Cadbury, *Making of Luke–Acts*, 254–73. The enduring interest in Luke's material on possessions and wealth even apart from the questions Degenhardt asks is represented by Jacques Dupont's *Les Beatitudes*, see esp. vol. 3, pp. 21–206.

placed upon them.[48] Subsequent studies similarly attempt to account for Luke's inconsistencies by supplying an audience that would not see the inconsistencies in the narrative as such.

Degenhardt's study, however, does not focus solely on dealing with apparent ethical contradictions. He also investigates the motives for charity (*die Wohltätigkeit*) in Luke's works.[49] On this matter, Degenhardt considers the possibility of eschatological influence and explicitly rejects it precisely because *Lukas eine eschatologische Naherwartung nicht unterstützt.*[50] Rather, Degenhardt sees *der Wille Gottes* and *die Worte Jesu* among others as the primary motivations for sharing possessions.[51] Here again we can see Conzelmann's influence.

Robert Karris's article, "Poor and Rich: The Lukan *Sitz im Leben,*" just over a decade after Degenhardt's study also seeks to give an account of Luke's audience in order to resolve ethical inconsistencies.[52] He concludes that "Luke is primarily taken up with the rich members, their concerns, and the problems which they pose for the community." The rich members' concerns, he says, "revolve around the question: do our possessions prevent us from being genuine Christians?" Jesus' answer is that riches are not an "infallible sign of God's favor" and that the rich should therefore repent before they lose their "invitation to the heavenly banquet."[53] Karris's conclusions imply that eschatological concerns influence Luke's ethics, but he says nothing more about it.[54] Karris's article represents a starting point of what Thomas E. Phillips calls "an emerging consensus" in studies of Lukan ethics.[55] Numerous scholars after Karris in the 1980s and 1990s have also concluded that Luke was directing his ethics to rich members of his congregation.[56]

48. Degenhardt, *Evangelist der Armen*, 31–39.

49. Degenhardt, *Evangelist der Armen*, 186.

50. Degenhardt, *Evangelist der Armen*, 187.

51. Degenhardt, *Evangelist der Armen*, 186–7.

52. While Karris expresses some reservations about Degenhardt's study, he says that Degenhardt's investigation of the Lukan community is "valuable," Karris, "Poor and Rich," 114–5.

53. Karris, "Poor and Rich," 124.

54. Schmithals, "Lukas—Evangelist Der Armen," 153–67, suggested a different thesis than Karris a few years earlier. He suggests that the Christian community to which Luke wrote was under constant threat of persecution, and persecution entailed potential dispossession of their property. Such an environment, he suggests, can make sense of Luke's ethics of wealth.

55. Phillips, "Wealth and Poverty," 239–40.

56. See e.g., Mealand, *Poverty and Expectation*; Schottroff and Stegemann, *Jesus*; Moxnes, *Economy*; Kim, *Stewardship*. Jonathan Marshall's work, *Jesus, Patrons, and Benefactors,* though it does not set out to reconcile contradictory ethical injunctions in

While solutions to the apparent inconsistency in Lukan ethics has largely been influenced by Degenhardt's attempt to reconstruct Luke's audience, there are some notable exceptions to this trend. Luke Timothy Johnson's study, for example, suggests a literary solution.[57] He argues that in order to deal with contradictions in the text, one must "place the passage within the dramatic flow of the narrative, recognizing that there is in all probability a good literary reason" for one passage containing the injunctions that it does in the place in the story in which it appears.[58] He concludes his study not by suggesting a *Sitz im Leben* of Luke's audience, but by arguing that possessions are for Luke "an indication, a symbol" of a person's interior disposition.[59]

Thomas E. Schmidt represents another exception. While he does not propose a literary solution to inconsistent ethical material in Luke, he nevertheless agrees with Johnson that it is unfruitful to search for a Lukan *Sitz im Leben*: "we observe little evidence . . . of the socio-economic circumstances of Luke's audience or of the situation described."[60] Rather, he suggests that Luke's works indicate only "Luke's active interest in communicating, in a consistent manner, dispossession of wealth as a way of expressing *Gottvertrauen*."[61]

In the studies considered so far eschatology plays almost no role in configuring the nature, consistency, and logic of Luke's ethics. But even around the time that Karris wrote his article about the link between Luke's audience and his ethics George W. E. Nickelsburg recognized the importance of eschatology for Luke's ethics. Nickelsburg's short study, "Riches, Rich, and God's Judgment in 1 Enoch 92–105 and the Gospel according to Luke," is not an exploration of Lukan ethics as such, but about the possibility that Luke was influenced by 1 Enoch.[62] Nevertheless, the point upon which Nickelsburg considers such a possible dependence is the link between judgment and riches that he sees both in 1 Enoch and in Luke. He concludes that in Luke as in 1 Enoch "the accumulation and holding of riches and

Luke, nevertheless implies a similar audience.

57. Johnson, *Literary*. Johnson's literary solution needs to be differentiated with what C. Hays calls the literary solution to Luke's ethics popular in Germany that sees the inconsistencies in Luke's ethics as a result of improperly integrated sources with an ascetic tendency. See Hays, *Luke's Wealth Ethics*, 10–16. For one such literary solution according to Hays's definition, see Theissen, "Wanderradikalismus," 245–71.

58. Johnson, *Literary*, 25.

59. Johnson, *Literary*, 148.

60. Schmidt, *Hostility*, 161.

61. Schmidt, *Hostility*, 161–2.

62 Nickelsburg, "Riches, the Rich, and God's Judgment," 324–44.

possession are inversely related to the possibility of salvation." Riches and possessions, he continues, are consistently "mentioned in the context of judgment or salvation."[63]

Peter David Seccombe also recognizes that eschatology plays a role in Luke's ethics. As others did before him, Seccombe concludes in his 1982 study that Luke does in fact have a consistent ethic. Luke is not an ascetic demanding that all divest themselves of all their possessions. Rather, he sees Luke demanding "positive engagement" with possessions: "money is to be used positively to good effect in accordance with the values of the Kingdom."[64] And as Degehardt and others also suggested, Seccombe says that Luke's ethics correlates with the *Sitz im Leben* of his audience. Luke's ethics is evidence that his readers were most likely "well-to-do Hellenistic God-fearers who were attracted to the Christian movement," but feared what it might cost them "socially and economically" for them to join Christianity.[65]

One of the key elements in Luke's consistent ethics, Seccombe says, is Luke's eschatological outlook. Luke's ethics is "determined at every point by the reality and imminence not only of the judgment, but also of the age to come."[66] Seccombe sees the eschatological determination of Luke's ethics, for example, in the summary statements at the beginning of Acts (2:42–47; 4:32–37). Though he admits that the summary statements do not state it explicitly, he suggests that they nevertheless indicate that the salvation of the eschatological future is embodied in the present through the common life of the community. They represent "a pattern of societal activity which is congruent with, and in some ways anticipates, the life of the age to come."[67] On Seccombe's account, in other words, Luke's eschatology informs his ethics.[68]

Just over a decade after Seccombe, Kyoung-Jin Kim offered another explanation of the underlying unity of Luke's ethical passages. He suggests that the category of discipleship on which scholars have typically focused is

---

63 Nickelsburg, "Riches, the Rich, and God's Judgment," 340.

64 Seccombe, *Possessions*, 228.

65. Seccombe, *Possessions*, 229.

66. He however adds that Luke "nonetheless looks forward to a perhaps lengthy continuance of the present age," *Possessions*, 138.

67. Seccombe, *Possessions*, 222; cf. 219–221. See also, Mealand, "Community of Goods," 96–99.

68. York, *Last Shall Be First*, also suggests that Luke's material on possession and wealth are related to his eschatology: "present reversals are portents of things to come," 162. But York conducts no investigation of Lukan ethics as such. He seeks rather to investigate the purpose of the literary theme of reversal in Luke's writing, 9–10.

insufficient to provide a complete picture of Luke's concern about wealth.[69] A "new paradigm," he says, needs to be offered, the category stewardship.[70] This supplementary paradigm, he suggests, emerges from several parables in Luke's Gospel such as the Parable of the Faithful and Wise servant (12:42–48), the Parable of the Unjust Steward (16:1–13), and the Parable of the Ten Minas (19:11–27). In his focus on these parables Kim indicates that eschatological expectation is linked with Luke's ethics.

According to Kim there are three characteristic elements in Luke's stewardship parables: first, the steward does not own what he is managing; second, the steward can be summoned for an account at any time; and finally, there is a guaranteed judgment of his work.[71] It is both with the imminence of giving an account and with the guarantee of judgment that Kim indicates that eschatological expectation is a central element in what he calls Luke's paradigm of stewardship. But despite acknowledging that eschatological expectation is central in these parables, he discusses Lukan eschatology at no length. This is perhaps because Kim assumes that "the *parousia* is also . . . delayed in Luke's Gospel so as to highlight a concern with the daily life of Christians."[72] Indeed, he suggests that one of the main reasons Luke wrote was not eschatological concern, but the more immediate concern of dealing with present-time matters such as famines: "with increased numbers of οἱ πτωχοὶ in [his] society" rich Christians needed "appropriate ethical teachings on how to deal with wealth."[73] While Kim never says it, his argument nevertheless suggests what Conzelmann argued, namely that eschatological delay occasions ethics.

Finally, there is C. Hays's recent systematic analysis of Luke's ethics.[74] As others before him, Hays has no extended discussion of Lukan eschatology and its relationship to Lukan ethics, but he does suggest that there is a

69. The focus on discipleship has likely been because of Luke 14:33 where Jesus says that one cannot be his disciple (μαθητής) unless all possessions are renounced.

70. Kim, *Stewardship*, 33, 111, 287.

71. Kim, *Stewardship*, 286.

72. Kim, *Stewardship*, 285.

73. Kim, *Stewardship*, 53.

74. Another recent study of Luke's ethics is James A. Metzger's *Consumption and Wealth*. While Metzger refreshingly suggests that "the various positions professed by each character or set of characters at separate stages in the story should be identified and preserved rather than conflated so as to squeeze a single perspective out of the narrative," his study is nevertheless limited in its usefulness since he focuses solely on Luke's Travel Narrative. As Metzger himself says, "further research would be required in order to place" his analysis "in conversation with wealth and possessions discourse elsewhere in the Gospel," 189–90. He moreover says nothing about the role eschatology plays in Luke's ethics.

relationship. He claims that in the apocalyptic discourse of Luke 17:22–37 "the second coming of Christ is a terrifying stimulus to a proper use of wealth."[75] The passage is "eschatologically motivated ethical teaching for the period between the crucifixion and the return of the Son of Man." Luke, he adds, is consistent with other NT writers on this point.[76] Hays also sees an eschatological aspect to ethical teaching in the Parable of the Unjust Steward (16:1–13). There, "the beneficiaries of charity become, not clients of the rich, but their eschatological patrons."[77] But these are only a few comments interspersed throughout a wider study in which Hays attempts to discover an underlying ethic behind Luke's various and apparently contradictory teachings. He attempts to demonstrate that discipleship is at the core of Lukan ethics and that Luke 14:33, in which Jesus commands the rejection of all possessions by his disciples, is worked out in different ways for Luke's audience throughout his two volumes.[78]

Scholars of Lukan ethics have thus recognized that eschatology is linked in some way with Luke's ethics, yet there has been no thorough treatment of the relationship. This may be in some instances because of the influence of Conzelmann's work. Degenhardt, Seccombe, and Kim all assume Conzelmann's suggestion that Luke accounted for the delay of the parousia in his theology. But, as Nicklesburg's work demonstrates, the eschatological context of Luke's ethics cannot be ignored.

Method

This study is a literary and theological analysis of Luke–Acts. Because Luke wrote a narrative, it will be read as such. This means most fundamentally that Luke did not intend to communicate reductive theological propositions or ethical principles to his audience.[79] Rather, what he intended to

75. He says this immediately after admitting that scholars have often considered Luke's to be the least "apocalyptic" of the Gospels, C. Hays, 160; cf. 159–66.

76. Hays, *Ethics*, 164.

77. Hays, *Ethics*, 146; cf. 144–48.

78. Hays, *Ethics*, 184–88; 261–63.

79. I am assuming that Luke's two books are deliberately and carefully crafted pieces of literature. Literary studies of Luke and Acts such as mine are commonplace in the academy. See e.g., Tannehill, *Narrative Unity*, "a comprehensive purpose . . . is being realized throughout the narrative," 1:1; and Luke Timothy Johnson, "Luke–Acts, Book of," in Freedman, *The Anchor Bible Dictionary*, "the development of plot in itself, in sequence, has persuasive force," 4:405.

communicate was his story. To use the words of Erich Auerbach, Luke's theology is "incarnate in . . . and inseparable from" the narrative.[80]

In order to investigate what Luke intended to communicate, this study proceeds first and foremost on the interpretive axiom standard in Western literary studies at least since Aristotle's *Poetics* that narrative is representation.[81] To say that narratives are representations is to make a distinction between the events that are related in the story and how those events are conveyed. Put concretely, Caesar's crossing of the Rubicon may be an event included in any number of narratives, but the way in which Caesar's crossing is told may be told in just as many different ways as there are authors who want to write narratives about those events. The different ways in which any story is told depends on what an author is attempting to persuade her readers of. The task in the present study is thus to investigate both Luke's techniques of persuasion and the goals of those techniques.

But to investigate authorial intent is at the same time to investigate Luke's reader(s).[82] What could Luke's reader(s) have understood from the text that he wrote? How one answers this question in each instance will influence how one configures the likely meaning of the text. Luke's readers must also therefore function as an interpretive control. One problem with this control, however, immediately presents itself: we have no access to Luke's original readers, nor do we know whether they were a diverse group with various levels of education. Nor do we know if Luke had a quantifiable original audience in mind. Because of this problem, Luke's readers must therefore be "built"—as John Darr has put it—even as one asks questions of how Luke's readers understood the text.[83] There must be a dialectic between

80. Auerbach, *Mimesis*, 15. Auerbach says this about the OT in general, giving the *Akedah* (Gen 22) as a particular example. Sternberg, *Poetics*, also suggests that it is the narrative itself that is the communicative act: "like all social discourse, biblical narrative is oriented to an addressee and regulated by a purpose or a set of purposes involving the addressee." But the author's purpose (or purposes) is not indicated explicitly: "the reticent narrator gives us no clue about his intentions except in and through his art of narrative," 1. Cf. Rowe, *Early Narrative Christology*, 9–13. For more on theology and biblical narrative generally, see Merenlahti, *Poetics for the Gospels*; and Alter, *Art of Biblical Narrative*.

81. See Abbott, *Cambridge Introduction to Narrative*, 12; Ryan, "Definition of Narrative," demonstrates the wide agreement in the academy, 23. Cf. Whitmarsh and Bartsch, "Narrative," 237–60, esp. 239; Cooper, *Poetics of Aristotle*; Halliwell, *Poetics of Aristotle*.

82. I am aware that it is likely that at least some of Luke's original "readers" were also made up of listeners and that this necessitates attention to the ways in which the narrative would have been heard by those who did not have the words before their own eyes. See Moore, *Literary Criticism*, 84–88.

83. Darr, *On Character Building*, 16–36. Joel Green, "Learning Theological Interpretation from Luke" in Bartholomew, Green, and Thiselton, uses the category of "Model

what a likely reader could have understood from the text and what kind of
reader the text demands for the text to be understood.[84]

Throughout this study, I draw on different and aggregate methodological resources, all of which are put in the service of enlightening Luke's
techniques of persuasion. Different resources are required at different points
in the narrative. Where text-critical or redactional-critical issues arise, for
example, they are addressed. Aggregate resources are required since interpreting later material in the story must take into account what has come
before it. Every methodological issue cannot therefore be addressed prior
to exegesis.[85] At the outset, however, there are three interrelated interpretive

---

Reader" who he says (following Umberto Eco) are "those who are able to deal with texts
in the act of interpreting in the same way as the author dealt with them in the act of writing." He continues, however, that it is the reader whom the text "not only presupposes
but also produces. This requires that readers enter cooperatively into the discursive dance
with the text, while leaving open the possibility that the text is hospitable to multiple
interpretations" (60, *italics mine*). Cf. Eco, *Role of the Reader*, 7–11.

84. The dating of Luke and Acts is difficult (if not impossible) to determine. As L.T.
Johnson notes, "any discussion of the circumstances accompanying the production of
Luke–Acts is inevitably circular. There are few external guideposts, so conclusions must
be based on internal evidence, which can—notoriously—be construed different ways,"
ABD 4:404 (cf. Pervo, *Acts*, "the notion that one can extract from a narrative data that
will indicate where it was written will now seem old-fashioned, for research must deal
with the concepts of an implied author and a principal narrator," 5). It is therefore im-
prudent to attempt to identify a date or community prior to extensive exegesis. But even
at the end of the exegetical process, this study refuses to attempt to identify a likely date,
author, and community, for the debate will never be settled. This study has therefore
attempted to exegete Luke–Acts in a way that would not change should a concrete date
be indisputably offered. Joel B. Green's commentary, *Gospel of Luke,* adopts this same
exegetical stance.

85. I have reservations about the adequacy of the interpretive tools offered by nar-
ratologists who suggest that "an infinite number of narrative texts can be described
using the finite number of concepts contained within the narrative system," [Bal, *Narratology*, 3; Cf. Genette, *Narrative Discourse Revisited*]. While basic concepts at play in
all narratives (questions and answers, foreshadowing, focalization, etc.) may be useful
in describing the general issues at stake when interpreting narratives, the goal of interpretation is never simply to analyze a text scientifically, but to understand the text.
The limitations of narratological descriptive systems is tacitly admitted by Irene J. F. de
Jong, who for celebrating both narratological tools and the fact that there is "a growing
number of people who know how to use them," admits that the techniques authors use
in narratives "change over time, are put to different uses and achieve different effects
in the hands of different authors, writing in different genres, and handling different
material," see Jong, Nünlist, and Bowie, *Narrators, Narratees, and Narratives*, xi–xii.
Narratalogical tools, in sum, are insufficient to describe narratives. As Meir Sternberg
says, the "listing of so-called forms and devices and configurations . . . is no substitute
for the proper business of reading," 2. Sternberg's assertion is in line with Rowe's suggestion that it is not that "theory matters little, but rather that an exegetical work is most
compelling when it moves actual exegesis up from an after dinner mint to the main

issues worth noting since they, in some respects, set this study apart from others: order, structure, and rhetoric.

Order

Luke's narrative is written καθεξῆς, "in sequence" (Luke 1:3).[86] A thematic, topical investigation that extracts "Luke's eschatology" or "Luke's ethic" by addressing passages synchronically without any regard for narrative time must therefore be excluded.[87] Neither Luke's eschatology nor his ethics is simply the sum total of everything he has to say about eschatology and ethics in the various passages that have something to say about those matters. Rather, the possibility must be considered that what he has to say about eschatology or ethics can develop as the plot develops. Peter's Pentecost preaching, for example, is not simply John the Baptist's preaching put on Peter's lips, even though it clearly recalls it. Rather, the outpouring of the Holy Spirit is the fulfillment (of at least part of) what John preached and, as Luke indicates later in Acts, is evidence that John's Baptism is now insufficient because it has been superseded by baptism in the name of the Lord Jesus (cf. Acts 19:5). Progression in the narrative demands a new posture toward the eschaton. Likewise, John the Baptist only demanded the sharing of possessions. In Acts, not only do they share possessions; they form a community around those possessions.[88]

---

course of the meal," Rowe, *Christology*, 9.

86. It should also be noted as Rowe, *Christology*, does that Luke wrote the narrative in a particular order that he believes to be correct. This is evidenced by the use of ἀκριβῶς to modify παρηκολουθηκότι, 12. The adverb καθεξῆς is used with a similar meaning throughout Luke's narrative. See esp. Acts 11:4 where Peter explains to the elders in Jerusalem "in order" everything that took place that led up to the inclusion of Gentiles in the movement (Cf. Luke 8:1; Acts 3:24, 18:23). Cf. Alexander, *Preface to Luke's Gospel*.

87. See e.g., Bock, *A Theology of Luke and Acts*, who, for example, appeals to individual verses separated at a distance in Luke's Gospel (e.g., Luke 11:20. 17:21) as evidence that Jesus' ministry is a "transitional period" in Luke's eschatology, 390.

88. As p. 58 demonstrates below, there is progression even between John the Baptist's and Jesus' preaching. John the Baptist preaches eschatology and ethics to point to the Christ who is judge; Jesus preaches eschatology and ethics to identify himself as the Christ who is judge. Likewise, the day of Pentecost represents a shift in the role of possessions: they are used to form a community (cf. Ch. 4). In Gentile contexts, the trope of possesssions is again used to demonstrate the inclusion of Gentiles into the restored tent of David (cf. Ch. 5). Gentile hospitality is not identical in form or function to the Jerusalem community's sharing of possessions, but it is clearly connected since it gains its logic from the Jerusalem community (which itself gains its logic from John the Baptist's preaching).

At the same time, the significance of Pentecost is only properly understood in light of John the Baptist's preaching. Luke himself reminds the reader of this (Acts 1:5). Just as Pentecost only makes sense in view of John the Baptist's preaching, so also does the outpouring of the Holy Spirit on the Gentiles in Acts 10 make sense only in light of Pentecost. Indeed, as is demonstrated in Ch. 5 of this study, it appears that Luke wants the reader to recall Pentecost precisely to demonstrate that Christians in Acts 10 are now in the position that Judeans were on the day of Pentecost: they stand by in amazement as others receive the Spirit.[89] Characterizing the Christians in Acts 10 as such suggests that the inclusion of the Gentiles is not only yet another sign that for Luke these are the last days (cf. Acts 2:17), but also that the last days have occasioned the inclusion of the Gentiles since they are now receiving the Spirit.[90] This is unnoticeable if one simply mines the outpouring in Acts 10 for indications of "Luke's eschatology."

Structure

In addition to following Luke's narrative in order, I also give attention to Luke's literary structures. To build on the previous example, one could suggest that because the outpouring of the Holy Spirit on the Gentiles so clearly recalls the original Pentecost event, Luke intends the reader to see this not only as a new chapter in the history of Christianity, but also a new stage in his narrative. And, indeed, from there onward Gentiles are present at almost every stage of the narrative.[91]

But what structural signals can be found in Luke's narratives? Luke frequently gives helpful transitional words like ἐγένετο (e.g., Luke 3:2; Acts 9:32). A change of geography might also indicate a transition (see e.g., Luke 4:14; Acts 13:1). This study, however, pays close attention to the ways in which Luke puts his individual stories into cohesive sequences.[92] Paul's mis-

---

89. Both Acts 2:7 and 10:45 use the verb ἐξίστημι to describe the onlookers' astonishment.

90. These characterizations are also a feature of rhetoric (for more on rhetoric, see below). As Rothschild, *Luke–Acts*, notes, "by alignment of more recent with more remote past events, through repetitions of pithy memorable phrases *and* alignment of historical characterizations, the author [of Luke–Acts] establishes the early history of the Jesus movement as a dynamic complex of interrelated series of reenactments," 140.

91. Finding structures within Luke's narrative is, of course, a necessity and is done by all interpreters. One must, at the very least, decide where a pericope begins and ends and whether those individual pericopae are to be interpreted on their own, or in conjunction with the context in which they appear.

92. As Roland Meynet points out, structural marks in biblical texts were originally linguistic in nature since the texts did not have chapter and verse divisions. See

sionary journeys are illustrative. Paul's first missionary journey, for example, is not only demarcated at the beginning by his sending from the Antioch church (Acts 13:3) and at the end by the transition to the Jerusalem council (Acts 15:1), but also geographically. Paul begins and ends his journey in Antioch, and on his way back to Antioch visits for a second time in reverse order the places he visited on his outward journey.[93] As a there-and-back-again story, the journey both gives the reader a clue that the journey is coming to an end with each place mentioned in reverse order and gives a sense of completion when the journey comes to an end with Paul's reappearance in Antioch. Structural indications can also be thematic. The series of three pericopae in Luke 15 are all about lost things being found. Structural indications may moreover be found in similar content and the similar ordering of that content. Acts 3–4, for example, mirrors Acts 1–2. In both sequences of stories, Peter announces Jesus' resurrection to a crowd following a miracle, which results in mass conversions and the sharing of possessions in communities. This could indicate that Acts 3–4 is supposed to be seen as an elaboration of Acts 1–2.

Such structural indications can be seen on a much larger scale as well. Luke, it appears, even gives literary markers to signal that both Luke and Acts are concluding. The Gospel begins with Simeon and Anna hoping for the restoration of Israel and ends with Joseph of Arimathea and the two disciples on the road to Emmaus hoping for the same.[94] Similarly, Acts both opens and closes with a challenge to Israel to see and to hear what God has done through Jesus' resurrection.[95] Luke signals, in other words, that both of his books are concluding via an *inclusio*.

Rhetorical Analysis, 182–83. Cf. Meynet, *Treatise on Biblical Rhetoric*. Meynet's commentary, *L'Évangile de Luc*, likewise emphasizes the sequencing of pericopae in Luke's Gospel. Cf. McComiskey, *Lukan Theology*.

93. Luke notes that after Derbe, Paul and Barnabas return to Lystra, Iconium, and Antioch (14:21). In v. 24, he adds that they passed through Pisidia and Pamphylia. The only differences between the outgoing journey and the return is that on their way back, they visit Attalia (near Perga) and do not revisit Cyprus.

94. Simeon and Anna look for the παράκλησιν of Israel (2:25) and the λύτρωσιν of Jerusalem (2:38), respectively. Joseph of Arimathea looks for the kingdom of God (23:51) and the disciples on the road to Emmaus were hoping that Jesus was the one to redeem (λυτροῦσθαι) Israel (24:21). Despite the fact that the same words are not used for each character, what brings them together is that they are all longing for some sort of national salvation and that longing is in no way invalidated by Luke. Meynet, *L'Évangile de Luc*, 984. Meynet also points out how the Gospel begins and ends in the Temple (1:9; 24:53), 988–90.

95. At the beginning of Acts, Peter appeals to the crowds to see and hear at both the miracle of Pentecost and of the healed cripple (Acts 2:33, 3:16 [here, to see only]). At the end of Acts, Paul quotes Isa 6:9–10, which speaks of both seeing and hearing

As we shall see, I suggest that every passage in Luke and Acts can be placed in what is in effect a mini-narrative. These mini-narratives allow the reader to take Luke's work in digestible portions.[96] Exploring these larger literary structures can shed light on the individual pericopae by seeing the function they play in those structures. None of these structures, however, are self-standing. Each mini-narrative itself plays a part in the larger narrative that Luke has written. And precisely because no structure is self-standing, the various parts of Luke's narrative resist any totalizing structural analysis. Any given passage may fit into multiple structural configurations of the text.

Rhetoric

The question of this thesis is occasioned by what is fundamentally an observation of Luke's rhetoric. By rhetoric, I mean specifically his "creative and discreet" use of language in his techniques of persuasion.[97] Luke uses not only topics (last days, repentance, etc.) in Peter's Pentecost proclamation that recall John the Baptist's preaching, but also similar language. For Peter, as for John the Baptist, salvation means forsaking crookedness ($\sigma \kappa o \lambda \iota \acute{o} \varsigma$, Luke 3:5; Acts 2:40). It is because of this observation that I have chosen to use John the Baptist's proclamation as a criterion for choosing the other passages included in this study. Most of the passages considered in this study either invoke John the Baptist by name or use language similar to his.

Because of this fundamental observation and its correlating methodological commitment, I pay attention to Luke's use of language. If Peter's Pentecost sermon can so clearly recall John the Baptist's preaching, then

---

(28:26–27).

96. The individual pericopae in Luke's work can be thought of as bite-sized pieces in the digestible portions of his mini-narratives. By structuring his work at these various levels, Luke gives the reader help in seeing how the parts fit into the whole of his narrative.

97. Rothschild, *Rhetoric*, 2. She says this of techniques of persuasion in general among ancient historians, including the author of Luke–Acts. But she also notes in the conclusion of her work that among historiographical techniques of persuasion that she does not address at length in her work, one could also consider Luke's imitation of the LXX. She points, for example, to the frequent use of the noun $\sigma \acute{\eta} \mu \varepsilon \rho o \nu$ in Luke's Gospel. It is used among other instances to refer to Jesus' birth (2:11), to the inauguration of his public ministry (4:21), and to the time when the thief next to him on the cross will be in paradise (23:43). She suggests that this "may represent a stylistic emphasis, possibly related to the LXX (e.g., Exod 19:10–11), on the reliability of the event recorded," 293–94. Rothschild's observation points not only to the importance of observing the ways in which Luke uses the LXX, but also to the ways in which word repetition (stretching the entirety of one of his books as the term $\sigma \acute{\eta} \mu \varepsilon \rho o \nu$ does) may be one of Luke's techniques of persuasion.

this suggests that Luke can use other language in similarly creative ways. Not only does Luke use language to recall previous scenes in the narrative, he also uses language in new contexts to give the language itself a different shade of meaning.

The problem with tracking Luke's use of language, however, is that there is no exact science to it. Luke, like any author, uses language creatively, not systematically. How is the reader to understand the word ἔξοδος in Luke 9:31? Does it simply refer to Jesus' departure in his death? Or does Luke intend to recall Israel's escape from Egypt? Or does he intend both?[98] Does the command to "rise" in both of Peter's healings of cripples in Acts indicate that Luke wishes these miracles to be symbolic, pointing to the promise of resurrection on the last day (Acts 3:6, 9:34)? Does the complete darkness right before the shipwreck in Acts 27 represent the loss of the eschatological hope (27:20)? Various possibilities must be weighed.[99]

The problem of interpreting Luke's language is intensified by the fact that in interpreting Luke and Acts it is not only the text itself that needs to be taken into account. Various other texts from the literary world of Luke–Acts need to be taken into account as well. So, for example, Joseph Fitzmyer has suggested that a reader would have noticed that Luke cut off his quotation of Isaiah 61:1–2 early, leaving out the phrase "and the day of vengeance of our Lord" (Luke 4:19). Having noticed this, he suggests, a reader would see that Luke was not interested in talking about judgment at this point in his narrative.[100] Fitzmyer assumes that in order to understand Luke properly, one needs to pay attention to his creative use of Scripture.[101] On the other hand, Steve Mason has suggested that "at least some of [Luke's] Greek-educated

98. Rowe's work, *Christology*, is instructive on this point. He details how in some instances the title κύριος is clearly applied to the Judean God, and in others is clearly applied to Jesus. Still, in other instances the referent of the title is ambiguous about whether it refers to the Judean God, Jesus, or some other character (such as in the parables). These varied uses develop the identity of the κύριος over the length of the whole Gospel, at the end of which the reader can conclude that "Jesus of Nazareth is the movement of God in one human life so much so that it is possible to speak of God and Jesus together as κύριος," 218.

99. As Sternberg, *Poetics*, notes, "biblical narrative emerges as a complex, because multifunctional, discourse. Functionally speaking, it is regulated by a set of three principles: ideological, historiographic, and aesthetic. How they *co*operate is a tricky question," 41.

100. See Fitzmyer, *Luke*, 1:526–39; Cf. Nolland, *Luke 1—9:20*, 1:191–203.

101. Scholars have noted not only that Luke appears to be quite competent with his use of the OT, but also that he writes in a way that mimics the OT. See e.g., Sterling, *Historiography and Self-Definition*. For more studies on the use of the OT in Luke and Acts see e.g., Lyons, "Paul and the Servant(s)"; Wendel, *Scriptural Interpretation*; Brawley, *Text to Text*; Pao, *New Exodus*; Mallen, *Reading and Transformation*.

audience" would have noticed that Paul uses the phrase "it is hard for you to kick against the goads" in his account of his conversion before Festus and Agrippa (Acts 26:14) in a similar context to that in which it appears in other Greek texts. The phrase often appears in the context of "obeying a divine being who must in any case be obeyed."[102] Scholars have thus argued that knowledge of at least some of the Old Testament and some Graeco-Roman literature would aid in understanding Luke's rhetoric.

Whether one locates Luke and his audience more in the Judean or in the Graeco-Roman world (or some combination of the two), the one matter that is agreed upon is that the reader is on some level expected to supply information that the text itself does not explicitly provide. This is an assumption that I also will make when reading the text.[103] But the role the reader has in meaning-making concerns not only other texts. Luke also appears to invite the reader to make meaning within the confines of his own narrative. To use an example I already mentioned, I suggest in Ch. 4 of this study that Luke intends the reader to see the cripple's healing in Acts 3:1—4:22 as a resurrection-mimicking miracle. Luke never says this explicitly, but pushes the reader in this direction rhetorically, via the repetition of words, imagery, and themes from the cripple's healing when he speaks of Jesus' resurrection.[104]

In sum, because it is impossible to speak in strict terms of what literary structures are or are not in Luke's narrative, because of the multivalent and creative nature of language, and because an identified reader or group of readers cannot be identified prior to reading the text, I will not suggest hard and fast meanings in my interpretations of Luke's theology. The goal will be instead to open meaning, allowing space for further investigation that may in the end further expand the meaning of any given passage. But

102. Mason, "Speech-Making", 156.

103. There are several notable studies on Luke–Acts that acknowledge the role the reader has in meaning-making. See Darr, *Character*; Longenecker, *Hearing the Silence*; Dinkler, *Narrative Representations*; and Rowe, *Christology*.

104. Longenecker, *Hearing the Silence*, points to Jesus' miraculous escape in Nazareth in this respect (Luke 4:30). Luke curiously understates how Jesus escaped. He says only that he "passed through" the crowd that was seeking to kill him. Longenecker suggests that this understatement invites the reader not only to supply divine intervention as the means of Jesus' escape, but also to consider whether Jesus' escape is not a fulfillment in part of Ps 91:11, which the Devil quoted to Jesus in his final temptation (Luke 4:10). It is possible to see it as a fulfillment of scripture precisely because the temptation involved the possibility of miraculous escape at the threat of being thrown down from a height. One may dispute Longenecker's configuration of Jesus' escape with the temptation scene, but the fact that Luke understates Jesus' escape from the Nazareth mob is undeniable. See pp. 1–23; 38–112. What Longanecker recognizes in this passage is what literary theorists call "gaps" in the narrative—places where the reader is required "to fill things in" in order to makes sense of the story (Abbott, 83–88).

this goal is set not simply because of the above-discussed issues. It is also because narratives themselves resist singular, totalizing interpretive paradigms. This goal therefore has implications for what sort of conclusions this study will draw.

Answers

It is clear from the above survey of scholarship that, at the very least, Lukan scholars who have written both on eschatology and on ethics have recognized a relationship between the two. But beyond making a similar general observation about the interrelatedness of eschatology and ethics in Luke and Acts, this study has little else in common with the studies conducted by the aforementioned scholars. I will not be asking if there is a way to reconcile apparently contradictory material about Luke's eschatology. I will also not be asking if there is a way to reconcile the apparently contradictory material in Luke's ethics. The reason I will not be asking these questions is because Luke's theology cannot be reduced to unadorned, systematic theological claims.

Because Luke wrote a narrative, to ask about the underlying unity of Luke's contradictory ethical material as some scholars have done is to read Luke's narrative not as a narrative. As David Herman puts it, "narrative . . . is a basic human strategy for coming to terms with time, process, and change—a strategy that contrasts with, but is in no way inferior to, 'scientific' modes of explanation that characterize phenomena as instances of general covering laws."[105] Narratives are not, in other words, scientifically-minded arguments governed by thesis statements. They do not function in the same way as argumentative essays or—to use Herman's example—dictionary definitions do, which are characterized by "paradigmatic" or "logico-deductive" reasoning.[106] Narratives do not define or sub-categorize material. Rather, narratives draw links "between the experiencing self and the world experienced" and build "causal-chronological connections."[107]

---

105. Herman, "Introduction," 3–21, 3.

106. Ibid., 6–7.

107. Ibid., 7–8, cf. 6–11. Mason, "Judaeans," has argued that Josephus's narrative of the Judean War is similarly irreducible. Josephus's *War* is particularly instructive on this point since it provides an instance where, unlike Luke, there actually does appear to be a thesis statement at the beginning of book 1, which, if it is a thesis statement, would indicate that Josephus is making a systematic claim at the beginning of his work for which he is then arguing with supporting evidence throughout the rest of the work. Most scholars have taken Josephus's prologue as such. Josephus is taken to claim that, in sum, there was a singular, isolated group of "troublemakers, whom he labels 'tyrants'"

Here again we are reminded of Erich Auerbach's suggestion that theology is "incarnate" in biblical narrative.[108] Form and content are inseparable. Rather than making systematic, reductive claims, Luke's theology is much more about drawing links between "the experiencing self and the world experienced." Yet this needs to be clear: Luke is indeed making theological claims—he is simply not making reductive ones. Luke is indeed claiming, for example, that Jesus came back from the dead. He is indeed claiming that the Holy Spirit was poured out on the day of Pentecost. And he is indeed claiming that the Gentiles are included in the people of God. But Luke's narrative is not reducible to one or several of these claims.

The way in which interpreting narratives propositionally violates the nature of the genre can be demonstrated concretely by demonstrating how a third literary genre is equally violated if it is interpreted propositionally. Consider Proverbs 26:4–5: "Do not answer fools according to their folly, or you will be a fool yourself. Answer fools according to their folly, or they will be wise in their own eyes (NRSV)." The proverb is a complete contradiction—and a completely intended one—and is therefore irreducible to any singular, summarizing, propositional claim. The two sayings cannot, for example, be reduced to "do not talk to fools," as if that is the unifying thought behind and beneath the two sayings, for the proverb assumes that one must and will talk to fools. And there is similarly no extractable lesson to be learned from the two sayings that one can take away after having studied them. Rather, the wisdom of the contradiction lies precisely in the contradiction. In its contradiction the proverb teaches multiple lessons. One may, for example, say that the proverb indicates that it is best to avoid talking with fools. One may moreover say that the proverb indicates that sometimes fools should be answered according to their folly, and other times not. But again, none of these are the singular, reduced, or extracted

---

bent on war, while "the nation, the aristocracy, and especially himself" are guiltless of any sedition (J.W. 1.9–1; Mason, "Judaeans," 162). But, Mason argues, if the prologue is taken as a thesis statement to Josephus's account of the war, then J.W. 2 is a "glaring contradiction" of it. "In War 2 those statesmen have no single group of adversaries." Rather, they are "torn by conflicting commitments to their people, to regional peace, and to foreign masters." Josephus thus emerges rather as an "urbane observer who watches events unfold with a tragic foreboding, from his avowedly retrospective position, which no one trapped in the story, including his own character, can do anything about" than as an accuser of a select group (Mason, 165–66). Both Josephus and Luke obviously organized their material in the way they did to communicate what they wanted to communicate to their audiences. But their organization of material was not to argue a thesis (or even a quantifiable group of theses); it was rather to tell a story. Those stories make both fewer claims and more claims than do thesis-driven arguments.

108. Auerbach, Mimesis, 15.

meaning of the proverb. In order to live by the proverb, one must learn the proverb, not its meaning.

Narratives and proverbs are equally different genres as narratives are to argumentative essays, but to the extant that Luke's narrative is productive of meaning, rather than restrictive, the example of Prov 26:4–5 is instructive. Any part of Luke's narrative may have multiple possible meanings and may fit into various configurations of the text.[109] Luke's Jesus may at some points demand complete divesture of possessions and at other times demand vigilant management. These are not necessarily contradictory injunctions. Indeed, the complexity of teachings on possessions may simply be an acknowledgment of the complexity of life. The way to live according to Luke's ethics of possessions may not be to learn the most fundamental demand that unifies the diversity of the teachings in his books, but to learn the teachings in all their diversity. And in addition to learning all the diverse things that Luke has to say about possessions, one must learn what he has to say about them in the complex relations he puts them with other equally important and complex matters—not least the announcement of the coming eschaton.

The conclusions of this study will therefore not be restrictive, but productive of meaning, indicating ways in which Luke's ethics of possessions come in the context of eschatological proclamation. Such an interpretive posture will not only be in accordance with the nature of Luke's communicative act, but may also be in accordance with the condition he himself sets for the narrative. His narrative is about the "things" ($\pi\rho\alpha\gamma\mu\acute{\alpha}\tau\omega\nu$)—in the plural—that have been accomplished (Luke 1:1). If Luke himself says that his narrative is not about a singular "thing," then it seems that the best interpretive posture is to assume that the parts of his narrative are similarly irreducible. At the very least, this approach will present the opportunity not to bring the study of eschatology and ethics in Luke–Acts to a conclusion, but to open further opportunities to explore the world of meaning in Luke's story.

---

109. So, for example, Luke's birth narrative of John the Baptist and Jesus (Luke 1–2) recalls the birth of Samuel (1 Sam 1—2:11). But Luke is—apparently—not precise in his topology. Elizabeth is in one way like Hannah, for it is Elizabeth who is barren and appears in the context of the Temple. Yet, it is Mary who sings a song like Hannah's (Luke 1:46–55; 1 Sam 2:1–10). Likewise, it is John the Baptist, like Samuel, who will be a prophet (Luke 1:17), but it is the boy Jesus, who, like Samuel, appears in the Temple (Luke 2:41–51; 1 Sam 1:21–28). These configurations resist the reductive conclusion either that Elizabeth or Mary *is* a new Hannah.

2

John the Baptist and Jesus

Opening Proclamations

Introduction

The opening proclamation of Luke's Gospel is both eschatological and ethical. John the Baptist asks the crowd before him, "who told you to flee the wrath about to be?" (τῆς μελλούσης ὀργῆς, 3:7).[1] He speaks of the coming fiery judgment: every tree that does not bear good fruit will be burned (3:9). And when the crowd asks "what therefore shall we do?" (τί οὖν ποιήσωμεν; 3:10), he responds with ethics. Those who have two cloaks ought to share with the one who has none. Those who have food should do likewise (3:11).

The first task of this chapter is to demonstrate that Luke brings eschatological announcement together with ethical exhortations that are concerned specifically with sharing possessions. This task is important because John the Baptist's eschatological and ethical preaching are recalled at key points in Luke's two volumes. Establishing the relationship of eschatology to ethics in John the Baptist's preaching thus lays the groundwork for everything else in this study. Some scholars, moreover, have doubted the relationship between eschatology and ethics in John the Baptist's preaching.[2]

1. There is proclamation in the infancy narrative as well, but the proclamation there is a) not public, and b) does not demand a decision on the part of the hearers. I am not saying here, in other words, that Luke 3 is the "beginning of the Lucan Gospel proper" (Fitzmyer, *Luke*, 1:450). Fitzmyer's words suggest that the John the Baptist's preaching can be interpreted in isolation from the infancy narratives. As I argue below, it appears that to the contrary John the Baptist's preaching builds on the themes begun in the infancy narratives.

2. See e.g., Conzelmann, *Theology*, 102; Fitzmyer, *Luke*, 1:459; Bovon, *Luke 1*, 123;

The second task is to investigate how John the Baptist's preaching fits into the larger opening narrative of Luke's Gospel and particularly how it functions to introduce Jesus' ministry.[3] Luke parallels John the Baptist's and Jesus' characters throughout the first four chapters of his Gospel. Both structure and content indicate that Jesus is intelligible only in view of John the Baptist.

In this chapter, I look at the two opening sequences of Luke's Gospel: the infancy narrative (Luke 1–2), and the opening proclamations of John the Baptist and Jesus (Luke 3–4). Both sequences of Luke 1–2 and Luke 3–4 are structured for rhetorical effect. The structure of these stories is detailed in general terms before engaging the passages in more detail. Throughout the analysis, eschatology and ethics will be highlighted to demonstrate how these matters fit within the story that Luke is telling.

The Infancy Narrative: Luke 1–2

Structure

I make all structural observations with caution. One reason for caution is simply that scholars disagree, and disagreement might mean that Luke did not give his narrative a rigid structure.[4] Another reason is that any total-izing structural analysis may violate the creative nature of the narrative. It is possible, for example, both that Luke intended multiple configurations of the text and that he deliberately made some structural elements inconsistent. Nevertheless, the many indications of structural intentions on the author's part deserve to be investigated. The infancy narrative in particular is a good example of intentional structuring on Luke's part since it is widely accepted

---

Cf. p. 6 above, and p. 53 below.

3. On the importance of John the Baptist for Luke's works, see e.g., Darr, *Character*, 60–84; and Böhlemann, *Jesus und der Taufer*. My work corroborates Böhlemann's findings that the motifs Luke presents in John the Baptist's infancy narrative and John the Baptist's opening proclamation (such as eschatology, ethics, election, etc.) will reappear throughout Luke–Acts. These motifs thus offer a hermeneutical key for reading Luke's two volumes. For more on John the Baptist generally, including historical investigations of John the Baptist and his ethical preaching see e.g., Rothschild, *Baptist Traditions and Q*; Bammel, "Baptist," 95–128; and Wink, *John the Baptist*.

4. For all of its helpful insights, the weakness of Meynet's work (*Luc*) is that he forces every part of Luke's narrative into a rigid structure, which (at times) ignores the possibility that Luke intended there to be multiple configurations of the text. The structure I propose finds close agreement with Wolter's, *Lukasevangelium*, 70–71. For various structural configurations of Luke's infancy narrative, see e.g., Bovon, *Luke 1*, 29; Fitzmyer, *Luke*, 1:313–4; Bock, *Luke*, 1:68–69; Nolland, *Luke 1—9:20*, 19–23; cf. Laurentin, *Structure et Theologie*.

both that the infancy narrative forms a structural unit and that there is, on a general level, a coherent structure in the rotating scenes between John the Baptist and Jesus' characters.[5]

Time demarcates Luke's infancy narrative from the rest of his Gospel. Between the end of Luke 2 and the first verse of ch. 3 the story jumps decades ahead from John the Baptist's and Jesus' childhood to John the Baptist's adult years. The leap in time suggests that Luke 1–2 is a literary unit that, while functioning as an introduction to the entire Gospel, is nevertheless a digestible, self-contained unit of the narrative.[6] Several literary features immanent to Luke 1–2 confirm this. To begin with, Luke 1–2 is demarcated by a geographical *inclusio*: it begins and ends in the temple in Jerusalem. The infancy narrative moreover begins and ends with an elderly man and an elderly woman in the Temple. Zachariah and Elizabeth are both "advanced in age" (προβεβηκότες ἐν ταῖς ἡμέραις αὐτῶν ἦσαν, Luke 1:7); Simeon is near death (2:26, 29), and Anna, like Elizabeth, is advanced in her years (2:36).[7] Finally, there is a sense of expectation that opens and concludes the first two chapters. Luke says that "all the multitude of the people" (πᾶν τὸ πλῆθος . . . τοῦ λαοῦ, 1:10) were waiting outside the place of Zachariah's sacrifice. The hyperbolic "*all* the people" seems synecdochic— Luke appears to suggest that all of Israel waits with the waiting people. At the close of the infancy narrative, Simeon and Anna are waiting for the "consolation" (παράκλησιν, 2:25) of Israel and the "redemption" (λύτρωσιν, 2:38) of Jerusalem, respectively.

There also appears to be two smaller literary sequences within the infancy narrative divided between Luke 1 and 2. The two sequences are

5. See e.g., Fitzmyer, *Luke*, 1:306; Green, *Luke*, 47; Wolter, *Lukasevangelium*, 69–71.

6. Some scholars have suggested that the infancy narrative was not part of Luke's original Gospel composition and that its theology is therefore not in harmony with the rest of the Gospel. Conzelmann, *Theology*, for example, excludes the infancy narrative from his analysis of Lukan eschatology. It is generally agreed that it was Luke who composed the infancy narrative of his Gospel (see e.g., Brown, *Birth*, 241). But Brown points out that Lukan authorship does not mean that the infancy narrative's theology is in harmony with the rest of the Gospel. Luke may have composed it after his Gospel was already written, and may have been heavily reliant on pre-Lukan sources (Brown, *Birth*, 241; cf. Fitzmyer, *Luke*, 1:306). It appears to me, however, that the theology of the infancy narrative is consonant with the rest of the Gospel. The tropes of sight and hearing that appear in the infancy narratives (which are detailed below; cf. e.g., 2:30) continue to appear both in Luke 3–4 (again, see below; cf. 3:6, 4:20), and at the end of the Gospel (see e.g., 24:31). And there is significant scholarly support for my claim, see e.g., Bock, *Luke*, 1:68–69; Green, *Luke*, 47; Fitzmyer, *Luke*, 1:306; Bovon, *Luke 1*, 28–30.

7. Anna, also like Elizabeth, is introduced as a θυγάτηρ of a tribe of Israel (2:36; cf. 1:5).

demarcated at Luke 2:1 both by the ἐγένετο in 2:1 and the mention of a political figure of the time. These two elements also appear at the beginning of Luke 1. The story of Zachariah and Elizabeth takes place "in the days of Herod, king of Judea" (ἐγένετο ἐν ταῖς ἡμέραις Ἡρῴδου βασιλέως τῆς Ἰουδαίας, 1:5); the story of Jesus' birth comes "in those days" when a decree went out from Caesar Augustus (ἐγένετο δὲ ἐν ταῖς ἡμέραις ἐκείναις ἐξῆλθεν δόγμα παρὰ Καίσαρος Αὐγούστου, 2:1).[8]

The first sequence in Luke 1 appears to be structured as a chiasm. The announcement of John the Baptist's birth is followed by the announcement of Jesus' birth (1:11–25; 1:26–45). The announcement of Jesus' birth is then followed by Mary's celebratory song (1:46–56). After John the Baptist is born, Zachariah sings another celebratory song (1:57–80). The characters make a chiasm: John the Baptist—Jesus—Jesus—John the Baptist. And the two halves of the chiasm contrast in literary form: annunciation—annunciation—song—song.[9]

The only event concerning John the Baptist in the first sequence for which there is no counterpart in Jesus' sequence is Jesus' birth.[10] The fact that every other event concerning the two characters has a counterpart makes Jesus' birth expected, and that is what opens second sequence. Like the first sequence (Luke 1), the second (Luke 2) can be subdivided into two parts. The two parts in this instance appear to be structured geographically and thematically. In Bethlehem, shepherds see "the glory of the Lord shine around them" (δόξα κυρίου περιέλαμψεν αὐτούς, 2:9), after which they say, "let us go see this thing" (ἴδωμεν τὸ ῥῆμα τοῦτο) which the Lord has made known to us" (2:15). After the shepherds visit, Luke says that Mary "treasured all these things, considering them in her heart" (πάντα συνετήρει τὰ ῥήματα ταῦτα συμβάλλουσα ἐν τῇ καρδίᾳ αὐτῆς, 2:19). In Jerusalem, Simeon speaks of the "word" (τὸ ῥῆμα) God had spoken to him and proclaims that

8. The endings of the two literary sequences are also parallel. At the end of the first, Luke says John the Baptist ηὔξανεν καὶ ἐκραταιοῦτο πνεύματι (1:80), and at the end of the second, Luke says Jesus ηὔξανεν καὶ ἐκραταιοῦτο πληρούμενον σοφίᾳ ˆ (2:40) and προέκοπτεν [ἐν τῇ] σοφίᾳ καὶ ἡλικίᾳ καὶ χάριτι παρὰ θεῷ καὶ ἀνθρώποις (2:52).

9. If this configuration is correct, then the meeting between Elizabeth and Mary (1:39–45) is a central point of overlap that relates and intertwines the two stories of John the Baptist and Jesus.

10. Meynet, Luc, 192–93, helpfully notes the numerous correspondences between the birth stories of John the Baptist and Jesus—e.g., Luke speaks in both instances of Elizabeth's and Mary's time of child bearing coming to fulfillment (1:57, 2:6), and both John the Baptist and Jesus are circumcised (1:59; 2:21). The correspondences between the two birth stories makes them parallel like the two annunciations. Yet, it seems clear that a new section has started in 2:1, as I have pointed out, because of the verb ἐγένετο and because of the political synopsis. The two birth stories appear therefore to be an instance in which Luke's narrative is intended to have multiple configurations.

his "eyes have seen" (εἶδον οἱ ὀφθαλμοί) God's salvation (2:30) and that what has happened will be a "light to the nations" (φῶς εἰς ἀποκάλυψιν ἐθνῶν, 2:32). The mention of things spoken by God and the tropes of eyesight and light all recall the experience of the shepherds. At the end of the Jerusalem scenes in Luke 2,[11] Luke says once again that Mary "treasured all these things in her heart" (διετήρει πάντα τὰ ῥήματα ἐν τῇ καρδίᾳ αὐτῆς, 2:51).

The theological themes of the infancy narrative begin to emerge with the literary structure in view, the most prominent of which is expectation. The old age of the four characters at the beginning and end evoke a sense that what is about to happen has been long expected: Zachariah himself says that the events that are about to take place are in fulfillment of God's promise to Abraham (1:73). The expectation moreover appears to be eschatological. It is salvation (τὸ σωτήριόν) that Simeon's eyes see (2:30); it is redemption (λύτρωσιν) that Anna sees in Jesus (2:38); and it is light that Zachariah and Simeon proclaim (1:78; 2:32) and that the Shepherds see (2:9). Perhaps it is significant that Isaiah also uses light to speak of eschatological fulfillment. Consider Isa 60:1, "Shine! Shine, Jerusalem, for your light (τὸ φῶς) has come, and the glory of the Lord has risen upon you!"[12] Isaiah features prominently in Luke 3–4, so it is reasonable to believe that Luke is already drawing on Isaiah's language and imagery in his infancy narrative.[13]

A second matter that emerges from the structure is that the development of John the Baptist's and Jesus' characters is intertwined. The chiastic structure of Luke 1 seems to suggest that John the Baptist is the context in which to understand Jesus. In what follows, I take a closer look at eschatological expectation, how John the Baptist's and Jesus' characters are related to that expectation, and how an ethics of possessions is introduced (however minimally) in this context.

11. Though there is a period of time between the two Jerusalem visits, it appears that the Jerusalem scenes are supposed to be seen together since one visit happens immediately after the other (2:40–41).

12. The Benedictus in particular might be drawing on this passage. Zachariah speaks of a sunrise visiting from on high (ἐπισκέψεται ἡμᾶς ἀνατολὴ ἐξ ὕψους, Luke 1:78) and Isa 60:1 speaks similarly of light rising (ἀνατέταλκεν).

13. In Acts, Paul quotes Isa 49:6 when he says that the Lord made him and his traveling companions a light (φῶς) to the nations (Acts 13:47). On Luke's use of Isa 49:6 in Acts 13:47, see Lyons, "Paul and the Servant(s)." Cf. Pao, *New Exodus*; and Mallen, *Isaiah in Luke–Acts*.

The Annunciation of John the Baptist

After Zachariah and Elizabeth are introduced (1:5–7), Luke says that Zachariah is chosen by lots to go before God and burn incense. Luke gives the impression that everything is going on as usual. Not only is Zachariah chosen "in the order of his division" (1:8), but the burning of the incense is also done "according to custom" (1:9). At the same time, Luke indicates the scene is one of expectation. All the people wait and pray outside at the hour of Zachariah's offering. Again, the hyperbole "*all* the people" seems to be synecdochic, which suggests that the praying people are representative of Israel.[14] But what are they praying for?[15] Luke does not say.

An angel appears to Zachariah in front of the altar. "Fear not," the angel says, "for your prayer has been heard" (1:13). Up until this point, no personal petition has been mentioned on Zachariah's part. If the angel had not continued speaking, the reader might be left to assume that the prayer that has been heard is the same prayer that the people outside of the altar room were praying since it was on their behalf that Zachariah was offering incense. But the angel's words then supply information previously unknown to the reader. Zachariah and Elizabeth have been praying for a child: "your wife Elizabeth will bear a son for you" (1:13). That is the prayer that has been heard. Nevertheless, the momentary ambiguity about which prayer the angel is referring to might be deliberate: though the reader is immediately informed that Zachariah and Elizabeth have been praying for a child, the angel goes on to announce that John the Baptist will be born for the sake of Israel.[16] He will "turn many of the sons of Israel to the Lord their God"

14. As Nolland, *Luke 1—9:20*, says, "here faithful Israel is pictured at worship, at the commencement of the fateful chain of events that will constitute Luke's story," 28. Cf. De Long, *Surprised by God*, who says the songs of praise in the infancy narrative are evoked by the "long awaited, eschatological visitation of God," 138, 152.

15. Though the verb προσεύχομαι often refers to petitionary prayer, it can also refer to doxological prayer (see BDAG, 879). In some instances in Luke, the nature of prayer is ambiguous, such as when Jesus goes into the wilderness to pray (see e.g., 5:16; cf. 3:21, 6:12, 9:18). In other instances, it clearly refers to petitionary prayer (i.e., when Jesus commands his listeners to pray [προσεύχεσθε] for their persecutors [6:28; cf. 11:2]). In the instance of the people outside the temple, it appears that the prayer of the people at least includes a petitionary aspect because the tenor of the infancy narrative as a whole suggests it. As will be seen, Simeon and Anna have both been awaiting Israel's restoration (2:25, 38). Even if the prayer of the people is supposed to be understood as primarily doxological, every doxology implies certain petitions. To praise the deity is to praise the deity for particular attributes that have been revealed through divine action. And the point of recalling past divine action (as will be seen in the Magnificat) is to articulate expectation of future, similar actions on the part of the deity.

16. While Bovon, *Luke 1*, does not see ambiguity in the angel's words, he nevertheless asserts that the answer to Zachariah's personal prayer "converges with the 'prayer'

(πολλοὺς τῶν υἱῶν Ἰσραὴλ ἐπιστρέψει ἐπὶ κύριον τὸν θεὸν αὐτῶν, 1:16). If the praying people are supposed to represent Israel, and if John the Baptist's work will be on behalf of Israel, then perhaps John the Baptist is also the answer to their prayer.[17]

John the Baptist's birth, according to the angel, is a portent of eschatological events. The angel concludes by saying that John the Baptist was prophesied from of old. No prophet is mentioned by name, and there is no formulaic "as it is written" (cf. Luke 3:4), but the angel's words are clearly drawn from Malachi.[18] The angel says that John the Baptist "will go before" the Lord his God "in the spirit and power of Elijah" (καὶ αὐτὸς προελεύσεται ἐνώπιον αὐτοῦ ἐν πνεύματι καὶ δυνάμει Ἡλίου). And he will "turn the hearts of fathers to children and the disobedient to the wisdom of righteousness" (ἐπιστρέψαι καρδίας πατέρων ἐπὶ τέκνα καὶ ἀπειθεῖς ἐν φρονήσει δικαίων). And this will all be done to "prepare for the Lord a people prepared" (ἑτοιμάσαι κυρίῳ λαὸν κατεσκευασμένον, 1:17). The book of Malachi closes with the promise of Elijah's coming. "Behold I send to you Elijah the Tishbite" (ἰδοὺ ἐγὼ ἀποστέλλω ὑμῖν Ηλιαν τὸν Θεσβίτην), who, Malachi says,

---

(προσευχή) of the nation, which according to Luke, awaits redemption (1:68). For, with John the Baptist, the new age dawns for the entire nation (vv. 16—17)," 35.

17. The status of Israel in Luke–Acts has been a matter of perennial debate. Does Luke tell the story of Israel's fulfillment? The repeated references to Israel's restoration might indicate so (see e.g., Luke 2:25, 32, 38; 24:21; Acts 28:20). Or does he narrate their rejection of the Christian announcement and thus their exclusion from the people of God? The ending of Acts has been taken this way (28:23—28). For an overview, see Tyson, *Luke–Acts and the Jewish People*. Richard Bauckham, "Restoration," argues that Luke's audience knew of Israel's hopes (which included "Israel's return to God in repentance, the liberation of Israel from pagan rule and the overthrow of Israel's enemies, Israel's repossession of the land of Israel, the return of the diaspora to the land of Israel, the rebuilding of Jerusalem and the Temple in splendor, the conversion of the nations to the worship of the God of Israel and their pilgrimage to the temple in Jerusalem, the reconstitution of Israel as an independent theocracy under the rule of a legitimate king of the line of David and a legitimate high priest of the line of Zadok, the supremacy of Israel in the world," 435) and that Luke wrote his narrative in such a way as to demonstrate that Israel's restoration had taken place in Jesus. Michael Fuller, *Restoration*, comes to similar conclusions as Bauckham (though he limits Israel's expectations to Israel's re-gathering, the defeat of the nations, and a new temple [12]). The question, however, is how much of Luke's audience would have known about these hopes of Israel. One has to propose an audience well versed in the OT who would look for these common motifs across the OT literature. But to the extant that Israel's hope is an issue in Luke's narrative and that this is a question of eschatology, it seems that Bauckham and Fuller are correct. For more on Luke–Acts and Israel, see e.g., Jervell, *Luke*; Sanders, *Jews in Luke–Acts*; Brawley, *Luke–Acts and the Jews*; Tannehill, "Israel in Luke–Acts"; and Carroll, *Response*, 51–3.

18. Bovon, *Luke 1*, 37–8; Wolter, *Lukasevangelium*, 79–81; Fitzmyer, *Luke*, 1:326–7; Green, *Luke*, 76–78.

will "turn the heart of a father to his son, and the heart of a man to his neigh-
bor" (ὃς ἀποκαταστήσει καρδίαν πατρὸς πρὸς υἱὸν καὶ καρδίαν ἀνθρώπου πρὸς
τὸν πλησίον αὐτοῦ, Mal 3:22–23 [Eng. 4:5–6]). The mention of Elijah and
the turning of fathers' hearts to children make it clear that Luke intends this
passage to be recalled.[19]

But it appears that Luke is using another passage from Malachi. Mal
3:22–23 (LXX) says nothing about preparation, but Mal 3:1 does. Mal 3:1
speaks of a "messenger" (τὸν ἄγγελόν) that God will send, who, he says,
"will prepare the way before my face" (ἐπιβλέψεται ὁδὸν πρὸ προσώπου μου).
The verb (ἐπιβλέπω) of Mal 3:1 is different from the ones used in Luke 1:17
(ἑτοιμάζω, κατασκευάζω),[20] but the meaning is similar.[21] Moreover, Luke
1:17 and Mal 3:1 both speak of someone going "before" the Lord. Again,
the prepositions are different (ἐνώπιον in Luke 1:17; πρὸ in Mal 3:1), but
the thought is the same. It appears therefore that Luke has identified the
messenger of Mal 3:1 with the Elijah of Mal 3:23 (LXX), and is saying that
John the Baptist is he.[22]

The portions of Malachi that Luke reuses come in the context of eschatological announcement. The messenger of Mal 3:1 arrives before the
Lord comes suddenly to his temple: "who can endure the day of his coming? . . . he is like the fire of a furnace," (τίς ὑπομενεῖ ἡμέραν εἰσόδου αὐτοῦ;
3:2). Likewise, Mal 3:22 (LXX) says that Elijah comes before the "great
and manifest day of the Lord" (ἡμέραν κυρίου τὴν μεγάλην καὶ ἐπιφανῆ). It

19. To say that Luke intended this prophecy to be recalled implies that at least
some of Luke's readers would have been familiar with this passage since, again, there is
no formulaic "it is written" or attribution to the prophet. It seems likely at least some
of Luke's audience would have been able to recognize this and other reuses of the OT
since, as commentators have often noted, even the character of Luke's prose in the infancy narrative imitates the LXX. See e.g., Bovon, *Luke 1*, 30; Wolter, *Lukasevangelium*,
70. As Gregory Sterling, *Historiography*, notes, "there is no point in writing in the style
of the LXX unless he thinks the readers would be able to see it and its significance." He
also points out that in order to understand the Nazareth scene in Luke 4:25–27 where
Jesus mentions Elijah and Elisha a "knowledge of the OT greater than what is immediately supplied" is necessary, 375. The same seems to be true of the infancy narratives
generally, and Luke 1:17 in particular.

20. It possible that Luke changes the verb to keep it consistent with his quotation of
Isa 40:3–5 in Luke 3:4, ἑτοιμάσατε τὴν ὁδὸν κυρίου.

21. ἐπιβλέπω is normally translated "to look upon" or "to observe," (see Lust,
Greek-English Lexicon, 168), but here probably has the meaning "to survey" in the
sense that the way is prepared by having looked over it before it is traversed. Only
some hexaplaric editions change the verb to αποσκευασει or ἑτοιμάζει, see Ziegler,
Duodecim Prophetae, ad loc.

22. Luke will explicitly identify John the Baptist as the messenger of Malachi in
Luke 7:27. The OT text-form does not parallel any extant version of the LXX, but it is
nevertheless clear that Luke has Malachi in mind.

appears that Luke intends the eschatological context of his reuse of Malachi to be in view in the angel's announcement, for he says that John the Baptist will go before "him" (αὐτοῦ, Luke 1:17). The referent of the pronoun "him" at this point in the narrative can only refer to the "Lord God" of the previous verse (1:16). The fact that John the Baptist will go before the Lord implies that the Lord is coming. And why else would the Lord come but to judge? Judgment must moreover be the reason why Israel needs to repent (1:16) and prepare (1:17) for the Lord's coming.

There are many similarities between Malachi's announcement about the coming Elijah and Luke's announcement of John the Baptist's birth and vocation, but there is also a potentially significant difference. Where Malachi speaks of preparing the "way" (ὁδὸν, 3:1), Luke speaks of preparing a "people" (λαὸν, Luke 1:17). Luke, it appears, knows that Malachi uses ὁδός since he will speak of the Lord's "way" being prepared in the Benedictus (1:76).[23] If Luke is making an intentional switch in vocabulary here, then it likely connects John the Baptist's annunciation with the people praying at the hour of incense and therefore again evokes a sense of national expectation. John the Baptist's ministry will be for Israel, and Israel's preparation involves not only turning to the Lord (1:16), but also a turning to one another: "the hearts of fathers will turn to their children" (1:17). Familial ties must be reasserted.

The Annunciation of Jesus

Both the form and content of Jesus' annunciation indicate that Jesus is supposed to be seen in the light of John the Baptist. The schematized form of both annunciations creates proportion between the two scenes and thus invites comparison between the two characters. In both annunciations, it is the angel Gabriel who makes the announcement (1:19, 26). In response to both Zachariah's and Mary's alarm at his appearance, Gabriel tells them not to fear (μὴ φοβοῦ, 1:13, 30). Gabriel also tells both characters the names of their future children with the same formulaic καὶ καλέσεις τὸ ὄνομα αὐτοῦ (1:13, 31). And both children, they are told, will be μέγας (1:15, 32). The Holy Spirit also plays a role while both are still unborn. John will be filled with the Holy Spirit from his mother's womb (1:15), and Jesus will be conceived by the power of the Holy Spirit (1:35). Finally, both Zachariah and Mary respond to the angel with a question about the possibility of

23. The term ὁδός in also used in Luke quotation of Isa 40:3–5 (Luke 3:4), which indicates again that Luke knows of the term and that he thinks John the Baptist comes to prepare the Lord's "way."

conception (1:18, 34). The angel takes away Zachariah's speech as a sign to him; Elizabeth's conception is a guarantee to Mary that nothing is impossible for God (1:20, 36–37).

At the center of Jesus' annunciation, as in John the Baptist's, is Israel. And it is in this common focus on Israel that we can see the eschatological outlook of Jesus' annunciation. Gabriel tells Mary that Jesus will "rule over the house of Jacob" (βασιλεύσει ἐπὶ τὸν οἶκον Ἰακὼβ, 1:33). And the throne from which he will rule is the throne of "David his father" (τὸν θρόνον Δαυὶδ τοῦ πατρὸς αὐτοῦ, 1:32). Again, like the annunciation of John the Baptist, it appears that Luke is drawing on the OT. In 2 Sam 7, God promises David that he will raise up a seed (τὸ σπέρμα) after David's death and will "prepare his kingdom" (καὶ ἑτοιμάσω τὴν βασιλείαν αὐτοῦ), which will be established "forever" (εἰς τὸν αἰῶνα, 7:12–13). Luke says that Jesus will sit on the Davidic throne "forever" (εἰς τοὺς αἰῶνας, Luke 1:33).[24] Jesus, according to Luke, is the eschatological Davidic king—his kingdom will have no end (τῆς βασιλείας αὐτοῦ οὐκ ἔσται τέλος, 1:33). Luke has not yet revealed what relationship Jesus' coronation to the Davidic throne has with the anticipated day of the Lord, but at the very least it is clear that Jesus is an eschatological figure.

Whereas the common form and content of the two annunciations suggest that Jesus' character is supposed to be seen in light of John the Baptist, the next scene takes it beyond suggestion. Mary goes to visit Elizabeth, and when Mary's greeting reaches Elizabeth's ear, John the Baptist leaps (ἐσκίρτησεν) in his mother's womb (1:41). In response to the leap, Elizabeth blesses Mary and the child within her (1:42), and then asks, "why has it been granted to me that the mother of my lord should come to me? (καὶ πόθεν μοι τοῦτο ἵνα ἔλθῃ ἡ μήτηρ τοῦ κυρίου μου πρὸς ἐμέ; 1:43). Do Elizabeth's words imply that Mary's fetus is the κύριος for whom John the Baptist will prepare the people (cf. 1:17)? If so, then this would imply that at this early stage in the narrative Luke is already identifying Jesus with the God of Israel. It is, however, likely that the personal pronoun "my" (μου) implies that Elizabeth simply means that Mary's child will be her "master." The angel did indeed say that Jesus will be Israel's king. No conclusions can therefore be drawn from the use of the title. However, it is worth noticing that the title κύριος has up until this point in the narrative been used exclusively to refer

24. Isaiah also looks forward to God placing someone on David's throne (Isa 9:7), which is worth noting given Luke's frequent use of Isaiah throughout his two volumes. For more on Davidic themes in Luke–Acts, see e.g., Strauss, *Davidic Messiah in Luke–Acts*; Bauckham, "Restoration"; and Hahn, "Kingdom and Church in Luke–Acts: From Davidic Christology to Kingdom Ecclesiology" in Bartholomew, Green, and Thiselton, eds., *Reading*, 294–326.

to the God of Israel, and that the next time the title is used is at the end of Elizabeth's address to Mary it again refers to Israel's God: "blessed is the one who believed that that which was spoken to her by the Lord (παρὰ κυρίου) would be fulfilled" (1:45).[25] Regardless of what the title implies at this point in the narrative, it is clear from John the Baptist's leap that he anticipates Jesus. And as a harbinger of the day of the Lord, John the Baptist's fetal leap indicates again that Jesus is an eschatological figure.

The Magnificat

Mary sings after Elizabeth declares her blessed. The song functions as a commentary on what has just taken place and, as such, expands on what has and will take place.[26] Its function can be seen in the way that it connects with the immediately preceding context.[27] John the Baptist leaps for joy (ἐν ἀγαλλιάσει, 1:44), and Elizabeth reacts with doxology and amazement (1:42–43). Likewise, Mary now praises God and declares her own joy at the events taking place (1:46–47). Mary "magnifies" (μεγαλύνει) the Lord (1:46), and she "rejoiced" (ἠγαλλίασεν) in God her savior (1:47). The past tense verb "rejoiced" evidently looks back on Mary's reaction when she received the news that she would conceive by the Holy Spirit.[28]

25. Cf. Rowe's discussion of the term κύριος in this passage, *Christology*, 34–49.

26. As Tannehill notes, Mary's song is like an aria in an opera: it stops the action "so that, through a poetic and musical development exceeding the possibilities of ordinary life, a deeper awareness of what is happening may be achieved," (265), "The Magnificat as Poem," 263–75. Bovon says, "the hymn is intended to interpret the events theologically," *Luke 1*, 64.

27. It seems likely to me that Luke wrote the Magnificat even though there is a broad consensus among scholars that the Magnificat is of pre-Lukan origin and existed before Luke's composition as an independent hymn (Wolter, *Lukasevangelium*, 99). Lukan authorship seems likely because of the numerous textual correlations between the song and its surrounding narrative. As Goulder points out, there are lexical and thematic connections between vv. 46 and 45; 47 and 44; 48 and 38; 49 and 37; 52 and 32; 54 and 33; 55 and 45; see Goulder, *Luke*, 230. See also Green's list of lexical and thematic correlations between the song and the narrative, *Luke*, 98–99. Cf. Johnson, *Luke*, 41. But arguing for or against a pre-Lukan origin is inconsequential, for even scholars who assume pre-Lukan origin (see e.g., Fitzmyer, *Luke*, 1:359; Bovon, *Luke 1*, 64; Brown, *Birth of the Messiah*, 347) all say that the song has been fully incorporated into Luke's narrative. Brown, for example, suggests that Luke added a few of his own lines to the song (348). Even if the song existed before Luke's narrative, once one admits Luke has so reworked it to the extent that he even added his own lines to the song, it seems to me difficult to claim the song's pre-Lukan existence (if it had one) has any bearing on the meaning of Luke's narrative.

28. The past tense verbs in vv. 51–55 have generated much debate among scholars. Are they gnomic aorists? Do they reflect an iterative perfect from the Hebrew? Are the

Mary says that God's name is holy (ἅγιον τὸ ὄνομα αὐτοῦ) and that his mercy is from generation to generation (τὸ ἔλεος αὐτοῦ εἰς γενεὰς καὶ γενεάς, 1:49–50). Both statements imply the present tense state of being verb (εἰμί), but Mary's song then curiously switches from the present tense to the aorist. The beginning of the song also did this, as I noted, but in this second instance there is no apparent correlate to the events of which she speaks in Luke's narrative thus far. She declares that God "has shown strength with his arm" (ἐποίησεν κράτος ἐν βραχίονι αὐτοῦ, 1:51), and that, among other things, God "cast down (καθεῖλεν) the powerful from their thrones and exalted (ὕψωσεν) the humble" and "filled (ἐνέπλησεν) the hungry with good things and sent (ἐξαπέστειλεν) the rich away empty" (1:52–53). Of what past events does Mary speak?

Since there is no clear historical referent in Mary's words, it is possible that no specific past events are in mind here.[29] Mary is perhaps speaking simply of God's iterative saving action throughout history. At the same time, Mary's word choices may indicate that a particular event is in view here. The first phrase in which the switch to the aorist verb occurs (1:51) may be telling. To say "God has shown strength with his arm" (ἐποίησεν κράτος ἐν βραχίονι αὐτοῦ) is similar to some of the OT's rhetoric concerning the exodus.[30] Consider Exod 6:6, "Go say to the sons of Israel saying, 'I am the Lord

---

prophetic aorists of God's future eschatological salvation? Or do they actually represent past events? It seems to me that these are not all mutually exclusive options. As I argue below, it appears to me that Mary recalls past events that represent what God habitually does in order in proleptic celebration of God's future eschatological salvation. For a discussion of these options, see e.g., Bock, *Luke*, 1:154–55.

29. Scholars have called Mary's song a "mosaic" of Scriptures (Brown, *Birth*, 348; Fitzmyer, *Luke*, 1:359). Both Brown and Fitzmyer note many verbal correspondences between Mary's song and Second Temple literature (biblical and non-biblical), but do not spend much time looking for how they fit together in Mary's song. As Goulder, *Luke*, says, it is "not at all illuminating" simply to assert that the song is a mosaic without any attempt to discover what controls the song and its selection of scriptures thematically, 225. Green, *Luke*, says the song is a "collage," but goes on to suggest there are two specific motifs held in balance in the song, that of God as the divine warrior and of God as the one who has favor on the lowly (101–2). Hannah's song (1 Sam 2:1–10), as Fitzmyer, *Luke*, says, is clearly a "principle model" for the song, but says nothing about why it is an appropriate model, 1:359. It seems to me that both Mary's miraculous conception and the fact that the angel told her that Jesus would sit on the Davidic throne make Hannah's song an appropriate model. Hannah's song concludes with mention of God giving strength to "our kings" (τοῖς βασιλεῦσιν ἡμῶν) and exalting the horn of "his anointed" (χριστοῦ αὐτοῦ, 1 Sam 1:10). Hannah's song moreover—like Mary's—speaks of God helping the poor (1 Sam 2:7–8; Luke 1:52–53). But this still does not answer the question of what past salvific event(s) Mary recalls, for Hannah's miraculous conception was hardly such.

30. Bovon suggests that "the prototype of such a [deliverance] by God, with his "arm," is the exodus from Egypt," 62. Cf. Acts 13:17, ὁ θεὸς τοῦ λαοῦ τούτου Ἰσραὴλ

and I will lead you from the power of the Egyptians and I will deliver you out of slavery and I will liberate you ἐν βραχίονι ὑψηλῷ καὶ κρίσει μεγάλη.'" When Moses pleads with God to allow him to enter the land in Deut 3:24, he tells God, "you began to show to your servant your strength and your power and τὴν χεῖρα τὴν κραταιὰν καὶ τὸν βραχίονα τὸν ὑψηλόν."[31]

If Mary's song is intended at this point to recall the exodus, then the other elements, all of which are also controlled by aorist verbs, could be configured to fit in with that theme. Mary says that the proud were "scattered in the thoughts of their hearts (1:51b)." Pharaoh's heart is frequently mentioned in the story of the exodus, and it is always "hardened" (see e.g., Exod 7:13, 22; 8:15; 9:35). The powerful who were cast down from their thrones and the humble who were exalted (1:52) might also be a way of speaking of Israel's liberation from their oppressors. The feeding of the hungry and the sending away of the rich empty might also recall the looting of the Egyptians by the Israelites (Exod 12:35–36). Perhaps most importantly, Mary says that God acts in remembrance (μνησθῆναι) of his mercy for Israel (Luke 1:54)[32] and in fulfillment of what God spoke to Abraham (1:55). The exodus, as well, occurred in remembrance (ἐμνήσθη) of God's covenant with Abraham (Exod 2:24).

If Mary is recalling any particular past event, the exodus is a likely candidate given the emphasis it receives throughout the OT.[33] We would, however, have to imagine a reader who is capable in the OT writings in order to pick up on some or all of the ways Mary's song might recall the exodus. Even if a reader knew of the exodus, the phrase κράτος ἐν βραχίονι αὐτοῦ might not recall the event unless the reader was familiar with the OT text. And even if Luke's readers were versed in the OT, that does not mean that the phrase ἐποίησεν κράτος ἐν βραχίονι αὐτοῦ (1:51) would make a reader think first and foremost about the exodus, for Isaiah uses similar language:

> Behold the Lord is coming with strength and ὁ βραχίων μετὰ κυριείας; behold his wages are with him and his work before him. (Isa 40:10)

ἐξελέξατο τοὺς πατέρας ἡμῶν καὶ τὸν λαὸν ὕψωσεν ἐν τῇ παροικίᾳ ἐν γῇ Αἰγύπτου καὶ μετὰ βραχίονος ὑψηλοῦ ἐξήγαγεν αὐτοὺς ἐξ αὐτῆς.

31. See also e.g., Exod 32:11; Deut 4:34, 5:15, 6:21, 7:8, 7:19, 9:26, 9:29, 11:2.

32. Ezek 20:6 uses the verb ἀντιλάμβανω (ἀντιλάμβανομαι) in reference to God's actions in the exodus, but the significance of this verb in Mary's song is hard to determine since the LXX uses it in numerous other instances without reference to the exodus.

33. The influence of the exodus events in the OT is impossible to underestimate. For just a sampling of references outside of the Pentateuch, see e.g., 1 Sam 10, 12; Ps 78; Isa 11:16; Hos 11:1.

And

> My righteousness draws near quickly, and my salvation will come out as a light, and εἰς τὸν βραχίονά μου the nation will hope; the coastlands wait for me and εἰς τὸν βραχίονά μου they hope. (Isa 51:5)[34]

It is possible that Isaiah is also using language that recalls the exodus in these verses and that Luke's readers would have recognized that, but we cannot be sure.[35] Finally, if the exodus is in view in Mary's song, it is a theological account of those events. To say that the powerful are cast down and the rich are sent away empty is to interpret the exodus events as being about those things. Luke's readers would have not only had to have been versed in the OT, but also would have had to have been able to understand Mary's words as an interpretation of the exodus.

Regardless, Mary's song recalls past salvific events in order to enlighten what is now taking place in the narrative. She sings this song in response both to the annunciation and to Elizabeth's words. And the present events, like the past ones, will lead to salvation (cf. 1:47), which gives the song an eschatological outlook.[36] If Mary is recalling the exodus, it remains unclear whether there will be some correlation between the exodus events and the salvific events that will follow beyond the fact that they are both salvific events.[37] But what does seem to be clear is that Mary's words to describe God's past salvific action—whether they are interpretations of the exodus event or not—will have some correlation to the coming events. When God acts, God debases the powerful and exalts the rich; he fills the hungry and

---

34. See also Isa 51:9, 52:10, 53:1, 59:16, 62:8, 63:5, 63:12.

35. For exodus imagery in Deutero-Isaiah, see e.g., Blenkinsopp's commentary on Isa 48:12–22, *Isaiah 40–55*, 291–96; see also *ABD* 3:490–501.

36. Scholars generally agree that Mary's song looks to the eschatological horizon. See e.g., Brown, who says that the Magnificat is a "commentary on how Mary 'has found favor with God' (1:30) and her resulting eschatological joy." He sees a sense of fulfillment most explicitly in vv. 54–55, *Birth*, 360. Bovon says the song extols "the eschatological fulfillment expected by faith," *Luke 1*, 64. Bauckham, "Restoration," says "the eschatological reversal of status" is the main theme of the Magnificat, 459. Cf. Nolland, *Luke 1—9:20*, 63, 76–77; Seccombe, *Possessions*, 70–83; Hays, *Ethics*, 101–6.

37. Jesus will speak of "the exodus" (τὴν ἔξοδον) which he "is about to accomplish in Jerusalem" (ἣν ἤμελλεν πληροῦν ἐν Ἰερουσαλήμ) with Elijah and Moses on the mount of transfiguration (9:31). For a discussion of this passage, see Ch. 3.

sends the rich away empty.[38] Here we get our first indication that the redistribution of possessions is part of the coming eschatological events.[39]

The Benedictus

The common elements between John the Baptist's and Jesus' annunciations create a sense of proportion between the two scenes. Zachariah's song is similarly proportionate to Mary's. Just as Mary remembered God's help for Israel (1:54), so also does Zachariah (1:68–69). Mary praised God her savior (τῷ θεῷ τῷ σωτῆρί, 1:47), and Zachariah announces salvation: God has "visited and redeemed his people; he raised a horn of salvation" for the house of David (ἤγειρεν κέρας σωτηρίας ἡμῖν ἐν οἴκῳ Δαυὶδ παιδὸς αὐτοῦ, 1:69). And God has done this according to both Mary and Zachariah because of his

38. There is a general consensus among scholars that Mary's song has ethical force. Nolland says, "the socio-political language of vv. 52–53 should not be spiritualized away," *Luke 1—9:20*, 72–73. According to Brown, "the poverty and hunger of the oppressed in the Magnificat are primarily spiritual, but we should not forget the physical realities faced by early Christians," 363. Nickelsburg, "Riches," comes to a similar conclusion as Brown.

39. Some scholars, however, do not see eschatology and ethics in the Magnificat. Charles H. Talbert, *Reading Luke*, thinks the song is ethical in a sense: it is an in-house ethic for the church, but it is not an ethic that advocates for "social action to transform culture, in the sense that we know such action today." Rather, Luke wished to call the poor and sinners into "a community whose life was to embody God's will." One of the reasons Luke is not an advocate for social action, Talbert says, is that Luke believes "only God . . . is able to achieve a just society on the Last Day." He adds that Stanley Hauerwas's claim that "the church therefore does not fulfill her social responsibility by attacking directly the social structures of society, but by being itself it indirectly has a tremendous significance for the ethical form of society," is an accurate description of Luke's view (25). Cf. Stanley Hauerwas, "The Nonresistant Church: The Theological Ethics of John Howard Yoder," in Hauerwas, *Vision and Virtue*.

Horsley, *Liberation of Christmas*, on the other hand believes the song has a "social revolutionary message." One of the reasons he says this is because the song, he claims, is not eschatological, but "historical." To say the song is eschatological serves only to "blunt" its ethical message (113–14). He claims moreover that "there is almost nothing in the Gospels that could be called eschatological in the sense of 'final' or 'end time,'" and that reading "apocalyptic imagery as eschatological is useful for those who want to avoid historical references and particularly the political implications of certain gospel traditions" (xiii).

Whereas Talbert suggests that eschatology undercuts the ethical force of the song, Horsley suggests that the song has ethical force precisely because it is not eschatological. Mary's song, however, uses past tense verbs, which means God has filled the poor and cast the rich away empty before. And if God has done these things before, then one cannot say, as Talbert does, that they are limited to the eschaton. Similarly, Horsley misses the fact that only if God will do these things again and once and for all (in e.g., the eternal rule of the Davidic king [cf. 1:32–33]) can the song's ethics have any force.

mercies (ἐλέους, 1:54, 78). Both Mary and Zachariah envisage the defeat of enemies when God's salvation comes. Whereas Mary calls them the rich and powerful (1:52), Zachariah simply calls them Israel's ἐχθροί (1:71–74). And finally, Mary and Zachariah both claim that God has acted in remembrance of what he spoke to Abraham (1:55, 73). Zachariah's song, in other words, echoes Mary's anticipation of God's eschatological action.

In addition to reiterating the themes of Mary's song, Zachariah's also serves to bring the reader back to John the Baptist's vocation. In 1:76, Zachariah turns to address the infant John the Baptist directly. The angel said that John the Baptist would go in the spirit and power of Elijah (1:17), so Zachariah proclaims that he will be a "prophet of the most high" (προφήτης ὑψίστου, 1:76). And just as the angel said that John's work would be preparatory, so also does Zachariah. But Zachariah uses slightly different vocabulary to describe John the Baptist's preparatory work. Whereas the angel said that John the Baptist would prepare a people for the Lord (ἑτοιμάσαι κυρίῳ λαὸν, 1:17), Zachariah here announces that he will prepare his "ways" (ἑτοιμάσαι ὁδοὺς αὐτοῦ, 1:76). The switch in vocabulary seems to indicate that Luke wants to identify the "ways" of the Lord with the people. Indeed, after Zachariah says that John the Baptist will prepare the Lord's ways, he says that we will "give knowledge of salvation" to the people: προπορεύσῃ γὰρ ἐνώπιον κυρίου ἑτοιμάσαι ὁδοὺς αὐτοῦ, τοῦ δοῦναι γνῶσιν σωτηρίας τῷ λαῷ αὐτοῦ. The infinitives ἑτοιμάσαι and τοῦ δοῦναι are both subordinate to the main verb προπορεύσῃ, which suggests that the two infinitival phrases are parallel. If they are parallel, then it is clear that Luke wants to identify the people with the "way(s)" of the Lord. This will be important to remember when Luke again speaks of John the Baptist preparing the "way" of the Lord when John the Baptist begins his ministry.

Luke brings a momentary sense of closure and completion by having Zachariah reiterate what the angel foretold about John the Baptist. John the Baptist is a sort of *inclusio* to this first sequence of stories in Luke 1. But Zachariah's song also serves to introduce the scenes that follow in the rest of the infancy narrative. Zachariah speaks of a "sunrise from on high to shine on those sitting in darkness and the shadow of death" (ἀνατολὴ ἐξ ὕψους ἐπιφᾶναι τοῖς ἐν σκότει καὶ σκιᾷ θανάτου καθημένοις, 1:78–79). Light comes in the next scene.

The annunciation scenes and their correlating celebratory songs clearly have an outlook to eschatological events. John the Baptist is Elijah who comes before the day of the Lord. Jesus' kingdom will have no end. The content of the first literary section of Luke's Gospel works in tandem with its structure to demonstrate that Jesus is supposed to be seen in the context of John the Baptist. The announcement of John the Baptist's preparatory work frames the announcement of Jesus' advent. John's birth is announced, then Jesus'. A song is sung about Jesus, then about John. Again, the ordering of characters is John—Jesus—Jesus—John. The structure of the passage along with the fact that John the Baptist leaps at the presence of Jesus suggests that it is Jesus for whom John the Baptist will prepare. And in order for John the Baptist to prepare for Jesus, a people must be prepared. This places not only Jesus, but also the people at the center of the eschatological stage.

The Birth of Jesus

Just as the parts of the first literary sequence in Luke 1 mirror each other, so the second literary sequence of Luke 2 mirrors Luke 1. Luke 2 begins, as does Luke 1, with a snapshot of the political landscape (2:1–2). Just as an angel enters the opening scene of Luke 1, so also an angel appears in the opening scene of Luke 2. As in Luke 1, the response to the appearance of an angel is fear (ἐφοβήθησαν φόβον μέγαν, 2:9; cf. 1:13, 30). The angel makes an announcement and gives a sign as evidence of that announcement. Zachariah was made silent (1:22); the angel now tells the shepherds that as a sign (τὸ σημεῖον) they will find Jesus in a manger (2:12). Finally, just as the events of Luke 1 direct the reader's eyes to coming eschatological events, so also do the events of Luke 2.

Joseph and Mary go to Bethlehem, the city of David. If Jesus will sit forever on the Davidic throne (1:32–33), then it is fitting for Jesus to be born in David's hometown. This is perhaps also why Luke chose to include shepherds in his story, since David himself was a shepherd. The eschatological overtones of the passage can already be seen from these small details, all of which recall the promise of Jesus' kingdom having no end (1:33). But there is another more telling theme of eschatological events in the geographical scenes of both Bethlehem and Jerusalem in Luke 2.

That theme is light. Zachariah's song ends on this note: he promises that God's "tender mercy" (σπλάγχνα ἐλέους) will result in the "sunrise" visiting "from on high" (ἀνατολὴ ἐξ ὕψους, 1:78). And this light will shine on those who "sit in darkness and the shadow of death" (τοῖς ἐν σκότει καὶ σκιᾷ θανάτου καθημένοις, 1:79). Jesus is born in Bethlehem and placed in a manger since there is no room in the inn. The scene then moves to a non-descript location not far from Bethlehem. Shepherds, Luke says, are watching their flocks in "watches of the night" (φυλάσσοντες φυλακὰς τῆς νυκτός, 2:8). Does Luke intend the darkness of the night of Jesus' arrival to be understood as symbol of the very darkness Zachariah said people are sitting in? Luke of course intends the reader to understand the darkness literally—it really was nighttime. But that the darkness is also symbolic might be suggested by the fact that light appears the very moment after Luke describes the shepherds' dark watches. The angel of the Lord appears, he says, and "the glory of the Lord shone around them" (δόξα κυρίου περιέλαμψεν αὐτούς, 2:9). It is, of course, natural for light to be associated with divine beings, as it is in all of the Gospels and throughout the NT.[40] But the fact that Luke is careful to mention that the shepherds are in the "watches" of the night (i.e., it is completely dark)[41] seems to indicate that the darkness and light are supposed to be understood in the context of Zechariah's words.[42]

That Zechariah's words are in view in this context is even more likely given the angels' doxology moments later. After the angel tells the shepherds where they will find the infant king, a host of angels appear singing "glory to God in the highest and peace on earth" (δόξα ἐν ὑψίστοις θεῷ καὶ ἐπὶ γῆς εἰρήνη, 2:14). If glory (δόξα) is supposed to be associated with light, and the glory is in "the highest" (ἐν ὑψίστοις), then it appears Luke has had the angels' words play off of Zechariah's. He spoke of the light of sunrise coming from "on high" (ἐξ ὕψους, 1:78). The angels' song, like Zechariah's, also speaks of peace for God's people. Zechariah said that God would lead the people's feet "in the way of peace" (εἰς ὁδὸν εἰρήνης, 1:79). The angels now sing of "peace among those with whom God is pleased" (εἰρήνη ἐν ἀνθρώποις εὐδοκίας, 2:14). With Jesus' birth, eschatological light has begun to dawn.

The shepherds find things just as the angel told them. Luke twice makes reference to the shepherds' eyesight. They say "let us go . . . and see (ἴδωμεν) this matter which has been made known to us by the Lord" (2:15). And after they meet Mary and Joseph with the child, they go glorifying and praising God "for all which they heard and saw (ἤκουσαν καὶ εἶδον, 2:20). The shepherds are eyewitnesses both of the divine light and of the infant Jesus. It is easy to see how the emphasis on light and eyesight fit together

40. See e.g., the Transfiguration scenes in the Synoptics (Matt 17:1–9; Mark 9:2–10; Luke 9:28–36); and John 1:5–14; 2 Cor 4:6; Jas 1:17; Rev 1:16.

41. In addition to stressing the fact that it was the middle of the night when the angels appear, the fact that they are watching in the watches of the night informs the reader why they are awake at such a time.

42. As Bovon, *Luke 1*, points out, "the dawn" (ἀνατολή) spoken of by Zechariah "denotes the appearing of the Messiah, ἐξ ὕψους ('from on high'), his origin." It likely denotes this, he says, because of—among other things—the importance of Num 24:17, which speaks of a star rising for Jacob (ἀνατελεῖ ἄστρον ἐξ Ιακωβ, καὶ ἀναστήσεται ἄνθρωπος ἐξ Ισραηλ) for the Qumran community (see 1QM 11:6–7; CD 7:18–21), 76. Bovon moreover sees the darkness of the Shepherds' watches in connection with Zechariah's words, 86–88. Green, *Luke*, thinks the manifestation of the angels to the shepherds is "reminiscent of Zechariah's Song," 132. Fitzmyer, *Luke*, on the other hand, draws no connection between Zechariah's words and the angels' appearance, 1:395–97; cf. Wolter, *Lukasevangelium*, 127–28.

thematically since light is necessary to be able to see. Sight of God's eschatological salvation symbolized by light is moreover what relates the next scene in Jerusalem with the events of Bethlehem.

Infant Jesus in Jerusalem

Like John the Baptist, Jesus is circumcised on the eighth day (Luke 2:21; cf. 1:59). Mary and Joseph take Jesus to Jerusalem where he is to be presented to the Lord (2:22). It is in Jerusalem at the temple—where Luke's narrative began—that infancy narratives are brought to a close. Just as the infancy narrative began with a godly elderly man and a godly elderly woman in the temple, so it also closes with two similar characters.[43] These two characters again confirm the eschatological outlook of the beginning of Luke's Gospel.

Simeon, Luke says, has been "expecting for the consolation of Israel" (προσδεχόμενος παράκλησιν τοῦ Ἰσραήλ, 2:25), and Anna speaks about Jesus to all those who are expecting for the redemption of Jerusalem (τοῖς προσδεχομένοις λύτρωσιν Ἰερουσαλήμ, 2:38). Just as the narrative began with people praying in the temple, the infancy narrative now closes with people praying.[44] But what resonance would παράκλησιν τοῦ Ἰσραήλ (2:25) and λύτρωσιν Ἰερουσαλήμ (2:38) have with Luke's audience? If Luke's readers were familiar with the OT, then these catch words might again relate Luke's narrative to portions of OT we have already suggested might be in view. Isaiah 40 begins with a command "'comfort, comfort my people,' says God! (παρακαλεῖτε παρακαλεῖτε τὸν λαόν μου, λέγει ὁ θεός, v. 1). In Exod 6:6, God tells Moses to say to the people of Israel, "I will redeem you with an outstretched arm" (λυτρώσομαι ὑμᾶς ἐν βραχίονι ὑψηλῷ). Both of these passages have to do with national formation (or reformation). Exodus 6:6 speaks of the exodus, and Isa 40 speaks of Israel's restoration after having paid double for its sins (Isa 40:1–2). It is likely that at least Luke had Isa 40 in mind given that he will quote Isa 40:3–5 in reference to John the Baptist in Luke 3:4–6. But we cannot be sure that Luke's readers would have been able to pick up on these references.

However that may be, it is clear that Luke, at least in the infancy narratives, has in mind an eschatological restoration of Israel.[45] Even without

---

43. As Bovon, *Luke 1*, points out, Simeon is δίκαιος καὶ εὐλαβής (2:25) like Zachariah and Elizabeth (1:6), 100. And, again, Anna, like Elizabeth, is introduced as a θυγάτηρ of a tribe of Israel (2:36; cf. 1:5).

44. Anna is said to be "fasting and praying" night and day in the temple (2:37).

45. The eschatological tone of Simeon's and Anna's expectation is widely

picking up on potential OT resonances, we cannot escape the fact that Simeon and Anna are hoping for Israel's restoration. Simeon and Anna's hopes moreover correlate with what I have suggested about the opening scenes of Luke's Gospel. The prayer of the people at the hour of incense and the prayer of Simeon and Anna are likely the same.

The scene in the Jerusalem temple functions not only to bring the reader back to the beginning of the narrative, but also to repeat and to confirm the significance of Jesus' birth. As I said above, Simeon's experience mirrors that of the shepherds. Simeon, Luke says, was told by the Holy Spirit that he would not "see death" (μὴ ἰδεῖν θάνατον) until he saw "the Lord's Christ" (ἴδῃ τὸν χριστὸν κυρίου, 2:26). And when he does see the infant Jesus, he embraces him and exclaims in praise to God, "my eyes have seen your salvation" (εἶδον οἱ ὀφθαλμοί μου τὸ σωτήριόν σου, 2:30). Both Simeon and the shepherds are promised a sign, and both see with their own eyes the fulfillment of that sign. They are both eyewitnesses of the coming salvation. Simeon's words moreover again play with the imagery of glory and light. The coming salvation, he says, will be "a light of revelation to the nations, and the glory of your people Israel" (φῶς εἰς ἀποκάλυψιν ἐθνῶν καὶ δόξαν λαοῦ σου Ἰσραήλ, 2:32).

Infancy Narratives: Conclusion

We can therefore see that the infancy narrative has an eschatological outlook, and that this is clear both from the structure and content of the two chapters. Elijah has been born; the day of the Lord is coming. Divine light has begun to dispel the shadows of death with Jesus' birth. At the center of eschatological hope in these two chapters is the hope of Israel. What Luke will make of the hope of Israel in the rest of the narrative is still yet to be seen, but there are already indications that the formation of the eschatological people of God will not be as easy as identifying who is of Israelite blood. Though some are eagerly anticipating God's salvation, John the Baptist must nevertheless prepare God's people. John the Baptist's coming preparatory work implies that the people by and large are currently unprepared. Simeon moreover tells Mary that Jesus will cause the "falling and

---

acknowledged. Nolland, *Luke 1—9:20*, sees the term παράκλησις on Simeon's lips as "rooted in the consolation language which in Isaiah is connected with God's eschatological restoration of his people," 118; Bovon, *Luke 1*, says that the term παράκλησις in 2:25 "has an unmistakably eschatological tenor," 100; cf. Bock, *Luke*, 1:238; Green, *Luke*, 145. Bovon, *Luke 1*, suggests λύτρωσις can denote "eschatological liberation" in a salvation-historical sense that recalls the exodus, 106; cf. Bock, *Luke*, 1:252–53; Green, *Luke*, 152.

rising of many in Israel" (πτῶσιν καὶ ἀνάστασιν πολλῶν ἐν τῷ Ἰσραὴλ, 2:34). Israel as it stands will not be the same Israel once John the Baptist and Jesus have completed their work.

Except for a few indications in the Magnificat, ethics of shared possessions is by and large not a prominent theme in the infancy narratives. We must await John the Baptist's ministry to see ethics come clearly in the context of eschatological proclamation. At the same time, the formation of a people, as has already been noted, is at the center of the infancy narratives. Though possessions do not feature in the infancy narratives, Luke's ethics of possessions, as will be seen, often comes in Luke and Acts around the question of the formation of a people. This is perhaps evidence that Luke is already preparing for his ethics in the infancy narratives.

The Preaching of John the Baptist and Jesus: Luke 3:1—4:44

Structure

Luke 3–4 relates the opening proclamations of John the Baptist and Jesus. The scenes parallel one another in both form and content in a manner analogous to the infancy narratives, which suggests that these two chapters form another digestible literary sequence in Luke's Gospel. The parallelisms moreover suggest that scenes that involve each character (John the Baptist, 3:1–20; Jesus, 3:21—4:44) are structured as smaller literary sequences.[46] As in the infancy narratives, the structure itself appears to hint at the theological themes of the literary section. Various corresponding elements between John the Baptist's and Jesus' first public appearances make their characters parallel and proportionate. In both of their first public appearances, eschatology and ethics are highlighted. But, again as in the infancy narrative, Jesus' character is not simply a mirror image of John the Baptist, nor is his preaching a mere repetition of John the Baptist's. John the Baptist declares eschatological imminence; Jesus declares eschatological arrival.[47]

---

46. Meynet, *Luc*, similarly sees a transition at the baptism scene (151–69), but sees a literary break after Jesus' wilderness temptations that I do not think is there. He sees 4:13 as a conclusion to literary sequence that began with the infancy narratives (see 189–207). Meynet, it appears, fails to see the themes that are carried over from Jesus' baptism and temptations into the scene in Nazareth. Most commentators, like Meynet, see a structural break between 4:13 and Jesus' appearance in Nazareth in 4:14. See e.g., Fitzmyer, *Luke*, 1:524–25; Bock, *Luke*, 1:386–88; Nolland, *Luke 1—9:20*, 183–84; Green, *Luke*, 196–97.

47. The eschatological nature of Jesus' Nazareth pronouncement is, however,

The Isaianic prophecies at the beginning of both John the Baptist's and Jesus' public appearances are the first literary feature that suggests that the literary sequences about each character are both distinct and parallel. The Isaiah quotations that preface their first public appearances in the Gospel are introduced by a formulaic "the book of the words of prophet Isaiah" (ἐν βίβλῳ λόγων Ἡσαΐου τοῦ προφήτου [3:4]// βιβλίον τοῦ προφήτου Ἡσαΐου [4:17]). Both John the Baptist and Jesus moreover come from being ἐν τῇ ἐρήμῳ when they make their first public appearances (3:2, 4:1).[48] Whereas Isa 40:3–5 is quoted only in reference to John the Baptist, Luke puts Isa 61:1–2 on Jesus' own lips, which makes the content of Jesus' and John the Baptist's preaching parallel as well. John the Baptist proclaims a baptism for the ἄφεσις of sins (3:3). Jesus announces through reading Isaiah that prisoners and the oppressed are sent into ἄφεσις (4:18). John the Baptist tells the crowds to share their possessions with the poor (3:11–14); Jesus announces good news for the poor (4:18).[49]

The conclusion of the first smaller literary sequence about John the Baptist is signaled not only by the switch from John the Baptist's to Jesus' character, but also by a summative "and with many other urgings he preached good news (εὐηγγελίζετο) to the people" (3:18). There also appears to be an *inclusio*. John the Baptist's ministry is prefaced by a synopsis of the political landscape, which includes mention of Herod and his brother Philip (Ἡρῴδου, Φιλίππου δὲ τοῦ ἀδελφοῦ αὐτοῦ, 3:1). The scenes about John the Baptist conclude by mentioning both Herod and his brother again. Their second mention explains to the reader why John the Baptist's character recedes from prominence in the narrative: he is arrested for rebuking Herod over the matter of Philip's wife (3:19).

The sequence of stories about Jesus ends similarly to the sequence about John the Baptist. Jesus tells the crowds that it is necessary for him to preach the good news about the kingdom of God in other cities (καὶ ταῖς

---

debated. See p. 58 below.

48. Jesus' genealogy appears to have no counterpart in the scenes about John the Baptist. Luke does remind the reader that John the Baptist is the son of Zachariah (3:2), which might be a deliberate correlation with Jesus' genealogy since at this point in the narrative the reader does not need to be reminded of whose son John the Baptist is. But the length of Jesus' genealogy makes a correlation with a brief mention of John the Baptist's father difficult. It seems best, therefore, simply to say that, again, Luke's narrative resists any totalizing structure. It may be that in having not counterpart in the John the Baptist scenes, Jesus' genealogy indicates Jesus' superiority over John the Baptist.

49. Both quotations of Isaiah are also followed by interactions with the crowd (3:7–17; 4:20–29). It is also worth noting that the two sequences in Luke 3–4 have a moment of overlap, as the two sequences in Luke 1 did. In Luke 1, Mary and Elizabeth meet (1:39–45). In Luke 3–4 John baptizes Jesus (3:21–22).

ἑτέραις πόλεσιν εὐαγγελίσασθαί με δεῖ τὴν βασιλείαν τοῦ θεοῦ, 4:43). Both Jesus and John the Baptist thus continue "to preach" (εὐαγγελίζω, cf. 3:18). The sequence about Jesus is also similarly demarcated by an *inclusio*. Jesus began by going into the desert before appearing in the Nazareth synagogue (4:1–21). At the end of the sequence, Jesus returns to the desert before again going to preach in synagogues (4:42–44).[50]

The sequence of scenes that makes up John the Baptist's ministry in 3:1–20 fits together logically. The crowd responds to John the Baptist's preaching with a question (3:10), which is clearly related to his eschatological announcement (3:7–9). John the Baptist's response to their question then causes them to wonder if he is the Christ, which occasions another announcement of imminent eschatological judgment. But what ties the material about Jesus from 3:21—4:44 together? The cohesion is not as obvious. Two factors seem to draw the material together. One is structural, the other thematic. Structurally, Jesus' opening proclamation is framed on either side by encounters with demonic forces. Before his Nazareth sermon, Jesus is tempted by the devil in the desert (4:1–13), and after the people of Nazareth make an attempt on his life (4:29–30), Jesus again encounters demonic forces in three subsequent scenes. In the first, Jesus casts a demon out of a man in a Capernaum synagogue (4:33–37). Jesus then heals Peter's mother in-law of a fever. The fever is "rebuked" (ἐπετίμησεν) just like the demon was in Capernaum, which makes the healing similar to an exorcism (4:39; cf. v. 35).[51] In a third scene, Jesus heals the masses, again "rebuking" (ἐπιτιμῶν) demonic forces (4:41).

Thematically, the sequence of scenes introducing Jesus' ministry are tied together by the question of whose son Jesus is. When the Spirit comes upon Jesus in his baptism, God says "you are my beloved son" (σὺ εἶ ὁ υἱός μου ὁ ἀγαπητός, 3:22). Jesus' genealogy begins by saying that Jesus was Joseph's "son, as it was supposed" (υἱός, ὡς ἐνομίζετο, 3:23).[52] The genealogy ends with "Adam, the son of God" (τοῦ Ἀδὰμ τοῦ θεοῦ, 3:38). In his temptations, the Devil tells Jesus twice, "if you are the son of God . . . " (εἰ υἱὸς εἶ τοῦ θεοῦ, 4:3, 9). Jesus then declares in Nazareth that the Spirit of the Lord is upon him, which recalls his baptism in which he was called God's son. After

---

50. In 5:1, we are met again with the transitional verb ἐγένετο, which likely signals a transition in the story.

51. Mark only mentions that Jesus took Peter's mother-in-law by the hand, making no mention of the manner in which Jesus healed her (1:29–32).

52. It appears that Bovon, *Luke 1*, misses this connection since he says that the "baptism account, which breaks off sharply, is linked only loosely with the genealogy by v. 23," 136. Contrast Wolter, *Lukasevangelium*, who entitles a section in his commentary running from 3:21—4:13 as "Die Präsentation Jesu als Sohn Gottes," 168–86.

Jesus tells the people of Nazareth that Isaiah's prophecy is fulfilled, they ask, "is this not the son of Joseph?" (οὐχὶ υἱός ἐστιν Ἰωσὴφ οὗτος; 4:22). The sequence then concludes with many demons crying out that Jesus is "the son of God" (σὺ εἶ ὁ υἱὸς τοῦ θεοῦ) when they are cast out (4:41).

The themes of Luke 3–4 thus already begin to emerge from a cursory structural analysis. The fact that John the Baptist is swept off the scene by Herod, coupled with the numerous thematic correspondences between John the Baptist's ministry and Jesus' seems to indicate that, as was the case in the infancy narratives, who Jesus is makes sense in light of John the Baptist.[53] Jesus, the Son of God, anointed with the Spirit, comes on the scene after John the Baptist declares that the Christ is coming to baptize in the "Holy Spirit and in fire" (3:16). That fire is the fire of judgment. Moreover, John the Baptist exhorts the people to share possessions. Jesus then appears announcing good news to the poor. This all seems to indicate not only that Jesus' arrival marks the arrival of eschatological events, but also that the redistribution of possessions is part of those eschatological events.

John the Baptist Preaches Eschatology and Ethics

Eschatology

Luke reintroduces John the Baptist's character by picking him up right where he left him: in the desert (3:2; cf. 1:80). John the Baptist proclaims that eschatological wrath is imminent (3:7)[54] and that his listeners ought therefore to share their possessions (3:11–14). But John the Baptist does not proclaim eschatological judgment alone; he also announces the coming salvation. Luke quotes Isaiah 40:3–5 in reference to John the Baptist. Through his preparatory work, "all flesh will see the salvation of God" (ὄψεται πᾶσα σὰρξ τὸ σωτήριον τοῦ θεοῦ, 3:6; cf. Isa 40:5). Moreover, John the Baptist comes from the desert announcing a baptism of "repentance for the forgiveness of sins" (μετανοίας εἰς ἄφεσιν ἁμαρτιῶν, 3:3). John the Baptist's announcement recalls Zechariah's words that John the Baptist would give the people knowledge of salvation (σωτηρίας) "in the forgive-

---

53. Scholars widely agree that it appears Luke may have changed the wording of the quotation of Isa 40:3–5 precisely to help make this point. Where as the LXX says εὐθείας ποιεῖτε τὰς τρίβους τοῦ θεοῦ ἡμῶν (Isa 40:3), Luke says εὐθείας ποιεῖτε τὰς τρίβους αὐτοῦ (Luke 3:4). Luke may have changed θεοῦ ἡμῶν to αὐτοῦ in order to apply the passage more easily to Jesus. See e.g., Bovon, *Luke 1*, 121; Bock, *Luke*, 1:293; Wolter, *Lukasevangelium*, 158.

54. Not only is the wrath "about-to-be" (τῆς μελλούσης, 3:7), but the "ax is already laid at the roof of the trees" (ἤδη δὲ καὶ ἡ ἀξίνη πρὸς τὴν ῥίζαν τῶν δένδρων κεῖται, 3:9).

ness of their sins" (ἐν ἀφέσει ἁμαρτιῶν αὐτῶν, 1:77). Several other features of John the Baptist's reintroduction recall the infancy narratives, all of which, again, identify John the Baptist as the announcer of eschatological wrath and salvation.[55]

It is perhaps significant that the quotation of Isaiah ends with the reappearance of the trope of sight.[56] All flesh will "see" (ὄψεται) the salvation of God. This, coupled with the fact that the Isaiah quotation begins with an emphasis on hearing (a voice is something that is heard), again recalls the infancy narratives.[57] The shepherds praised God for all they had "heard and seen" (ἤκουσαν καὶ εἶδον, 2:20), and Simeon says that his eyes have seen God's salvation at the sight of the infant Jesus (εἶδον οἱ ὀφθαλμοί μου τὸ σωτήριόν σου, 2:30). The reappearance of the tropes of sight and hearing coheres with John the Baptist's role in bringing knowledge of salvation to the people, for if they hear his voice, then according to the Isaiah quotation, they will see God's salvation. To hear of and to see God's salvation is to have knowledge of it.

But identifying John the Baptist as the voice of Isa 40:3 also makes him the harbinger of the coming wrath. Luke apparently identifies the voice of Isa 40:3–5 with the Elijah of Mal 3:22–23 (Eng 4:5–6), and he has identified this single figure with John the Baptist.[58] If the voice in the wilderness is the same figure as Elijah, and according to Malachi, Elijah comes before the "great and manifest day of the Lord" (ἡμέραν κυρίου τὴν μεγάλην καὶ ἐπιφανῆ, Mal 3:22 LXX [Eng 4:5]), then it makes sense for John the

55. Cf. Ferda, "John the Baptist," 154–88, who argues that Isa 40 would have been understood by at least some of Luke's readers as an announcement of Israel's return from exile. Ferda's conclusions at the very least might confirm my contention that John the Baptist's announcement was not only about judgment, but might also indicate another correlation with the infancy narratives where, again, Simeon and Anna are said to be awaiting the "comfort" and "redemption" of Israel (Luke 2:25, 38).

56. Luke is unique among the Gospel writers in including this part of Isa 40 in reference to John the Baptist (see Matt 3:3; Mark 1:2; John 1:23).

57. Luke's phrase "rough places into smooth ways" is inconsistent with Rahlf's LXX. Whereas Rahlf's LXX says ἡ τραχεῖα εἰς πεδία (Isa 40:4), Luke says αἱ τραχεῖαι εἰς ὁδοὺς λείας (Luke 3:5). It is possible that Luke changed the phrase also to make his quotation consistent with the infancy narrative (προπορεύσῃ γὰρ ἐνώπιον κυρίου ἑτοιμάσαι ὁδοὺς αὐτοῦ, Luke 1:76). But there are sufficient witnesses to suggest that Luke may have inherited this phrase as he has it. See Ziegler, Isaias, ad loc.

58. Mark's Gospel does the same at the very beginning of his Gospel. He begins his Gospel by announcing that what follows is in fulfillment of what was foretold by the prophet Isaiah (1:2), but then goes on to quote Mal 3:1 before Isa 40:3. If Mark inherited the hybrid quotation, then this is evidence that there was some agreement at the time of the Gospel's writing that the voice of Isa 40:3 is the same figure as the messenger of Mal 3:1. For more on Elijah and John the Baptist in Luke, see Rindos, It Is Written.

Baptist to then announce the coming judgment. John asks the crowd, "who told you to flee the wrath that is about to be?" (τίς ὑπέδειξεν ὑμῖν φυγεῖν ἀπὸ τῆς μελλούσης ὀργῆς; 3:7). He goes on to tell them that they must "do works worthy of repentance" (ποιήσατε οὖν καρποὺς ἀξίους τῆς μετανοίας), for they cannot simply assert their Abrahamic heritage to gain salvation (3:8). Those who do not perform works of repentance, he says, will be cast into the fire of judgment: "every tree that does not bear good fruit will be cut down and cast into the fire" (πᾶν οὖν δένδρον μὴ ποιοῦν καρπὸν καλὸν ἐκκόπτεται καὶ εἰς πῦρ βάλλεται, 3:9).

The people are not to rely on their Abrahamic heritage to escape the coming wrath. But that does not mean that God's promise to Abraham has been forgotten. On the contrary, both Mary and Zechariah sang of God remembering his promise to Abraham (1:55, 73). And John the Baptist affirms in his own preaching that Abraham will indeed have children—even if that means raising them from the stones beneath John the Baptist's feet (3:8). This is important to note, for as with the other aspects of eschatological announcement, John the Baptist's preaching is again consistent with the infancy narratives. The only difference is that whereas the infancy narratives announce the restoration of Israel without any qualification, John the Baptist says that the Israel to whom God will fulfill his promise is not simply those who can trace their family tree back to Abraham. The Israelites who will escape the coming wrath and inherit salvation are those who do works worthy of repentance.

Ethics

After announcing the coming judgment, John the Baptist tells the crowd to share their possessions. Ethics follows eschatology. The connection John's ethical exhortations have with the eschatological proclamation leading up to them is made clear by the crowd's question. They ask, "what therefore shall we do?" (τί οὖν ποιήσωμεν; 3:10). The narrative flow demands that this question be seen as an outgrowth of what John the Baptist just said.[59]

59. We can recall here Conzelmann's interpretation of this passage, that John is no longer proclaiming an "eschatological call to repentance," but "timeless ethical exhortation," *Theology*, 102. Fitzmyer, *Luke*, many years later maintained that John the Baptist's ethics lack "eschatological motivation" and is "not related to the coming of the Messiah." He admits that Luke's narrative ordering might color John the Baptist's ethics with eschatology, but John the Baptist's announcement of the end "yields" to a different emphasis. John the Baptist's ethics, Fitzmyer says, is Luke's attempt to relate the kerygma to "ordinary life," 1:465. Bovon, *Luke 1*, like Conzelmann, calls John the Baptist's exhortations "timeless ethical instruction," 123. Nolland, *Luke 1—9:20*, and

But not only that, the crowds ask specifically about what they should do (ποιήσωμεν), which recalls John the Baptist's words. He said that they needed to "do" or "bear" (ποιήσατε) fruit worthy of repentance. Likewise, he said that any tree that "does not bear" (μὴ ποιοῦν) good fruit will be cast into the fire (3:9).[60]

In response to the crowd's question, John the Baptist tells those who have two cloaks to share with the one who has none. The one who has food ought to do likewise (3:11). The scene then progresses with both tax collectors and soldiers asking the same question as the crowd: "what shall we do?" (3:12, 14). John the Baptist's response to these two groups is to do the inverse of what he told the crowd to do. Whereas he told the crowds to share actively with those who have none, he tells the tax collectors and soldiers not to take from those who have. Tax collectors are not to collect "more than that which is assigned" (μηδὲν πλέον παρὰ τὸ διατεταγμένον, 3:13), and soldiers are not to "extort" (διασείσητε) or take by false accusation (συκοφαντήσητε, 3:14).

John the Baptist's ethical exhortations are irreducible to a single command since one commands an action while the other prohibits. Yet, at the root, everything John the Baptist has to say is about possessions and about proper distribution of those possessions. But why focus on possessions in the context of eschatological proclamation? The question cannot yet be answered, but one suggestion presents itself in view of the narrative thus far. John the Baptist's ethics might be consistent with his role of preparing a people for the Lord's coming. John the Baptist, we will recall, was to facilitate the turning of fathers' hearts to their children (1:17). John the Baptist's ethics is an ethics of encounter. His audience must consider their fellow human beings in order to heed his instructions. And the person who shares and the one who receives are, as a result, brought into relationship.[61] Not

---

Green, *Luke*, on the other hand, see John the Baptist's ethics in the context of eschatological proclamation. For Nolland, John the Baptist's ethics answer the question "how, then, is life supposed to be lived in these last moments?" 154. Green says that even though what John the Baptist says one can already find in the OT Scriptures, his ethics are distinguished by its "eschatological edge," 178.

60. Wolter, *Lukasevangelium*, also sees the connection between the verbs, 161.

61. It was widely recognized in the ancient world, as in the modern, that a relationship is formed when possessions are shared. The patron-client relationship in Roman society, for example, has become a common category employed by NT scholars to analyze relationships in NT texts. In the patron-client relationship, the patron "provided legal and financial aid to their clients and received public honor and loyalty in return," Marshall, *Jesus, Patrons, and Benefactors*, 5. I am not saying that Luke was addressing patron-client relationships or any other social convention of the Mediterranean world directly. Rather, the existence of patron-client relationships serve to point out that it is clear that the exchange of goods was understood to be able to create a relationship

taking more than one is assigned to take and not extorting might have a similar effect since not doing these things might prevent fragmentation, the alienation of one from another. Perhaps "nation" is too strong a word to describe what John the Baptist's ethics seek, but the movement of the narrative prevents us from denying that this might be what Luke is implying. Perhaps the point of following eschatology with ethics is that the one who shares is a true child of Abraham, a member of an Israel prepared.

Interpreting John the Baptist's ethics this way assumes that one cannot attain salvation alone.[62] But this is nothing new to Luke's narrative.[63] Again, the angel did tell Zechariah that in order for the people to be prepared, fathers and children must turn to one another even as they turn to the Lord (1:16–17). But none of this is said explicitly. The most that can be said with any assurance at this point is that ethics follows logically from eschatology.

The Christ?

Just as eschatology leads into ethics in John the Baptist's preaching, the narrative then moves from ethics back to eschatology. Luke says that after John the Baptist preached the crowds were "considering all these things in their hearts concerning John, whether he might be the Christ" (διαλογιζομένων πάντων ἐν ταῖς καρδίαις αὐτῶν περὶ τοῦ Ἰωάννου, μήποτε αὐτὸς εἴη ὁ χριστός, 3:15). The fact that the crowd only asks this after John the Baptist's ethical exhortations might be suggestive. Does the crowd

---

between two (or more) human beings. For more on patron-client relationships in Luke–Acts, see Marshall, *Jesus, Patrons, Clients*; and Moxnes, *Economy*. For more on patron-client relationships and the NT, see e.g., Wheatley, *Patronage in Early Christianity*; DeSilva, *Honor, Patronage, Kinship and Purity*; and Neyrey, "God, Benefactor and Patron," 465–92. For more on the extant of Roman patron-client conventions in the ancient world, see Eilers, *Roman Patrons*.

62. That Luke envisions a corporate salvation of the people of God seems to not be given due attention by some commentators. E.g., Bovon, *Luke 1*, says "water baptism seals a personal decision to accept that one's entire life past is under God's judgment, and to wait solely for his forgiveness." Moreover, in John the Baptist's preaching, "the unique eschatological event is no longer the primary issue; the personal responsibility of the individual is underscored," 121. Nolland, *Luke 1—9:20*, says that John the Baptist's preaching is about "individual readiness," 144. To be sure, individual readiness is important for Luke, but it is not the whole picture. It seems to me that Böhlemann, *der Täufer*, is more on point when he says, "es scheint ihm gerade nicht um ein Almosen der Reichen an die Armen zu gehen, sondern um die Solidarität unter den Armen," 179.

63. Corporate salvation is also nothing new to an understanding of Jewish covenant, as indicated by God's election of a nation in the exodus.

think that both John the Baptist's eschatological announcement and his ethical exhortations indicate that he might be the Christ?[64] Jesus' Nazareth sermon might confirm this reading.

John the Baptist's ethics are framed by the warning of eschatological fire. John the Baptist has already warned that those who do not produce good fruit will be "cast into the fire" (3:9). After John the Baptist denies that he is the Christ, he informs the people that the Christ is coming and that he is the one who bears the eschatological tree-cutting ax. He is the one who executes the eschatological harvest. The Christ will "clean out his threshing floor," gathering the grain into his barn and burning up the chaff "with unquenchable fire" (πυρὶ ἀσβέστῳ, 3:17).

Jesus Preaches Eschatology and Ethics

After his wilderness temptation, Jesus comes to Nazareth of Galilee (4:14–16). There, as Luke says was his custom, Jesus enters a synagogue (4:16). He is asked to read Scripture, so he opens to the place where Isaiah says, "the Spirit of the Lord is upon me because he has anointed me to preach good news to the poor" (πνεῦμα κυρίου ἐπ' ἐμὲ οὗ εἵνεκεν ἔχρισέν με εὐαγγελίσασθαι πτωχοῖς, 4:18). The verb ἔχρισέν, a cognate of χριστός, appears to identify Jesus as ὁ χριστός of whom John the Baptist spoke—the Christ, that is, who comes at harvest time save the grain and burn the chaff (3:15–17).[65] Jesus moreover claims that he is anointed (ἔχρισέν) "to proclaim good news to the poor" (εὐαγγελίσασθαι πτωχοῖς). This, too, seems to recall John the Baptist's preaching since he instructed both those who have to share with the poor and the powerful to stop abusing the poor. John the Baptist's ethics, in other words, are indeed "good news" for the poor. If indeed this quotation of Isaiah is intended to recall John the Baptist's preaching, then it might also corroborate what I suggested before. The people wonder if John the Baptist is ὁ χριστός immediately after his ethical exhortations. Jesus' reading

64. The question here is not "what were people expecting of the Messiah in the Second Temple period?" but "what does Luke want his reader to think people expected of the Messiah?" These are two different questions since we cannot assume that Luke was aware of and responding to the diverse expectations concerning the Messiah in the Second Temple period. For more on the Messiah in the Second Temple period, see e.g., Porter, *Messiah*; Chester, *Messiah and Exaltation*; and Collins and Collins, *King and Messiah*.

65. The verb χρίω and its cognates have a wide usage in the ancient world (see TDNT, "χρίω κτλ," 9:493–580). Given that Luke has just had John the Baptist speak of the coming ὁ χριστός, and given that it is best to base word usage on context, it seems that Luke thinks the verb in 4:18 designates Jesus as ὁ χριστός.

of Isaiah might just validate the people's logic.[66] Most importantly, however, it appears that like John the Baptist, Jesus' preaches eschatology and ethics.

If Luke quotes Isa 61:1–2 here in order to recall John the Baptist's eschatological and ethical preaching, then we must first demonstrate that Luke's use of Isa 61:1–2 is careful and deliberate. We must demonstrate, in other words, that the Isaiah quotation is integrated at every level into his narrative.[67] If we can demonstrate that Luke's quotation is careful and deliberate, then we can investigate each part of the quotation, including, for example, what Luke thinks it might mean for Jesus to proclaim freedom to prisoners (κηρύξαι αἰχμαλώτοις ἄφεσιν, 4:18).[68]

66. Cf. Böhlemann, *der Täufer*, 181–84.

67. As Seccombe, *Possessions,* points out in reference to Luke's use of Isa 61, "it is possible for a NT writer to use an OT text with very little regard to its origins, meaning or context," 35.

68. Luke's use of Isaiah in this instance has determined the discussion about the eschatological nature of Jesus' announcement in Nazareth. Fitzmyer, *Luke,* sees the absence of the phrase "and the day of vengeance" (καὶ ἡμέραν ἀνταποδόσεως) from Isa 61:1–2 in Luke 4:19 as indicative of an eschatological shift Luke makes in his theology from earlier Christians. After he reads Isaiah, Jesus claims that "today" (σήμερον) Isaiah prophecy is fulfilled (Luke 4:21). Fitzmyer takes the "today" Jesus speaks of as indicative of the eschatological shift in Lukan theology. Luke has shifted the emphasis from *eschaton* to the *sēmeron*: he has "dulled the eschatological edge of some of the sayings of Jesus," 1:234. Nolland, *Luke 1—9:20,* as well, sees Luke's omission of "the day of vengeance" as part of Luke's characteristic two-stage eschatology: salvation now, judgment later, 1:198. Others, while not necessarily seeing the absence of the phrase as indicative of a shift in Lukan eschatology, think it is a deliberate omission on Luke's part. Bovon, *Luke 1,* says "the day of vengeance would have been inappropriate," 153; Goulder, *Luke,* says Luke wants "to keep the atmosphere positive," 302; Cf. Kimball, *Jesus' Exposition,* 110. Green, *Luke,* says it has probably been omitted "to suppress what would have been taken as a negative aspect of the Isaianic message," 210. Evans and Sanders, *Luke and Scripture,* on the other hand, suggest that the reason Luke omits the phrase is because Luke's audience held to a hermeneutical axiom that can also be seen in the writings of Qumran, namely that the end-time fulfillment of the scriptures meant blessings for the in-group on the one hand, and woe for their enemies on the other. The omission of the "day of vengeance" is Jesus' effort to proclaim blessings on all, not only an in-group. Jesus' omission according to Evans and Sanders constitutes a challenge "to Israel's covenantal self-understanding in any generation." This is why, they claim, the people of Nazareth react the way they do to Jesus' pronouncement, 57–65. All of these arguments, however, are based on what Luke does not say, rather than what he does, which makes these conclusions suspect.

Jesus and Isaiah 61:1–2

If Luke's Greek version of Isaiah 61:1–2 was the same as ours—and according to the best evidence we have, it was[69]—then it appears that Luke has made several changes to his text to suit his purposes.[70] First, he ends the quotation early. Isa 61:2 reads, "to proclaim the acceptable year of the Lord and the day of vengeance, to comfort all those who mourn." Luke cuts out "and the day of vengeance, to comfort all those who mourn."[71] Second, he has removed the phrase "to heal those broken in heart" from Isa 61:1 (ἰάσασθαι τοὺς συντετριμμένους τῇ καρδίᾳ) and replaced it with a phrase from Isa 58:6, "to send in freedom those who are oppressed" (ἀπόστελλε τεθραυσμένους ἐν ἀφέσει). And finally, he changes the final verb of his quotation from καλέω to κηρύσσω.

It appears all of these changes are deliberate manipulations of the text because each one of the changes gives Luke's quotation of Isaiah a structure.[72]

69. It appears that Luke is working foremost with a Greek version. The text and critical apparatus of the Göttingen LXX demonstrates no significant differences with Rahlfs's LXX [only MS 534 changes the infinitive καλέσαι to κηρύξαι, which is likely a result of the influence of Luke's text, as the critical apparatus of the Göttingen text suggests], see Ziegler, *Isaias*. It is because of the method by which Luke includes Isa 58:6 in Isa 61:1–2 that it is most likely that he was using a Greek version. One of the reasons it appears he included Isaiah 58:6 is that it, like Isaiah 61:1, uses the noun ἄφεσις. The noun ἄφεσις that connects the two passages, however, is two different terms in the Hebrew (דְּרוֹר in Isa 61:1 and חָפְשִׁי in Isa 58:6). Since the noun ἄφεσις appears to be key in connecting Isa 58:6 and Isa 61:1, and since this connection is possible only in the Greek, it appears that Luke was primarily using a Greek version of Isaiah.

70. The insights of this section are expounded at greater length in my article "The Hybrid Isaiah Quotation in Luke 4:18–19" in Allen and Dunne, *Ancient Readers*.

71. I say that Luke's quotation of Isa 61:2 ends early because the words "and the day of vengeance" are part of the infinitival phrase καλέσαι ἐνιαυτὸν κυρίου δεκτὸν καὶ ἡμέραν ἀνταποδόσεως.

72. It appears that Luke is concerned with the aesthetics of his scriptural quotations. Luke's quotation of Joel 3:1–5 LXX (2:28–32 Eng) in Acts 2:17–21 offers another example. The Greek versions of the OT Joel 3:3 read "and I will give wonders in the heavens and on the earth" (καὶ δώσω τέρατα ἐν τῷ οὐρανῷ καὶ ἐπὶ τῆς γῆς). Luke's version, however, reads "I will give wonders in the heavens above and signs on the earth below" (καὶ δώσω τέρατα ἐν τῷ οὐρανῷ ἄνω καὶ σημεῖα ἐπὶ τῆς γῆς κάτω, Acts 2:19). Luke makes three adjustments to this phrase: he adds the noun σημεῖα and he adds two prepositions ἄνω and κάτω. It appears that Luke made these changes himself since he will use the words σημεῖον and τέρας together several times in the narrative that follows. In his quotation of Joel, Luke not only adds the noun σημεῖα parallel to the noun τέρατα, which could have easily been done with out making any other adjustments, but he also adds the two prepositions at the end of each clause. The addition of the two prepositions, if nothing else, makes the parallelism more clear. Further study is needed to explore Luke's reuse of Joel 3:1–5, but it appears at the very least that Luke is attentive to the aesthetics of this scriptural quotation.

The final three lines of Luke's reworking of Isaiah are made up of three infinitival clauses (κηρύξαι, ἀποστεῖλαι, κηρύξαι), which are all dependent on the finite verb ἀπέσταλκέν. The final four verbs thus alternate between the two verbs ἀποστέλλω and κηρύσσω, giving it an aesthetic quality:

Luke 4:18b–19
ἀπέσταλκέν με,
  κηρύξαι αἰχμαλώτοις ἄφεσιν
    καὶ τυφλοῖς ἀνάβλεψιν,
  ἀποστεῖλαι τεθραυσμένους ἐν ἀφέσει,
  κηρύξαι ἐνιαυτὸν κυρίου δεκτόν.

Isa 61:1b–2
ἀπέσταλκέν με,
  ἰάσασθαι τοὺς συντετριμμένους τῇ
    καρδίᾳ,
  κηρύξαι αἰχμαλώτοις ἄφεσιν καὶ
    τυφλοῖς ἀνάβλεψιν,
  καλέσαι ἐνιαυτὸν κυρίου δεκτὸν καὶ
    ἡμέραν ἀνταποδόσεως,
  παρακαλέσαι πάντας τοὺς
    πενθοῦντας

The word ἄφεσις moreover makes the central two verbal phrases controlled by κηρύξαι and ἀποστεῖλαι parallel.[73] By replacing the clause about healing the brokenhearted from Isa 61:1 with the one about sending (from Isa 58:6), and by changing the final verb from καλέω to κηρύσσω, Luke creates a more pleasing alternation between the two verbs ἀποστέλλω and κηρύσσω, while connecting and the central two panels via ἄφεσις.[74] Similarly, changing the final verb makes the rotating verb structure possible. The one structural inconsistency is that the first phrase controlled by the infinitive κηρύξαι is a compound phrase: "to proclaim release to prisoners *and* sight to the blind," whereas the second phrase controlled by the infinitive κηρύξαι—the final phrase of the quotation—is not compound. It says only "to proclaim the acceptable year of the Lord." The LXX, on the other hand, has a compound phrase: "to proclaim the acceptable year of the Lord *and* the day

73. Commentators widely agree that the word ἄφεσις is a catch-word that brings the two lines together, though no one discusses why Luke thought it was necessary to import a phrase from a foreign context in the first place. See e.g., Fitzmyer, *Luke*, 1:533. Cf. Seccombe, *Possessions*, 46; Koet, *Five Studies*, 29–30.

74. Isa 61:1 and Isa 58:6 are the only two instances the noun ἄφεσις appears in the Isaian corpus. It also appears that Luke also noticed common themes between the two passages. Isa 58:6 comes in the context of speaking of proper fasts. Isaiah says, "will you call this an acceptable fast?" (Isa 58:5). In Luke's narrative, Jesus had just fasted for forty days before reading Isa 61:1–2 in the Nazareth synagogue (4:1–13). Moreover, the appropriate fast that the Lord looks for according to Isa 58:7 is to "share bread with the hungry and to bring the poor into your house" (διάθρυπτε πεινῶντι τὸν ἄρτον σου καὶ πτωχοὺς ἀστέγους εἴσαγε εἰς τὸν οἶκόν σου). The injunction to share bread with the poor (πτωχοὺς) coheres thematically with Jesus proclaiming good news to the poor (πτωχοῖς) in Nazareth.

of vengeance" (Isa 61:2). The lack of a correlating compound phrase in an otherwise structured quotation is noticeable and hence probably deliberate, as I shall argue below.

While it is possible that Luke is not the one who made these changes to his text and that he took his version of Isa 61:1–2 from a source that had already made these changes, it appears more likely that he is the one who made these changes. This is likely because both the first and the last lines of his quotation of Isaiah fit thematically with the surrounding narrative.

As I said above, Luke knits the literary sequence stretching from Luke 3:21—4:44 together thematically. The theme that unifies it is the question of whose son Jesus is. The first line of the Isaiah quotation fits with the theme of Jesus' sonship. If the first time in this literary sequence Jesus is called the son of God is when he receives the Spirit,[75] then for Jesus to say that the Spirit of the Lord has come upon him is another way to claim that Jesus is the son of God. Reading it this way fits both with the immediate context in which the people of Nazareth question whose son Jesus is and with the end of the literary sequence. When Jesus casts out many demons, they come out crying "you are the son of God" (σὺ εἶ ὁ υἱὸς τοῦ θεοῦ). And the reason they do this, according to Luke, is that "they knew that he was the Christ" (ὅτι ᾔδεισαν τὸν χριστὸν αὐτὸν εἶναι, 4:41). Luke thereby appears to link the titles "son of God" and "Christ."

The final line of Luke's reworked passage from Isaiah, like the first line, also fits thematically with the immediate narrative. The final line says that the one anointed with the Spirit has been sent to "proclaim the acceptable year of the Lord" (κηρύξαι ἐνιαυτὸν κυρίου δεκτόν, 4:19). In the following scene, Jesus says to the people of Nazareth, "a prophet is not acceptable (δεκτός) in his hometown" (4:24).[76] Jesus says this immediately after the people of Nazareth say "is this not Joseph's son?" which implies that they have either missed—or if they understood, doubted—Jesus' claim to be anointed with the Spirit and thereby to be God's son. By not "accepting" the son of God, Luke appears to suggest they might also miss the "acceptable" year of the Lord.

If Luke deliberately ended his quotation on the word δεκτός in order to draw attention to the word, then this can perhaps corroborate the claim that it was Luke himself that made all of the changes to the text of Isa 61:1–2. In the extant Greek versions of Isa 61:1–2, the main verb ἀπέσταλκέν

75. I say "in this literary sequence" because Jesus is called the "son of the most high" (υἱὸς ὑψίστου) in the infancy narrative (1:32).

76. Scholars have noted the reuse of the word δεκτός in the narrative that follows the quotation (Luke 4:24). See e.g., Bovon, *Luke 1*, 153; Fitzmyer, *Luke*, 1:528; Kimball, *Exposition*, 110–11.

is followed by four infinitives (ἰάσασθαι, κηρύξαι, καλέσαι, παρακαλέσαι). By ending on the word δεκτός, Luke excludes the final infinitival phrase controlled by παρακαλέσαι and would have been left with only three infinitives, which would disrupt the literary structure of Isaiah 61:1–2 since the four original infinitives themselves create a structure. The central two infinitives are parallel: both have compound clauses, "to proclaim liberty to prisoners *and* sight to the blind," and "to declare the acceptable year of the Lord *and* the day of recompense." The central two infinitives are also parallel semantically: "to proclaim" (κηρύξαι) has approximately the same meaning as "to declare" (καλέσαι). The first and fourth infinitival clauses are also parallel. Grammatically, both infinitives are followed by substantive participles. Semantically, "to heal those broken in heart," is similar to "to comfort all those who mourn."

Isa 61:1–2

πνεῦμα κυρίου ἐπ’ ἐμὲ,

οὗ εἴνεκεν ἔχρισέν με

    εὐαγγελίσασθαι πτωχοῖς

ἀπέσταλκέν με

    ἰάσασθαι τοὺς συντετριμμένους τῇ καρδίᾳ

        κηρύξαι αἰχμαλώτοις ἄφεσιν

            καὶ τυφλοῖς ἀνάβλεψιν

        καλέσαι ἐνιαυτὸν κυρίου δεκτὸν

            καὶ ἡμέραν ἀνταποδόσεως

        παρακαλέσαι πάντας τοὺς πενθοῦντας

It appears therefore that Luke made all of these changes, as I have said, to create a literary structure in his Isaiah quotation, which it otherwise would not have had after ending the quotation on the word δεκτός.[77]

---

77. It is worth noting that a reader would not have had to investigate the ways in which Luke has manipulated the text in order to get Luke's meaning. Luke's readers, in other words, did not need a scroll of Isaiah in order to see the structure of the quotation and how the quotation fits into the narrative. Scholars who have suggested that Luke's readers would have noticed the absence of the phrase "and the day of vengeance," on the other hand, must suggest that Luke's readers either had a scroll with Isa 61:1–2 on it, or that they knew the passage well enough to realize that one phrase was missing.

Eschatology and Ethics in Nazareth

It thus appears that Luke manipulates his quotation of Isa 61:1–2 in order to integrate it into his narrative. The first and last lines of the quotation clearly connect it with the wider narrative. Jesus also claims to be anointed (ἔχρισέν) with the Spirit of the Lord, which connects him with ὁ χριστός of whom John the Baptist spoke. As the Christ, he proclaims good news to the poor (πτωχοῖς), which again connects Jesus' announcement with John the Baptist's preaching. As we already noted, this alone might indicate that Luke is framing Jesus' ministry with eschatology and ethics. As the Christ, he executes judgment, and as judge, he executes it on behalf of the poor. Those who do not want to be cast in the fire, it appears, ought—among other things—to care about the poor.

If Luke has used his quotation of Isa 61:1–2 for his own purposes, then it is not unlikely that every phrase of the quotation aligns with Luke's purposes. But what does it mean for Jesus "to proclaim liberty for the prisoners and sight for the blind" (κηρύξαι αἰχμαλώτοις ἄφεσιν καὶ τυφλοῖς ἀνάβλεψιν)? And what does it mean for Jesus "to send those who are oppressed in freedom" (ἀποστεῖλαι τεθραυσμένους ἐν ἀφέσει, 4:18)? The literary structure of the quotation might indicate that these two phrases are parallel in meaning. Again, "to send those who are oppressed into liberty" is linked with the previous phrase "to proclaim liberty for the prisoners" via the noun ἄφεσις. Similarly, the structure might also indicate that the main verb ἀπέσταλκέν and the three infinitival phrases subordinate to it are parallel to the other finite verb in the quotation, ἔχρισέν and the infinitival phrase subordinate to it, εὐαγγελίσασθαι πτωχοῖς:

> ἔχρισέν με
> > εὐαγγελίσασθαι πτωχοῖς,
> ἀπέσταλκέν με,
> > κηρύξαι αἰχμαλώτοις ἄφεσιν
> > > καὶ τυφλοῖς ἀνάβλεψιν,
> > ἀποστεῖλαι τεθραυσμένους ἐν ἀφέσει,
> > κηρύξαι ἐνιαυτὸν κυρίου δεκτόν.

If that is the case, then the three infinitival phrases subordinate to ἀπέσταλκέν might expound what it means "to preach good news to the poor."[78]

---

78. Bovon, *Luke 1*, notes that it is possible that εὐαγγελίσασθαι πτωχοῖς is subordinate to ἀπέσταλκέν με and that, in his opinion, this is the more likely reading, 154. But it seems to me more likely that Luke reads the passage as saying that he is anointed to preach good news to the poor given the literary structure I have already pointed out.

If Luke's use of Isaiah in this instance demonstrates him to be a capable user of the Isaian writings, then it is worth considering what "to proclaim liberty for the prisoners and sight for the blind" and "to send those who are oppressed into liberty" might signify in their original context. In Isaiah, both being a prisoner and being blind might refer to being in exile.[79] Isa 5:13, says, for example, "therefore my people become exiles (αἰχμάλωτος) because they did not know the Lord, and the multitude become as of the dead because of famine and thirst for water." Other instances in Isaiah carry a similar meaning.[80] Blindness likewise seems to be a metaphor for exile. Isa 42:16 says, "and I will lead the blind in the way (τυφλοὺς ἐν ὁδῷ) which they do not know, and paths (τρίβους) which they do not know, I will cause them to march; I will make the darkness to them into light, and the crooked into straight (τὰ σκολιὰ εἰς εὐθεῖαν)."[81]

The phrase "to send those who are oppressed into liberty" might also signify the release from exile in the Isaian writings. The verb θραύω appears infrequently in the Isaian corpus, and is nowhere used in the same was as it is in Isa 58:6. But one instance might nevertheless be instructive.[82] In Isa 42:4, God says of the servant that he will "rise and not be oppressed (θραυσθήσεται) until he has established justice on the earth. The passage then goes on to speak of God calling the servant "to open the eyes of the blind and to lead out of bonds those who have been bound and out of the house of prison those who sit in darkness" (ἀνοῖξαι ὀφθαλμοὺς τυφλῶν, ἐξαγαγεῖν ἐκ δεσμῶν δεδεμένους καὶ ἐξ οἴκου φυλακῆς καθημένους ἐν σκότει, 42:7). If the darkness refers to exile, then it might be significant that the verb θραύω appears in this context.

It is one thing to suggest that Luke could have seen the meaning of these terms in their Isaian context. It is, however, another matter to suggest that Luke's readers would also have been able to do the same. It may be that at least some of Luke's educated audience would have been able to see the meaning of these phrases in their original context, but even if they could, we simply do not know if Luke's readers had access to Isaiah. It may very well be that they did, but because we cannot be sure, it is best to rely on what we

79. "By the NT period captives are more likely to have been seen in terms of the overall spiritual-political oppression of Israel, than as literal prisoners," Seccombe, *Possessions,* 58. Cf. Gregory, "Postexilic Exile," 475–96; TDNT "αἰχμάλωτος," 1:195–96.

80. See Isa 14:2, 23:2, 46:2, 52:2.

81. Cf. also Isa 29:18–19, 43:8, 59:10. Blindness as a metaphor for exile makes sense as well if we consider 2 Kings 25:7. The Babylonians conquer Jerusalem. The king is captured, and the Babylonians slaughter King Zedekiah's sons in front of him just before they gouge his eyes out and take him blind into captivity.

82. The only other instances of the verb are in Isa 2:10, 19, 21.

do know Luke's audience did in fact have. Is there, in other words, a way to make sense of prisoners, blindness, and those who are oppressed within Luke's own narrative? It appears that there is.

Ἄφεσις is proclaimed to the "prisoners" (αἰχμαλώτοις) according to Isaiah 61:1. Luke evidently wants to draw attention to the word ἄφεσις and what it signifies because, again, he integrates Isa 58:6 into his quotation as a catch-word. And it is Luke's emphasis on the term ἄφεσις that provides a possible link with his broader narrative. Interestingly, both previous instances of the term in Luke's narrative, as with the other aspects of Jesus' proclamation, appear in reference to John the Baptist. Zechariah proclaimed that John the Baptist would give "knowledge of salvation" to the people "in the forgiveness (ἐν ἀφέσει) of their sins" (1:77). When John the Baptist preaches in the regions of the Jordan, he proclaims a baptism "for the forgiveness (εἰς ἄφεσιν) of their sins" (3:3). This might mean that to be a "prisoner" (αἰχμαλώτοις) and to be one that is "oppressed" (τεθραυσμένους) is be one who is not free from and is oppressed by sin.

Giving sight to the blind fits with a trope that has already appeared a couple of times in Luke's narrative. The shepherds and Simeon both "see" salvation (2:20, 30). Similarly, Isaiah 40:3–5 speaks of all people being able to "see" God's salvation through John the Baptist's preaching (3:6). Eyesight is also emphasized immediately after Jesus reads the Isaiah scroll in Nazareth. Luke says that "all eyes" (πάντων οἱ ὀφθαλμοὶ) in the synagogue were "looking steadfastly" (ἀτενίζοντες) at him (4:20). Jesus then tells his audience that the Isaian writing is fulfilled "in their ears" (4:21). Hearing, we will remember, repeatedly appears in conjunction with the trope of eyesight. The shepherds glorified God because of all they had "heard and seen" (ἤκουσαν καὶ εἶδον, 2:20). And John the Baptist was a voice in the wilderness (3:4). To give sight to the blind, in other words, might mean to give them the ability to see God's salvation.[83]

Every element of Luke's quotation of Isa 61:1–2 therefore recalls various tropes and themes already established in the narrative. Jesus is the anointed one (ἔχρισέν) who, according to John the Baptist, will execute judgment. Jesus proclaims good news to the poor, just as John the Baptist did. Jesus is the one who will open people's eyes to see eschatological salvation. And Jesus proclaims the forgiveness (ἄφεσις) of sins. But two matters are left to be resolved.

First, if the verb ἀπέσταλκέν and its three infinitival clauses are parallel to the previous main verb, ἔχρισέν, and its accompanying infinitival phrase,

83. Jesus will, of course, also heal the eyes of those who are literally blind (see e.g., Luke 7:22), but up until this point in that narrative, eyesight is used only in reference to seeing God's salvation

does this mean that the "poor" (πτωχός) are not the literal poor?[84] The parallels with John the Baptist's preaching resist such a conclusion. But it also appears that Luke does not understand "prisoners" (αἰχμαλώτοις), the "blind" (τυφλοῖς), and the "oppressed" (τεθραυσμένους) in a purely metaphorical sense either. Luke believes people are actually oppressed by the devil, as Jesus' temptations and exorcisms indicate. Luke likewise believes Israel really does sit oppressed in the shadow of death (cf. 1:79). And Luke believes that though people can see with their eyes, they are in fact blind to what is right in front of them. The son of God stands before the people of Nazareth and they marvel, but they see him only as the son of Joseph.

Second, if Luke made all of the changes to his quotation of Isaiah, leaving in what he thought needed to be said and adjusting the structure to make it aesthetically pleasing (and thereby adding a phrase from a foreign context), is there any significance to the fact that Luke left out the second phrase of the compound sentence in Isa 61:2, "and the day of recompense" (καὶ ἡμέραν ἀνταποδόσεως)? Does its omission mean that Luke wants to mute the theme of judgment at this point in his narrative?[85]

There are several reasons this is likely not the case. First, as I have already pointed out, it appears that Luke ends his quotation of Isaiah where he does, not because he wants to exclude what comes thereafter, but because he wants to emphasize the word δεκτός. Second, we would have to suggest not only that Luke's readers were very capable in the OT scriptures, but also that they would have taken the omission of the phrase to be significant for what Luke wanted to say. It may well be that Luke's readers were very capable in the OT Scriptures, but it seems unlikely that any reader would have taken a lot of stock in what Luke did not say—especially

---

84. There is some debate over who the "poor" of whom Jesus speaks are precisely because, as Bovon, *Luke 1*, notes, "Luke hardly understands the various categories of people [in the quotation] in a merely literal sense," 154. Fitzmyer, *Luke*, thinks the term πτωχός functions here to introduce Luke's focus on "this social class," 1:532. Bock, *Luke*, on the other hand, does not exclude a "material and political" interpretation of the word, but thinks that "poor should be understood first and foremost as a way of speaking of those "who are open to God," 1:408–9. Green, *Luke*, says it is neither the spiritually poor nor the materially poor; rather it refers to a category of people who had diminished honor—i.e., those who were "excluded according to normal canons of status honor in the Mediterranean world," 211. Seccombe, *Possessions*, sees the term as an alternative moniker for oppressed Israel, 39 (cf. 24–43); cf. Hays, *Ethics*, 107–10. As I argue in the following, it seems best to me to see each categorical term Luke includes in the Isaiah quotation in light of his narrative thus far. Given that John the Baptist has already had to say something about giving to the poor, there is no way to exclude an economic understanding of the term "poor."

85. On this matter, see fn. 62 above.

when there is way to account for what he did say (i.e., that he wanted to emphasize the word δεκτός).

Finally, there is also the scene that follows. The people of Nazareth do not respond positively to Jesus' proclamation. Rather than recognizing him for who he is, they say "is this not the son of Joseph?" It may appear in isolation as an innocent question, but in context, it is incriminating. The last character in Luke's narrative to doubt that Jesus is the son of God was the devil ("*If* you are the son of God . . . " [4:3, 9]).[86] The people of Nazareth then also attempt to throw Jesus from a cliff, which might also be an eerie reminder of the devil's final temptation. The devil, too, wanted Jesus to fall from a height (4:9). However, it is ultimately Jesus' own words that convict them. If he, the prophet, is not acceptable (δεκτός), then it seems that the people of Nazareth might also be missing the acceptable (δεκτός) year of the Lord. If they reject Jesus the Christ then what will happen to them when the Christ does what he comes to do? So far, they do not appear to be the grain that will be gathered into his eschatological barn.

Conclusion

The first task of this chapter was to establish that Luke brings eschatology together with ethics in the opening proclamations of his Gospel. This connection should now be clearly established. John the Baptist tells the crowd that judgment is coming, so they ask what they must do. John the Baptist counsels that they distribute possessions. The crowd's question "what shall we do (τί οὖν ποιήσωμεν;)?" (3:10) is clearly connected to John the Baptist's eschatological warnings, for, as I pointed out, John the Baptist had just told them to "bear" (ποιοῦν) good fruit (3:9). After John the Baptist counsels sharing possessions, the people wonder if he is the Christ. I have suggested that this might indicate that Luke wants the reader to think that the Christ was expected to say the kinds of things John the Baptist was saying.[87] Jesus' Naza-

86. There is some disagreement among scholars on how the people of Nazareth's question is supposed to be understood. Green, *Luke*, suggests that the question is not a negative response to Jesus' announcement. It is in fact a response of "admiration" and their error is a "joke between narrator and reader," 215. Talbert, *Reading*, suggests that the question represents a negative response. The people are in effect saying "he is our boy, therefore he should do miracles among us," 56. Bovon, *Luke 1*, on the other hand, seems to suggest that the question is neutral, representing the fact that they have come only half way in their faith, 155. But, as I have pointed out, this question comes in a series of stories about whose son Jesus is. In this context, the reader knows that the people of Nazareth have completely missed what Jesus has just said.

87. In order to substantiate such a claim, however, we would have to, among other things, identify who Luke wanted his audience to think was expecting a Messiah of this

reth sermon might just confirm this. The Christ, the one who will execute the judgment, says that he comes first and foremost for the poor. The numerous connections Jesus' reading of Isaiah has with the narrative, seen most clearly in the announcement of ἄφεσις, necessitates that we see Jesus' Nazareth announcement in the context of John the Baptist's preaching.

The second task of this chapter was to show how John the Baptist's and Jesus' opening proclamations fit within Luke's larger narrative. Eschatological proclamation is what ties the opening proclamations to the narrative. This can be seen in the tropes that link the various scenes together. Sight and hearing is one of these tropes. The shepherds glorify God for all they had "seen and heard" (2:20). Simeon rejoices because his eyes have now seen salvation (2:30). John the Baptist is the voice in the wilderness that announces that all flesh will be able to see God's salvation (3:6). And when Jesus tells the people of Nazareth that the Scripture is fulfilled in their ears, all eyes are fixed steadfastly on him (4:20–21).

In addition to sight and hearing, the other theme that ties the opening proclamations to Luke's first four chapters is the question of the people of God. The infancy narrative imagines an expectant Israel. John the Baptist tells the crowds that Abraham will have children. Jesus is rejected in his homeland by his own people. As I have suggested, the question of the eschatologically prepared people of God may be what connects eschatology with ethics in Luke's theology. The people, it appears, must share possessions because in order to be a people prepared, they must not turn to God alone, but also to one another. If this is the logic of eschatology and ethics in Luke's theology, then we can see how even though ethics does not feature prominently in the infancy narratives (except for perhaps in the Magnificat), it is part of Luke's theological interests from the beginning of his narrative.

Luke's paralleling of John the Baptist's and Jesus' characters throughout the first four chapters of his Gospel indicates that John the Baptist sets the context in which to understand Jesus. If this is especially the case in their opening proclamations, then it seems likely that eschatology and ethics will continue to be themes of Jesus' public ministry.

---

nature and investigate why Luke would want them to think that.

3

Received and Rejected in Luke

The Way to Jerusalem

Introduction

J ohn the Baptist's preaching in Luke's Gospel is both eschatological and ethical. As I argued in Chapter Two, Jesus' first public announcement is likewise both eschatological and ethical, and makes sense in light of John the Baptist's preaching. Luke parallels John the Baptist's and Jesus' characters throughout the first four chapters of his Gospel. I suggested that since the paralleling culminates in their similar opening proclamations, it would seem likely that Jesus' public ministry will continue to emphasize eschatology and ethics. The task of this chapter is to demonstrate that Jesus' public ministry does indeed continue to highlight these two, apparently related, matters.

This chapter focuses on three passages: the sending of the Seventy (10:1–12); Jesus' accusations against the Pharisees (16:1–31); and the Zacchaeus episode (19:1–10). Much larger passages, however, form the context within which these pericopae should be seen. As we saw in Chapter Two, Luke writes in digestible sequences that are bound together by common lexemes, imagery, and themes. I will investigate how each of these passages fit within their larger literary sequences to see how Luke has integrated eschatology and ethics into his narrative.[1]

The first and third passages come at the beginning and the end, respectively, of the so-called "Travel Narrative" of Luke's Gospel, and thus at key

---

1. The larger passages are Luke 9:28—10:24; 16:1–16; and 18:31—19:48. On the character of Luke's digestible literary sequences, see p. 29 above.

transition points in Luke's Gospel.[2] Since these are passages come at structurally significant markers, they seem particularly promising places to consider the relationship of ethics and eschatology in Luke's Gospel. The sending of the Seventy sets the tone for Jesus' mission to Jerusalem, and his entry into Jerusalem suggests one of the reasons Luke thinks Jesus and his mission are rejected. The middle passage (16:1–31) merits attention because of Jesus' declaration that appears in the middle of two parables about money: "the Law and the Prophets were until John, since then the kingdom of God is proclaimed and each person forces one's way into it" (16:16).[3]

Each of the passages I address moreover reuses themes, imagery, and lexemes from John the Baptist's opening proclamation. In the sending of the Seventy, Jesus calls his mission a harvest (10:2), a metaphor John the Baptist used of the coming Christ's vocation (3:17). In Luke 16, John the

2. While scholars agree that the Travel Narrative begins in 9:51, they disagree about where it ends. Nolland, *Luke 9:21—18:34*, suggests Jesus' final prediction of his death in 18:31–34 as the concluding pericope, 529; both Fitzmyer and Bovon locate it at 19:28, when Jesus begins his final ascent to the city (see Fitzmyer, *Luke*, xv, 2:1242; Bovon, *Luke 2*, xi, 605); Bock places it at the conclusion of Jesus' foretelling of the destruction of Jerusalem in 19:44, 2:959. Apart from the fact that each one of these scholars' configuration misses the structure of Luke 18:31—19:44 I have identified (see p. 90 below), it seems to me that Luke does not intend formally to conclude his "Travel Narrative." Rather, what is important is simply that Jesus arrives in Jerusalem. The term "Travel Narrative," we should remember, is itself a modern scholarly construction. Perhaps scholars disagree about where the Travel Narrative ends because Luke never thought of the central section of his Gospel as a travel narrative with a clear beginning and ending. Indeed, the reader already knows that Jesus is on his way to Jerusalem before 9:51 when Luke says that Jesus will accomplish his exodus in Jerusalem (9:31). Remembering the fact that the term Travel Narrative is not something that the author of the Gospel came up with might relieve some scholars' angst about why for supposedly having a travel narrative, there is almost no perceivable journey taking place between 9:51 and 19:48 (see e.g., Nolland's discussion, *Luke 9:21—18:34*, 527–28). Thus, when I say that the story of Zacchaeus is important because it comes at "end" of the Travel Narrative, I mean only that it comes immediately before Jesus comes to the place where Luke said he would in 9:31 and 9:51.

3. Other passages in Luke's central section might also demonstrate the relationship between eschatology and ethics. Luke 12:13–46 and 14:1–35 in particular might be relevant. In order to add to my argument, however, these passages must be placed within the digestible narrative sequences Luke has constructed. The parable of the rich fool (ἄφρων, Luke 12:16–21), for example, cannot be read apart from Jesus' question about who the faithful and wise (φρόνιμος) manager is (12:42). And Jesus' challenge that a disciple must complete (ἐκτελέσαι) what he started in 14:30 cannot be read apart Jesus' promise to finish (τελειοῦμαι) his work in Jerusalem (13:32). On both of these passages, cf. Meynet, *ad loc*. Not noticing these structural arrangements (and those outlined below) is a weakness of previous studies on Lukan ethics. On the Luke 12, for example, see e.g., C. Hays, *Ethics*, 125–39; and Seccombe, *Possessions*, 135–58; Cf. Rindge, *Jesus' Parable*; on Luke 13–14, see e.g., C. Hays, *Ethics*, 129–39; Seccombe, *Possessions*, 97–114.

Baptist is invoked by name (16:16). Zacchaeus is called a son of Abraham for divesting himself of wealth (19:9), a title that John the Baptist himself was evidently willing to give to those who behaved in Zacchaeus's manner (cf. Luke 3:8–14).

The Sending of the Seventy: Luke 9:28—10:24

Introduction

At the beginning of Luke 10, Jesus, ὁ κύριος, selects and sends messengers, two by two, before his face (πρὸ προσώπου αὐτοῦ) into every place he himself is about to go (10:1).[4] The textual witnesses are divided over whether Jesus sent out seventy or seventy-two messengers. The likely significance of the number—whether it was seventy or seventy-two—is addressed below (see p. 78). Without assuming that it was the original figure, I will use the number seventy to designate those sent out in Luke 10:1. When Jesus sends out his messengers, they are to have no money, no bag for extra possessions, and no shoes. He sends them in haste: "greet no one on the way" (10:4). And whether or not they are accepted in all the "places which he himself was about to go" there is a singular message: the kingdom of God has come near (ἤγγικεν ἐφ' ὑμᾶς ἡ βασιλεία τοῦ θεοῦ, 10:9, 11).[5]

4. It might be significant that Luke calls Jesus ὁ κύριος right before Jesus tells the disciples to pray to the κύριος of the harvest (10:2). Jesus and the Lord of the harvest appear not to be one and the same person precisely because Jesus tells his disciples to pray to the Lord of harvest that he might send out workers. Yet, Luke calls Jesus ὁ κύριος and Jesus is the one sending workers out (cf. v. 7). Jesus, ὁ κύριος and ὁ κύριος of the harvest thus appear simultaneously to be different people and the same person. If Luke intends an identification of the Lord of the harvest with Jesus, then Jesus appears more and more likely to be ὁ κύριος announced and prepared for by John the Baptist (cf. Luke 3:4). The other elements of John the Baptist's character and preaching Luke recalls in this context might corrborate this suggestion (see below). Cf. Rowe, *Christology*, 133–36.

5. The phrase might have been taken from Mark 1:15 (ἤγγικεν ἡ βασιλεία τοῦ θεοῦ). Here we can see that those who think Luke has tempered Mark's eschatology because Jesus' quotes the prophet Isaiah (Luke 4:17–19) in the Nazareth synagogue instead of saying "the kingdom of God has drawn near" may not have looked far enough (cf. p. 58 above). Simply because Luke has rearranged his sources and delayed the use of the phrase until the sending of the Seventy(-two) does not mean it is any less important of a proclamation to him. Indeed, precisely because he puts it at this key moment in the narrative—the moment after he has set his face to Jerusalem to die there—evidences the importance of the phrase for Luke's purposes. Fitzmyer notes that the episode in Luke 10 is "important for Lucan eschatology" (*Luke*, 2:845). According to him, Luke has here retained the futurist orientation from the earliest Christian kerygma. Yet, Fitzmyer maintains that Luke has shifted his eschatological emphasis from the *eschaton* to *sēmeron* (*Luke*, 1:234). This one episode does not prove Fitzmyer's analysis is

Jesus sends out the Seventy looking for hospitality. The people they visit are to receive (δέχωνται, 10:8) them, sharing shelter and food. To those who share their possessions, the message of the nearness of the kingdom is good news. To those who do not receive (μὴ δέχωνται, 10:10), on the other hand, it is a message of coming judgment: "it will be better for Sodom in that day than for that city," (10:12). The "day" to which Luke refers is the day of judgment (cf. 10:14). The Seventy are therefore on an eschatological mission. And evidence of their hearer's readiness to receive ὁ κύριος is their hospitality—their sharing of goods with poor messengers.[6]

Structure

The sending of the Seventy comes in a sequence of related pericopae that stretches from Jesus' transfiguration (9:28) to his rejoicing at the return of the Seventy (10:24).[7] After the transfiguration and immediately before the sending of the Seventy, Luke makes a major transition in the narrative. In 9:51, Luke says that the days of Jesus "taking up" (τῆς ἀναλήμψεως) had been fulfilled. Jesus takes a prophetic stance towards Jerusalem: he "sets his face" (αὐτὸς τὸ πρόσωπον ἐστήρισεν) to go to the city and prophesy against it.[8]

Two related tropes knit the sequence of scenes together in Luke 9:28—10:24.[9] The first trope is sight and hearing, which, as we saw in Chapter Two, is a pervasive motif in the first four chapters of Luke's Gospel. In 9:28, Jesus takes three disciples up a mountain with him to pray. There, Jesus is transfigured. Moses and Elijah appear and speak with him about the ἔξοδος

---

incorrect, but it does make it less convincing.

6. I say that they receive ὁ κύριος, leaving the identity of ὁ κύριος ambiguous, for as Jesus himself says, to receive him is to receive the one who sent him (10:16).

7. Luke may also have wanted the mission of the Twelve (9:1–6) to be recalled in the sending of the Seventy since Jesus' instructions to both groups are similar. It is moreover possible that the rejection (οὐκ ἐδέξαντο αὐτόν, 9:53) by a Samaritan village (κώμην, v. 52) is supposed to be recalled when Martha receives Jesus (Μάρθα ὑπεδέξατο αὐτόν) in a certain village (κώμην, 10:38). For more on the possible connections, see Meynet, Luc, ad loc. These sort of connections again confirm that no structural analysis should be totalizing and that Luke may have intended multiple configurations of his narrative. Cf. p. 29 above.

8. Cf. Ezek 6:2, υἱὲ ἀνθρώπου, στήρισον τὸ πρόσωπόν σου ἐπὶ τὰ ὄρη Ισραηλ καὶ προφήτευσον ἐπ᾽ αὐτά.

9. Commentators generally seem to miss the way in which Luke has knit these scenes together. This is most likely because commentators wish to emphasize the transition in 9:51 when Jesus turns his face toward Jerusalem. See e.g., multivolume commentaries that break the volumes at 9:51 such as Fitzmyer, Luke; Bovon, Luke 1 and Luke 2; and Bock, Luke, 9:51 is a transition in the narrative, but as I demonstrate below, the break is not as radical as commentators often make it out to be.

he is "about to fulfill in Jerusalem" (ἤμελλεν πληροῦν ἐν Ἰερουσαλήμ, 9:31). A cloud then appears, and from it God's voice says, "this is my chosen one, listen to him!" (αὐτοῦ ἀκούετε). After Jesus casts a demon out of a boy in the next scene (9:37–43), Jesus turns to his disciples and says "put these words in your ears" (θέσθε ὑμεῖς εἰς τὰ ὦτα ὑμῶν τοὺς λόγους τούτους). He says that the son of man is "about to be given into the hands of men" (ὁ γὰρ υἱὸς τοῦ ἀνθρώπου μέλλει παραδίδοσθαι εἰς χεῖρας ἀνθρώπων, 9:44). Both the emphasis on hearing and the verb μέλλω recall the transfiguration scene. The ἔξοδος Jesus is "about to" (μέλλω) accomplish will evidently involve him being given into the hands of men. But though the disciples have heard these things, they do not understand (9:45).

When Jesus sends out the Seventy, he tells them, "the one who hears you, hears me, and the one who rejects you, rejects me; the one who rejects me, rejects the one who sent me (ὁ ἀκούων ὑμῶν ἐμοῦ ἀκούει, καὶ ὁ ἀθετῶν ὑμᾶς ἐμὲ ἀθετεῖ· ὁ δὲ ἐμὲ ἀθετῶν ἀθετεῖ τὸν ἀποστείλαντά με, 10:16). And when they return, he tells them, "I say to you that many prophets and kings desired to see what you see and did not see, and to hear what you hear and did not hear" (λέγω γὰρ ὑμῖν ὅτι πολλοὶ προφῆται καὶ βασιλεῖς ἠθέλησαν ἰδεῖν ἃ ὑμεῖς βλέπετε καὶ οὐκ εἶδαν, καὶ ἀκοῦσαι ἃ ἀκούετε καὶ οὐκ ἤκουσαν, 10:24).

Related to the trope of hearing/sight is the second trope of acceptance/rejection. Just before Jesus sets his face to Jerusalem (9:51) and immediately after he foretells his death, the disciples quarrel about who is the greatest. Jesus sets a child before them and says "he who receives this child in my name, receives me, and he who receives me, receives the one who sent me" (ὃς ἐὰν δέξηται τοῦτο τὸ παιδίον ἐπὶ τῷ ὀνόματί μου, ἐμὲ δέχεται· καὶ ὃς ἂν ἐμὲ δέξηται, δέχεται τὸν ἀποστείλαντά με, 9:48). Immediately after Jesus sets his face toward Jerusalem, Luke says that Jesus sent messengers "before his face" (πρὸ προσώπου αὐτοῦ, 9:52). Messengers go to a village so as "to prepare" for him, but, Luke says, the town does not receive him (οὐκ ἐδέξαντο αὐτόν, 9:53).

When the Seventy go to all the places where Jesus himself was "about to go" (ἤμελλεν αὐτὸς ἔρχεσθαι, 10:1), Jesus instructs them to heal the sick among those who "receive" (δέχωνται) them and proclaim that the kingdom of God "has come near" upon them (ἤγγικεν ἐφ' ὑμᾶς ἡ βασιλεία τοῦ θεοῦ, 10:9). The announcement is the same to those who "do not receive" (μὴ δέχωνται, 10:10–12). Finally, just before Jesus sends out the Seventy, he tells them—as we have already seen—"the one who hears you, hears me, and the one who rejects you, rejects me; the one who rejects me, rejects the one who sent me (ὁ ἀκούων ὑμῶν ἐμοῦ ἀκούει, καὶ ὁ ἀθετῶν ὑμᾶς ἐμὲ ἀθετεῖ· ὁ δὲ ἐμὲ ἀθετῶν ἀθετεῖ τὸν ἀποστείλαντά με, 10:16). This saying demonstrates how the trope of hearing/seeing relates to the trope of acceptance/rejection. To hear is to receive; not to hear is to reject.

These two recurrent tropes give the sequence of scenes an eschatological outlook. Hearing and sight recall the hearing and sight of eschatological salvation in the first four chapters of the Gospel. The acceptance/rejection motif functions similarly. It will be worse for those who do not receive Jesus' messengers than it will be for Sodom (10:12), since to reject them is ultimately to reject the one who sent Jesus (10:16).

These two tropes may give the entire sequence an eschatological outlook, but why are they important for Luke's purposes at this point in his narrative? Part of the answer is that, as we have already noted, Luke is playing with imagery he has already used in his Gospel. As we shall see, Luke plays with other imagery in this passage he has already employed. But it appears that Luke also wishes to characterize Jesus and the messengers he sends by reusing these tropes. Luke, it appears, wants to characterize Jesus as the prophet like Moses foretold in Deut 18:15.[10] And it appears that he wants to characterize the messengers as those who, like John the Baptist, prepare the way of the Lord.

Jesus, the Prophet Like Moses

The first clue that Luke wants to characterize Jesus as the prophet like Moses foretold in Deut 18:15 is that when he is on the mount of transfiguration, Jesus speaks with Moses and Elijah about the ἔξοδος he is "about to accomplish in Jerusalem" (ἤμελλεν πληροῦν ἐν Ἰερουσαλήμ, 9:31).[11] The term ἔξοδος can simply mean "departure" in the sense that someone "departs" when they die.[12] And this meaning must be retained since it appears that death is what Jesus has in mind when moments later in the narrative he will tell his disciples that he is "about to be given into the hands of men" (μέλλει παραδίδοσθαι εἰς χεῖρας ἀνθρώπων, 9:44).[13]

10. For more on the prophetic characterization of Jesus in Luke–Acts, see McWhirter, *Rejected Prophets*.

11. A fuller analysis of Luke's use of the Old Testament in Luke 9:28-10:24 can be found in my article "Luke's Use of the Old Testament in the Sending of the Seventy(-Two): A Compositional Study" in Nielsen and Müller, *Luke's Literary Creativity*, 160-184.

12. BDAG, 350–51.

13. Most commentators agree that Jesus' exodus is not the journey itself, but his death and subsequent resurrection and ascension. See Nolland, *Luke 9:21—18:34*, 499–500; L.T. Johnson, *Luke*, 153, 156; Goulder, *Luke*, 441; Fitzmyer, *Luke*, 1:800; Green, *Luke*, 382. That his exodus includes his ascension is probably signified in the use of the

But Luke might also intend a secondary, symbolic meaning. To speak of what Jesus is going to accomplish in Jerusalem as an ἔξοδος might also recall Israel's liberation from Egypt.[14] This might be the case first and foremost because his ἔξοδος is something that he is about to "fulfill" (πληροῦν). One does not normally speak of "fulfilling" one's death. Secondly, we can also consider the events in Jerusalem that immediately precede his death. Jesus eats the Passover with his disicples the night before he is killed. When he addresses his disciples over the meal, he tells them that he will not eat the meal again with them until "it is fulfilled (πληρωθῇ) in the kingdom of God" (22:16). The use of the verb πληρόω along with the mention of the kingdom of God (which the Seventy will announce soon after the transfiguration, 10:9, 11) might indicate Luke is picking up language from the transfiguration when Jesus is commemorating Israel's liberation in the moments before he completes his ἔξοδος. But even if Luke intends to characterize Jesus' death as an exodus that recalls Israel's liberation, none of this is stated explicitly in the transfiguration scene. The reader must await the progression of the narrative to see the fuller meaning of the term ἔξοδος.

Luke may also be characterizing Jesus as the prophet like Moses through the use of Deut 18:15 itself, the passage in which Moses tells Israel that God will some day raise up a prophet like him.[15] God's words from the cloud might be taken from the passage:

οὗτός ἐστιν ὁ υἱός μου ὁ ἐκλελεγμένος, αὐτοῦ ἀκούετε.

This is my chosen son, listen to him!   Luke 9:35

---

hapax legeomenon ἀνάλημψις in Luke 9:51. Jesus is referred to as ὁ ἀναλημφθείς after his ascension in Acts 1:11 (cf. Acts 1:2). This, however, cannot be known in 9:51. The reader is thus forced to await what his ἀνάλημψις consists of.

14. According to Green, Luke has in the Travel Narrative "built up a series of reminiscences, some linguistic, and others conceptual, of Exodus material, but he has done so in a way that mimics the Deuteronomic portrayal of Exodus journey as a series of speeches delivered by Moses to the people of God," *Luke*, 398. This follows the work of Moessner, *Lord of the Banquet*, who says Luke "tells his readers in 9:1–50 that the story of the Prophet like Moses is about to unfold in a New Exodus journey to the promised salvation," 69; cf. C.F. Evans, "The Central Section of St. Luke's Gospel" in Nineham, *Studies in the Gospels*, 37–54. However much one chooses to see exodus traditions influencing Luke's construction of Luke 9 and the Travel Narrative, one must at the very least admit, as Nolland does, that Jesus' exodus will not be entirely analogous to the ancient Israelites', for the exodus Jesus will accomplish is something he will go on alone, not something on which he will lead other people, see Nolland, *Luke 9:21–18:34*, 500.

15. Scholars have recognized the likely influence of Deut 18:15 on Luke 9:35. See e.g., Bovon, *Luke 1*, 379–80; Fitzmyer, *Luke*, 1:803; Wolter, *Lukasevangelium*, 354; Nolland, *Luke 9:21–18:34*, notes the possible influence, but does not think the language should be pressed for a Moses typology: "Everything serves the end of getting Jesus listened to!" 502.

προφήτην ἐκ τῶν ἀδελφῶν σου ὡς ἐμὲ ἀναστήσει σοι κύριος ὁ θεός
σου, αὐτοῦ ἀκούσεσθε.

The Lord your God will raise a prophet from out of your brother
like me, listen to him! Deut 18:15

These words also appear in Mark, one of Luke's sources (see Mark 9:7),
which might mean that Luke is simply preserving his source material. But
Luke is clearly using his sources reflectively. Luke preserves the scene from
Mark in its general details: God speaks from a cloud to Jesus on a mountain
top. These preserved elements might evoke Moses' experience (cf. Mark 9:7)
since Moses, too, ascended a cloudy mountain where he heard God's voice
(Exod 19.9–16, cf. Deut 18.16).[16] It might also be significant that Moses
himself is on the mountain with Jesus (Luke 9:30; cf. Mark 9:4). It is reasonable to think that Luke noted the similarities in the transfiguration scene
with Moses' experience and added the term ἔξοδος (which Mark does not
have) since it will serve his purposes in the coming narrative.[17]

16. Exod 19.9, 16: "Behold I myself come to you in a pillar of cloud (νεφέλης) in
order that the people might hear what I speak to you (ἵνα ἀκούσῃ ὁ λαὸς λαλοῦντός μου
πρὸς σὲ) . . . and on the third day near dawn there was a voice and lightening and a dark
cloud on Mount Sinai."

17. After the transfiguration scene, Luke tells a story of the disciples being unable to
cast a demon out of a boy. Jesus responds to the news of the disciples' inability saying, "o
faithless and twisted generation!" (ὦ γενεὰ ἄπιστος καὶ διεστραμμένη, 9:41). The words
Luke puts on Jesus' mouth might be another instance where he is trying to characterize
Jesus as the prophet like Moses from Deut 18:15. Jesus' words look very similar to Moses' words in Deut 32:5. Moses called Israel a "twisted and perverted generation" (γενεὰ
σκολιὰ καὶ διεστραμμένη) in his final song to the nation (31.30—32.47; cf. Moessner,
Banquet, 63–64). These words moreover come immediately after the author of Deuteronomy says "Moses spoke in the ears of all the assembly of Israel the words of this song
until the end," (Deut 31:30). The reappearance of the trope of hearing may have motivated Luke's choice of the words from Deut 32:5. Luke has the term ἄπιστος where Deut
32:5 has σκολιά. Luke may be following Mark in the choice of words (cf. Mark9:19),
but the context of Deuteronomy might itself allow ἄπιστος to be seen as a synonym
of σκολιά. Moses says to the Israelites that they are a γενεὰ σκολιὰ καὶ διεστραμμένη
immediately after Moses describes God's character. God's works, Moses says, are 'true'
(ἀληθινὰ), and he is 'a faithful God' (θεὸς πιστός) and 'not unrighteous' (Deut 32.4). The
force of Moses' words appears not only to be what he says, but also the order in which
he says them: the Israelites' character is opposite to God's, and this is put into stark relief
by its juxtaposition with God's character. If this is the case, then it seems likely that Luke
could think ἄπιστος was an appropriate synonym for σκολιά. Moreover, the Markan
Jesus calls the disciples only a "faithless generation" (ὦ γενεὰ ἄπιστος, 9:19), which may
demonstrate that Luke has modified Jesus' words to make them more easily recall Deut
32:4. It is, of course, also possible that Luke took the phrase over from Matthew if
he was indeed using him as a source since Matthew has the same compound phrase
(ἄπιστος καὶ διεστραμμένη, Matt 17.17). But this does not exclude the possibility that
Luke is still using Deuteronomy as a source since he continues to reuse Deuteronomy

A third instance in which Luke may be characterizing Jesus as the prophet like Moses comes at the moment when Jesus sets his face toward Jerusalem. Luke says, "sent messengers before his face" (ἀπέστειλεν ἀγγέλους πρὸ προσώπου αὐτοῦ, 9:52). Luke's words might be intended to recall Exod 23:20:

> καὶ ἀπέστειλεν ἀγγέλους πρὸ προσώπου αὐτοῦ. καὶ πορευθέντες εἰσῆλθον εἰς κώμην Σαμαριτῶν ὡς ἑτοιμάσαι αὐτῷ.

> And he sent messengers before his face. And going they went into a village of Samaria to prepare for him. Luke 9:52

> Καὶ ἰδοὺ ἐγὼ ἀποστέλλω τὸν ἄγγελόν μου πρὸ προσώπου σου, ἵνα φυλάξῃ σε ἐν τῇ ὁδῷ, ὅπως εἰσαγάγῃ σε εἰς τὴν γῆν, ἣν ἡτοίμασά σοι.[18]

> And behold I send my messenger before your face, in order to keep you in the way, so that he might lead you into the land, which I prepared for you. Exod 23:20

In addition to the sending of messengers before his face, the verb ἑτοιμάζω makes it likely that Luke is reusing Exod 23:20. But most importantly, the words of Exod 23:20 are spoken to Moses, which would seem to indicate, again, that Luke is characterizing Jesus as the prophet like Moses.

We may have to propose an audience versed in the passages and motifs Luke employs in this section in order to make plausible the claim that Luke intended through these several scenes to characterize Jesus as the prophet like Moses for his audience. But, Luke will reference Deut 18:15 explicitly in Acts 3:22–23, both identifying the foretold prophet like Moses as an eschatological figure and claiming that Jesus is he.[19] Acts 3:22–23 demonstrates both that Luke was familiar with the passage and that it was an important passage to him. It moreover demonstrates that even if Luke's audience did not see the ways in which the sequence of scenes begins to identify Jesus

---

in the next moment of the narrative whereas Matthew does not (see Matt 17.22–23).

18. As I shall note below, the verse also looks very much like Mal 3:1—ἰδοὺ ἐγὼ ἐξαποστέλλω τὸν ἄγγελόν μου, καὶ ἐπιβλέψεται ὁδὸν πρὸ προσώπου μου, καὶ ἐξαίφνης ἥξει εἰς τὸν ναὸν ἑαυτοῦ κύριος, ὃν ὑμεῖς ζητεῖτε, καὶ ὁ ἄγγελος τῆς διαθήκης, ὃν ὑμεῖς θέλετε· ἰδοὺ ἔρχεται, λέγει κύριος παντοκράτωρ. Mal 3:1 is itself likely recalling Exod 23:20. However, the appearance of ἑτοιμάζω in Luke 9:52 makes it more likely Luke is thinking here first of Exod 23:20. Scholars generally miss this as a reuse first and foremost of Exod 23:20 and instead appeal directly to Mal 3:1. See e.g., Fitzmyer, *Luke*, 1:828; Green, *Luke*, 404; Nolland, *Luke 9:21—18:34*, 535; Bock, *Luke*, however, thinks that a reference to Mal 3:1 is "less than clear," 2:969.

19. For more on this passage, see Ch. 4 of this study.

as the prophet like Moses, they would nevertheless eventually find out that there was such a foretold prophet and that—again—Jesus is he.

Messengers Like John the Baptist

As I already mentioned, the moment Jesus turns his face toward Jerusalem where he will accomplish his ἔξοδος, he sends messengers before him to prepare for his arrival (9:51–52). As we also already noted, Luke's words appear to be a reuse of Exod 23:20, which characterizes Jesus as the prophet like Moses. But it appears that Luke may intend a double scriptural reference here since the words also look very similar to Mal3:1, which itself is a reuse of Exod 23:20.

> ἀπέστειλεν ἀγγέλους πρὸ προσώπου αὐτοῦ. καὶ πορευθέντες εἰσῆλθον εἰς κώμην Σαμαριτῶν ὡς ἑτοιμάσαι αὐτῷ Luke 9:52

> ἰδοὺ ἐγὼ ἐξαποστέλλω τὸν ἄγγελόν μου, καὶ ἐπιβλέψεται ὁδὸν πρὸ προσώπου μου Mal 3:1

As I argued in Chapter Two, Luke references Malachi, including Mal 3:1, in John the Baptist's annunciation.[20] And, as the Zechariah's song about John the Baptist said, his role would be to go before the Lord "to prepare his ways" (ἑτοιμάσαι ὁδοὺς αὐτοῦ, 1:76).

In addition, the Lukan Jesus himself has already quoted a passage of Scripture that looks very similar to Mal 3:1 and Exod 23:20 in reference to John the Baptist. Immediately before Jesus calls John the Baptist "great" (μέγας) and says that ὁ μικρότερος is still greater (μείζων) than John the Baptist, and immediately before he compares John the Baptist to a child, he says that John the Baptist is "he of whom it is written,"

> ἰδοὺ ἀποστέλλω τὸν ἄγγελόν μου πρὸ προσώπου σου, ὃς κατασκευάσει τὴν ὁδόν σου ἔμπροσθέν σου.

> Behold I send my messenger before your face, he will prepare the way before you. Luke 7:27

The quotation is not entirely consistent with the extant Greek versions of Mal 3:1,[21] and appears to be reliant on Mark's quotation of the passage (Mark1:2). But it nevertheless seems that Luke intends the passage to be

---

20. Scholars have generally recognized that Luke intends to recall John the Baptist's ministry in 9:52. See e.g., Bovon, *Luke 2*, 7; Wolter, *Lukasevangelium*, 370; Nolland, *Luke 9:21—18:34*, 535; Green, *Luke*, 404–5.

21. See the Göttingen LXX, Ziegler, *Duodecim Prophetae, ad loc.*

attributed to Malachi since he has clearly applied Malachi's prophecies to John the Baptist in the infancy narratives. Regardless of where the quotation comes from, it is clear from Luke's narrative that it is applied to John the Baptist and that its reuse in 9:52 characterizes Jesus' messengers as those who carry on John the Baptist's preparatory work.[22]

The mission of the Seventy thus comes in the context of a carefully constructed and richly symbolic narrative. Jesus, the new prophet like Moses, is on an ἔξοδος. He sends messengers before his face, who, like John the Baptist, prepare the people. And the tropes of hearing/sight and acceptance/rejection highlight these characterizations of both Jesus and his messengers.

The Seventy

If Luke intends to characterize Jesus as the prophet like Moses, then we can make sense of why Jesus sends the number of messengers that he does in 10:1. The manuscript tradition is split over whether Jesus sent seventy or seventy-two,[23] but the original number is irrelevant because, whether it was seventy or seventy-two, the number again characterizes Jesus as the prophet like Moses.[24] In Numbers 11, God instructed Moses to select seventy elders to help him bear the burden of the people (v. 16). Now, Jesus, as the new Mosaic prophet, does the same. The likely reason the number seventy-two

22. It is worth noting that Luke says it was specifically a village of Samaritans to which Jesus sends his ἀγγέλους (9:52). To speak of Samaria might bring to mind the prophet of Samaria *par excellence*, Elijah (see 1 Kgs 17:1-21:29). If to speak of John the Baptist is to speak of Malachi's Elijah (cf. Luke 1:17), then it makes sense to invoke Samaria here. Immediately following rejection in the Samaritan village, Luke puts the words of 2 Kgs 1:10, 12 on James and John's lips. They want to call fire down from heaven as Elijah did (Luke 9:54). They evidently think that they have the spirit and power of Elijah as Jesus sends them before his face to prepare.

23. See e.g., Bovon, *Luke 2*, 26; Fitzmyer, *Luke*, 2:845; Bock, *Luke*, 2:994; Metzger,"Seventy or Seventy-Two Disciples?" 299–306.

24. Bock, *Luke*, says there is no symbolism in the number, 2:944 (cf. Wolter, *Lukasevangelium*, 377); Nolland, *Luke 9:21—18:34*, suggests the table of nations in Gen 10 which has seventy in the MT and seventy-two in the LXX is in view and rejects an allusion to Num 11 because "Luke is less likely . . . [to] suggest that Jesus, like Moses, had a limited capacity to cope with the situation in which God had placed him," 549–50 (cf. Bovon, *Luke 2*, 26); Fitzmyer, *Luke*, considers both Num 11 and Gen 10 as possibilities, 2:846. But, as Marshall, *Gospel of Luke,* points out, if the number was intended to represent the table of nations of Gen 10, then it only did in a pre-Lukan tradition that Luke chose not to develop. If Luke was intending to say that the nations were in view, then he would not have sent them out two by two, which makes them thirty-five pairs, 415. Gen 10 moreover never explicitly counts the nations in the MT or LXX, which would make it less likely that either Luke or a later scribe thought this is what the number was supposed to represent.

is equally part of the manuscript tradition is because of the ending of Num 11. Two men, Eldad and Medad, who were not invited to be part of the original Seventy also received the Spirit and prophesied in the camp (Num 11:26–30). Luke may have counted them, or a later manuscript copyist may have counted them,[25] but, either way, the Seventy(-two) represent Jesus' action to present himself as the prophet like Moses.[26]

Luke says that Jesus sends the Seventy πρὸ προσώπου αὐτοῦ (10:1). As we have already noted, this language is simultaneously reminiscent of God's words to Moses in Exod 23:20 and of John the Baptist's ministry. If the Seventy, like the original messengers who went to Samaria (9:52), are carrying on the work of John the Baptist, we can now see why this characterization is important for Luke's purposes. Jesus tells his messengers that he sends the Seventy out into a harvest (θερισμὸς, 10:2).[27] This harvest is necessary, Jesus says, because "the kingdom of God has drawn near" (ἤγγικεν ἡ βασιλεία τοῦ θεοῦ, 10:9, 11). And the harvest comes before judgment: it will be worse for the city that rejects Jesus' messengers than for Sodom (10:12). All of this recalls John the Baptist's announcement about the coming χριστός. John the Baptist said that ὁ χριστός comes to carry out a harvest. He would have a

25. It is worth noting that Luke has established that those who are not part of the chosen group can also be part of the prophet's mission. In Luke 9:49–50 Luke tells of John saying that some others who were not included in Jesus' immediate following. Jesus responds, "do not prevent (μὴ κωλύετε) them, for he who is not against us is for us" (9:50). Similarly, in Num 11, Joshua son of Nun asks Moses to prevent (κώλυσον) Eldad and Medad from prophesying (11:28). Moses, like Jesus, refuses (11:29). Marshall, *Luke*, thinks this explanation is "forced," but does not explain why he thinks it is, 415.

26. If the number of messengers that Jesus sent out has significance then is there also significance in sending them two by two? Luke might in this instance be recalling the Sodom traditions when two angels were sent ahead of God's judgment to the city (Gen 18–19; esp. 19:1). Luke both mentions Sodom explicitly (10:12) and calls Jesus messengers ἀγγέλους (Luke 9:52; cf. Gen 19:1). Later interpreters moreover interpreted the sin of Sodom as inhospitality (see Ezek 16:48–49; Wis 19:1–16; Josephus, *Ant.* 1.194–200; Philo, *On Abraham* 119–66; Heb 13:2; *T. Levi* 14:6; *T. Naph.* 3:4, 4:1; *T. Benj.* 9:1; *Jub.* 16:5–9, 20:5–6; cf. Jipp, *Hospitality*, 145), which may have made it a likely narrative for Luke to draw upon in this instance. The author of the Wisdom of Solomon moreover parallels Sodom's sins with Egypt's sin against the Israelites before the exodus, which would make the reuse of Sodom imagery fit with the broader context of Luke's narrative. If Luke is indeed drawing on the Sodom narrative, then this again shows Luke's interest in bringing eschatology and ethics together. Cf. Green, *Luke*, 416; Goulder, *Luke*, 462; Jipp, *Hospitality*, 190.

27. Nolland, *Luke 9:21—18:34*, says the use of harvest imagery "draws its force as an image for the eschatological calling of people into the kingdom of God" from the OT (e.g., Mic 4:11–13; Isa 63:1–6; Jer 25:30–31; Joel 3:13 and Isa 27:12–13), 550–51; cf. Bock, 2:995, fn. 16. This may be so, but a reference to John the Baptist's preaching is more likely the primary referent since John the Baptist's preaching is so central to Luke's narrative.

winnowing fork in his hand, and he would separate the grain from the chaff (Luke 3:17). The grain would be gathered into his barn, but the chaff will be burned with "unquenchable fire" (πυρὶ ἀσβέστῳ, 3:17). Sodom, we should remember, was consumed by fire from heaven (Gen 19:24).

As it did in John the Baptist's preaching, the ethics of shared possessions appears in the context of eschatological proclamation. Jesus sends his disciples out poor. And three times Luke emphasizes the importance of hospitality on the part of the cities Jesus' messengers visit. Jesus tells them to speak peace to any house they come upon, and if a son of peace is there, he will receive them, placing food and drink before them and giving them a place to stay (10:5–7).[28] Likewise, whatever city receives (δέχωνται) them will give them food and shelter (10:8–9). Those who do not receive (μὴ δέχωνται) are evidently those who do not give them food and shelter. The messengers in the final instance are to shake the dust off of their feet as a sign of those cities' divine rejection on the last day (10:11).

Summary: The Seventy

At a key transition in his narrative Luke again brings eschatology and ethics together. Jesus sets his face to Jerusalem where he will accomplish his ἔξοδος. At the moment of the turning of his face, Luke characterizes Jesus as the prophet like Moses foretold in Deut 18:15. His messengers go before him, doing the preparatory work like John the Baptist, announcing the nearness of eschatological events. Those who are ready for the coming judgment share their possessions with the poor. The two characterizations of Jesus and his messengers overlap thematically via the two tropes that bind the broader narrative together. The people must hear the prophet like Moses. And to hear him, they must receive his messengers with hospitality.

The Law and the Prophets and
the Kingdom: Luke 16:1–31

Introduction

In Luke 16 Jesus again preaches eschatology and ethics. As he did in Nazareth, he tells his listeners that the kingdom is now proclaimed: "the Law and the Prophets were until John, since then the kingdom of God is

---

28. The title "son of peace" (υἱὸς εἰρήνης) might recall Zachariah's prophecy in reference to John the Baptist about the peoples' feet being guided "into the way of peace" (εἰς ὁδὸν εἰρήνης, Luke 1:79).

proclaimed and everyone forces his way into it" (ὁ νόμος καὶ οἱ προφῆται μέχρι Ἰωάννου· ἀπὸ τότε ἡ βασιλεία τοῦ θεοῦ εὐαγγελίζεται καὶ πᾶς εἰς αὐτὴν βιάζεται, 16:16; cf. 4:17–21, 43).[29] Jesus says this immediately after he criticizes the Pharisees for being "lovers of money" (16:14). Jesus' eschatological pronouncement moreover comes in the context of two parables concerned with the use of possessions. An unjust manager makes friends by reducing debts (16:1–9), and a rich man is condemned to fiery torture because he ignored the poor (16:19–31).

But why does Jesus appeal to the Law and the Prophets? And what does it mean to "force one's way" into the kingdom? As we shall see, the parables on either side appear to shed light on the saying. To "force one's way" into the kingdom, it appears, is to use one's possessions to secure entry into it.[30] And the Law and the Prophets are invoked because they corroborate Jesus' directive to make friends with unrighteous mammon.

Structure

Luke 16 comes in the context of Jesus' explaining his association with tax collectors and sinners. At the beginning of ch. 15, Luke says that the Pharisees and the scribes were "grumbling" (διεγόγγυζον) because Jesus was receiving and eating with such people. Jesus then tells three parables about lost things being found (15:3–32), culminating in the parable of the prodigal son, all of which explain in part his association with sinners. Even though there is a small transition between the end of final parable of Luke 15 and the parable of the unjust manager (Jesus turns to address his disciples, 16:1), Jesus' parable about the unjust manager in Luke 16:1–9 appears to

29. Luke likely sees Jesus' reading of Isaiah in the Nazareth synagogue as the announcement of the kingdom since his summary of Jesus' continued preaching ministry at the end of that literary sequence recalls the Nazareth sermon through the reuse of several lexemes. After Jesus heals many (4:40–41), Luke says Jesus said to his hearers "it is necessary for me to preach (εὐαγγελίσασθαί) the kingdom of God (τὴν βασιλείαν τοῦ θεοῦ) because for this I was sent (ἀπεστάλην)." Luke then says that Jesus was "proclaiming (κηρύσσων) in the synagogues of Judea" (4:43–44). The verbs εὐαγγελίζω, ἀποστέλλω, and κηρύσσων along with the fact that Jesus continues to do these thing in synagogues all recalls the Nazareth scene.

30. The verb βιάζεται can be taken either as a passive (cf. Matt 11:12) or as a middle. The middle is more likely, as Bovon, Luke 2, says, since it likely refers to the "the same struggles as those carried on by those competitors who are invited to enter through the narrow door in 13:24." He goes on to note that "it may seem incongruous to speak of violence in connection with a faith decision, but we should take this expression in the figurative sense . . . those who have welcomed the good news of the kingdom put all their moral and spiritual strength into entering it," 466–67. The unjust manager, it seems to me, appears as a model (though a complex one) of just such resolve.

continue to explain his association with sinners because of thematic correlations with the parable of the prodigal son. Both the prodigal son and the
unjust manager are guilty of squandering (διασκορπίζω, 15:13; 16:1). Like
the prodigal son, when the unjust manager realizes that he is in trouble, he
thinks to himself (ἔγνων τί ποιήσω, 16:4) and devises a plan.[31] Both stories
of the prodigal son and the unjust manager moreover end with a "certain
person" (ἄνθρωπός τις, 16:1; 15:11) acting in a way that was not anticipated
given the squandering activities of the main characters.[32]

But the change in audience in 16:1 to Jesus' disciples nevertheless offers a break in the material and suggests the beginning of a new digestible
portion of Luke's narrative. It appears that the parable of the unjust manager
(16:1–9) and the parable of the rich man and Lazarus bracket Jesus' pro-
nouncements about the kingdom and possessions. The two parables parallel each other in form and content.[33] Both parables begin with the phrase
"a certain rich man" (ἄνθρωπός τις ἦν πλούσιος, vv. 1, 19), and both speak
about the proper use of possessions. The unjust manager secures a future
for himself by cancelling debts, thus using possessions in the way that Jesus
counsels them to be used—i.e., they are to be used to make friends (16:9).
The rich man, however, is condemned to fiery torture because of his lack of
concern for the poor man Lazarus.

We can again see how the structure of the narrative already begins to
illumine Jesus' central pronouncement about the Law and the Prophets, and
forcing one's way into the kingdom. If we see the unjust manager as manipu-
lating his resources to secure by any means possible a future for himself,
then this might be an instance of what Jesus' means by "forcing one's way"
into the kingdom. And the Law and the Prophets appear to be highlighted
because, according to Abraham in the parable of the rich man and Lazarus,
if the rich man had listened to "Moses and the Prophets" (16:29), then he
would have not found himself in a fiery torment.

31. Cf. the prodigal son: εἰς ἑαυτὸν δὲ ἐλθὼν ἔφη (15:17).

32. Green, *Luke*, notes the similarities between the parables, but does not make
much of the connections. He says that it only creates an "organic" connection and reminds the reader that the context is the issue of table fellowship, 587; cf. Bovon, *Luke*
2, 446.

33. Commentators generally recognize that these two parables ought to be read together. See Bovon, *Luke* 2, 443–44; Wolter, *Lukasevangelium*, 542; Green, *Luke*, 586–88;
Fitzmyer, *Luke*, 2:1095; C. Hays, *Ethics*, 140.

The Unjust Manager

The first parable Jesus tells after turning to address his disciples concerns a rich man who has a household manager. This manager, the reader is informed, has been squandering the rich man's possessions (τὰ ὑπάρχοντα, 16:1), so the rich man notifies the manager that he is no longer able to manage the rich man's possessions. Fearful at the thought of losing his employment, since he is both too feeble to dig and too ashamed to beg (16:3), he devises a plan that will guarantee his reception (δέξωνταί, 16:4) into others' homes after his employment is terminated. He calls his lord's debtors and cuts what they owe on the official record. The end of the parable is shocking. The squandering manager, who has now readjusted the debt records, is not condemned, but praised (ἐπήνεσεν) by his lord.[34] To be fair, he readjusts the records while he still has the title of "manager" (οἰκονόμος) so he does nothing outside of the bounds of his authority.[35] But the shock comes from

34. The lord's praise has puzzled interpreters. For a history of various way of understanding this parable see Landry and May, "Honor Restored," 287–94; and Ireland, *Stewardship*, 5–35. Cf. Kim, *Stewardship*, 145–60.

35. Recent interpretations have hinged on how one configures the manager's actions. Are they unethical or not? Goodrich, "Voluntary Debt Remission," 547–66, suggests that the manager's debt-reduction ought to be seen in the context of lease adjustment in the early empire. Debts were often reduced in order to encourage payback. The manager, in other words, did himself *and* his lord a favor by reducing people's debts. The lord would benefit from the repayment that would now begin (553, 565). But the question still remains: why is he called the house-manager of *unrighteousness* at the very end of the parable (v.8)? Udoh, "Unrighteous Slave," 311–35, suggests that the parable ought to be seen in the context of the "social and ideological world of chattel slavery" and concludes that the parable does not fit into Luke's narrative neatly, so the praise that the lord gives is retained from his source simply so Jesus can go on to urge the children of light to be wise in the own generation (Ireland, *Stewardship*, comes to a similar conclusion that the parable is told simply to make the point that Jesus' hearers ought to be wise—though he comes to this conclusion via a different route than Udoh does [see 114–15, 217]). Udoh is correct to the extent that Jesus counsels wisdom (indeed this is said plainly in the text [cf. 16:8]), but he appears to miss the way in which Luke plays with the language and imagery of the parable in the coming verses (Luke 16:10–13). We must also not miss the fact that the manager is wise with possessions in particular, just as Jesus counsels his hearers to be. Metzger, *Consumption*, on the other hand, suggests that the reason the lord praises the manager is because he has done nothing corrupt at all. He suggests that the possessions the manager has been squandering are his own—i.e., the commission that was his from his work (111, 130). When the manager cuts the debts of others, he cuts only his commission. The manger's shrewd generosity thus impresses the lord and secures friendship from those who will receive him (130–31). The problem with Metzger's interpretation, as with Goodrich's, is that we are still left wondering why at the end of the parable the manger is still called unrighteous. Moreover, the terms of the story do not indicate that the lord cares what the manager does with the manager's own possessions, and it is not

the fact that it is still something unprincipled. Still more shocking is that Jesus' voice appears to overlap with that of the manager's lord. After the lord praises the manager, Jesus adds, "because the sons of this age are wiser than the sons of light in their own generation" (16:8).[36]

It is not difficult to see why Luke would have Jesus tell this story at this point in that narrative. Jesus has just told three parables about lost things being found to explain why he is eating with sinners. The lost things evidently refer to the sinners with whom he is sharing meals. The unjust manager is likewise a sinner precisely because he is called an "un-just manager" (τὸν οἰκονόμον τῆς ἀδικίας, 16:8). The genitive τῆς ἀδικίας, it should be clear, is a noun, not an adjective, and thus could be translated "manager of unrighteousness." But the term is likely a description of his character, not the things he is managing, since he has just done something that, while well within his bounds as manager of his lord's possessions, is nevertheless underhanded.

But why is it that the lord of the parable, and thereby Jesus, praises the manager for his actions? Part of the answer comes in Jesus' pronouncement that immediately follows the parable. There is an eschatological lesson to be learned: "make friends for yourselves by means of unjust mammon in order that when you die, they might receive you into eternal dwellings" (ἑαυτοῖς ποιήσατε φίλους ἐκ τοῦ μαμωνᾶ τῆς ἀδικίας, ἵνα ὅταν ἐκλίπῃ δέξωνται ὑμᾶς εἰς τὰς αἰωνίους σκηνάς, 16:9). It is clear that the eschatological lesson is to be learned from the parable not only from the reuse of the term ἀδικία but

---

clear that the possessions are the manager's, not the lord's. In sum, each one of these interpretations misses the fact that the manager is not sacked immediately: he still has the power of manager of the lord's possessions when he considers what he ought to do to secure a future for himself. This is clear from the fact that he asks himself what he shall do since his lord "is taking away" (ἀφαιρεῖται) his management duties from him (16:3). The present tense of the verb indicates that he has not yet been fired. He still has the authority to cancel debts. The lord's praise thus makes sense precisely because, while underhanded, the manager's actions were in fact wise.

36. As Green says, "interpretations that assume the need for locating references to characters outside the parable have faltered on attempts to correlate, e.g., "God" with "a rich man" (v. 1), since the wealthy are negatively characterized in the Luke's Gospel, and "Jesus" with "his master/lord" (v. 8), since this would entail having Jesus commend the manager for apparently criminal activity." He thus rejects that the characters in the parable correspond to anyone outside of it (589). Cf. C. Hays, 142. Rowe says of the parable in Luke 12:35–48 that "the story world created by the narration of the parable is intertwined with the Gospel narrative through the word κύριος as it is read on both levels, as "master" in the world of the parable, and as "Lord" along the allegorical lines that Luke so clearly provides," (154). He says of all Luke's parables that though they "refuse to be tidy," Luke nevertheless "uses the word [κύριος] to bring to the fore the allegorical significations of the parable by means of a connection to the larger narrative," (155–57). The "allegorical lines Luke so clearly provides" in Luke 16 comes in v. 13.

also because the action Jesus recommends mirrors that of the manager's: the disciples are to make friends in order to be "received" (δέξωνται 16:9) just as the manager made friends in order to be "received" (δέξωνταί, 16:4). And in order to be received by others, the disciples must use possessions just as the manager did.

Luke thus makes the manager a model for action, albeit in a limited way. To be sure, no one ought to mimic his squandering activities. But the manager nevertheless assesses the gravity of his situation and does whatever is within his power to secure a future dwelling for himself. The key rhetorical move in the lesson comes with the switch from talking about an οἰκονόμος τῆς ἀδικίας to μαμωνᾶς τῆς ἀδικίας. In this rhtorical move, Luke says that, while not all are sinners in the manner that the unjust manager was, all are managers of μαμωνᾶς. And μαμωνᾶς is, according to Jesus, μαμωνᾶς τῆς ἀδικίας.[37] The unrighteousness of mammon sets the terms for the final pronouncement Jesus makes in reference to mammon. No "servant" (οἰκέτης), he says, is able to serve "two lords" (δυσὶ κυρίοις, 16:13). Here again the Lukan Jesus is again playing with the terminology of the parable about an οἰκονόμος and his κύριός. The two lords, he goes on, are God and mammon. One is not "able to serve" (δύναται . . . δουλεύειν) two lords, so "you are not able to serve" (οὐ δύνασθε . . . δουλεύειν) God and money (16:13).

In the next moment, the reader is informed that while these sayings have been directed at Jesus' disciples (cf. 16:1), Pharisees have been listening to what Jesus has to say. Luke says that the Pharisees are φιλάργυροι, lovers of money, and therefore mock (ἐξεμυκτήριζον) Jesus for what he has said (16:14). Jesus' response indicts them for their love of money. They may appear righteous before men, but God knows their hearts (16:15).

The scene then culminates with the saying with which we began this section: "the Law and the Prophets were until John; since then the kingdom of God is proclaimed and everyone forces his way into it" (16:16).[38] The flow

37. Scholars have noticed this rhetorical switch. See Nolland, *Luke 9:21—18:34*, 805; Wolter, *Lukasevangelium*, 548–49; C. Hays, *Ethics*, suggests as I do that this ultimately means that all money is unrighteous—though he adds that it is only so insofar as it leads one away from God, 144.

38. Luke 16:16 was central to Conzelmann's argument that Luke had divided salvation history into three periods, *Theology*, 16–17, 112; cf. 95–136. Fitzmyer, *Luke*, maintains this threefold division and likewise appeals to this saying, 2:1115–16. But few scholars have continued to place so much emphasis on it (see Bock's discussion, *Luke*, 2:1351). Scholars have continued to discuss whether John the Baptist is supposed to be grouped with the prophets or with the proclamation of the kingdom (see e.g., Wolter, *Lukasevangelium*, 554–55). But, as Bovon, *Luke 2*, says, what is important for Luke is not identifying which group John the Baptist falls into, but that salvation history has now entered its final phase, 465.

of the narrative, particularly in the way in which Jesus has reused terminology from the parable of the unjust manager suggests that Luke intends the example of the unjust manager to be in view in order to understand what it means to "force one's way" into the kingdom. The manager knew his job was going to be taken from him imminently, so he did whatever was necessary to secure his future. Likewise, those who wish to secure eternal dwellings for themselves must force their way into them by shrewdly calculating what it will take. The kingdom of God is now proclaimed, which means time is running out.[39] It is time to forsake mammon for itself and begin using it to make eternal friends.

The Rich Man and Lazarus

Jesus' pronouncement about the proclamation of the kingdom and people entering by force appears to come not only as a culmination of the parable of the unjust manager and the sayings associated with it, but also to introduce what follows it. Despite saying that the Law and the Prophets were "until John" (16:16), Jesus goes on to say that nothing of the Law will be forgotten. It is "easier for heaven and earth to pass away than for one small stroke of the Law to become void" (16:17). The parable of the rich man and Lazarus appears to shed light not only on why the Law will not pass away, but also how the Law will hold people to account for the use of their possessions.[40]

The Lukan Jesus says nothing of the characters of his parable other than their economic standing.[41] Lazarus is poor; the rich man is rich. The

---

39. Seccombe, *Possessions*, 163; Ireland, *Stewardship*, 214–15; and C. Hays, *Ethics*, 144–46, also note the eschatological context of this parable.

40. Immediately after Jesus says that not one small stroke of the law will pass away, he says, "each one who divorces his wife and marries another commits adultery, and the one who leaves her husband and marrying another commits adultery," (16:18). Why does Luke insert this saying here? The law did not prohibit divorce so it appears on the one hand that the verse does not follow from the preceding context (Fitzmyer, *Luke*, 2:1119). On the other hand, Jesus does not here strictly speaking prohibit divorce; he prohibits marrying another after having been divorced. The matter of adultery is what is in focus. The "one small stroke" of the Law that will not pass away is that even divorce, which was permitted in Mosaic law, does not give one an excuse to commit adultery. It is not clear if anyone would have accepted Jesus' definition of adultery, but that might be the point of the saying. Still, why appeal to the Law on the matter of adultery in this context? Meynet, *Luc*, has suggested that Luke intends an allegorical meaning. The one who is divorced is God and adultery is committed when one marries another—money, 651–52. Adultery, we should remember, was a common way of referring to Israel's turning to other gods in the OT (see e.g., Hosea).

41. As Bauckham, "Rich Man," 225–46. Though the parable has some similarities to the Egyptian folktale about a rich man and a poor man dying, the differences are too

rich man wears purple and fine linen and always parties (16:19).[42] Lazarus, on the other hand, is destitute. He sits by the rich man's gate covered in sores, wishing only to eat something that might fall from the rich man's table. Dogs lick his wounds (16:20–21).

The story progresses quickly with both men dying. Lazarus, Luke says, is taken to the bosom of Abraham by angels, while the rich man is sent to a fiery torture. Luke does not here explicitly call Lazarus a child of Abraham, but nevertheless seems to suggest that he is. The rich man will twice call Abraham "father" (πάτερ, 16:24, 27). Luke thus appears to be playing with imagery first seen in John the Baptist's preaching. John the Baptist, too, spoke of children of Abraham in the context of one's use of possessions. The fact Jesus has just invoked John the Baptist by name might mean that Luke intends John the Baptist's preaching to be recalled by the reader. The rich man is himself explicitly called "child" (τέκνον, 16:25), which might be intended ironically if John the Baptist's preaching is in view. The rich man might have been a child of Abraham by blood, but he is now obviously not since he finds himself in a postmortem torture.

In death, the radical separation that existed between the rich man and Lazarus while they were alive is mirrored, though inversely. Abraham points this out to the rich man: "remember that you received your good things in your life, and Lazarus likewise evil things; but now here he is comforted and you are in pain" (16:25). Lazarus groveled below the rich man's table looking for crumbs; now it is the rich man who lifts his eyes to Lazarus looking similarly for some relief. The rich man asks if Lazarus could dip a finger in water to cool his tongue (16:24). At Abraham's response, the rich man concedes that Lazarus can give him no relief—the chasm is too wide (16:26). So the rich man instead submits another, seemingly altruistic, request: he asks father Abraham to send Lazarus into the house of his father and his five brothers. They still have a chance to avoid fiery punishment (16:28).[43] Abraham responds that not only can this not

great to claim Luke (or Luke's source) was using the folktale (contrary to Seccombe, *Possessions*, who says "there is no question of literary dependence of the parable on this [Egyptian] story," 174). For example, in the parable of the rich man and Lazarus, there is no revelation to someone outside of the dead which was characteristic of the Egyptian folktale and related stories: "the story in effect deprives itself of any claim to offer an apocalyptic glimpse of the secrets of the world beyond the grave. It cannot claim eyewitness authority as a literal description of the fate of the dead. It has only the status of parable." Cf. Bovon's discussion, *Luke 2*, 476–78.

42. As Bovon, *Luke 2*, points out, the description of the rich man parallels the negative portrayal of other rich people in Luke's narrative. See e.g., Luke 12:19.

43. Here I disagree with Bauckham, "Rich Man." He claims that there is no moral critique in the parable. "What is not stated," he says, "is not relevant," 232. He suggests

happen, but also that they already have all they need to know how to avoid the rich man's postmortem torture. They have Moses and the Prophets: "let them listen to them!" (ἀκουσάτωσαν αὐτῶν, 16:29). The rich man is not satisfied with the answer, so he presses the question: surely a dead man raised will convince them (16:30). But Abraham only reasserts his answer: they have Moses and the Prophets (16:31).

We can now see why the Lukan Jesus invokes the Law and the Prophets in the context of talking about God and mammon. The Law and the Prophets, evidently, demonstrate everything he has said about God and money in this context. The Law and the Prophets demonstrate that you can only serve God or money, and the Law and the Prophets demonstrate that the way to serve God and not money is to make friends with the money one has. The Lukan Jesus does not use the language of friendship to describe the relationship the rich man and Lazarus lacked, but the context suggests it should be seen in that light. The bosom of Abraham is likely Lazarus' eternal dwelling (cf. 16:9) since the chasm between Lazarus and the rich man cannot be traversed.[44] The implication might therefore be that, had the rich man heeded Moses and the Prophets and considered the plight of Lazarus before he had died, Lazarus would not only have given him a drop of water, but hospitably received him into his dwelling.

Summary: The Law and the Prophets and The Kingdom

The kingdom of God is now proclaimed, and the kingdom is a matter of urgency. The unjust manager is about to lose his position so he makes friends before it is too late. He tells them to write quickly (ταχέως γράψον, 16:6) so that their obligation to him is secured before the moment of his dismissal. Jesus' words immediately thereafter are in the imperative: "make (ποιήσατε) friends for yourselves!" (16:9). In the parable of the rich man and Lazarus, there is another imperative: "let them listen!" (ἀκουσάτωσαν) to Moses and the Prophets (16:29). And the threat of judgment looms: disregard of the poor guarantees a place of torment.

Ethics yet again appears in the context of eschatological proclamation. Here perhaps we can see in part the logic of eschatology and ethics for

---

that the fact that Luke does not say that the rich man was wicked means that his moral standing is not in view. He claims that the only thing Luke wishes to emphasize is the inequality of situations. But, why then, we must ask, does the rich man speak of repentance (16:30)?

44. As Lehtipuu, *Afterlife*, argues, a description of the afterlife is not the point of the parable, but, nevertheless, "the fate of the dead *is* revealed," 6.

Luke. To say that one must make friends in order to be received into those friends' eternal dwellings assumes that those friends both go before their benefactors and have a say about who will enter those eternal dwellings. The social nature of salvation in Lukan theology again emerges. John the Baptist looked for a prepared people. The Seventy looked for hospitality. But something slightly different emerges here. Whereas in previous passages we have addressed it is God and his Christ who judge who is grain and who is chaff, here it appears that others will be involved deciding who is in and who is out. It is from Lazarus that the rich man asks for a drop of water.

Zacchaeus, Jerusalem, Rejection:
Luke 18:31—19:48

Introduction

Before Jesus completes his journey to Jerusalem that he had begun when he had "set his face" toward the city (9:51), he stops in Jericho. As he is passing through the city a man named Zacchaeus notices a commotion and "seeks to see (ἐζήτει ἰδεῖν) who Jesus is" (19:3). Zacchaeus, Luke mentions, is both a tax collector and rich (αὐτὸς ἦν ἀρχιτελώνης καὶ αὐτὸς πλούσιος, 19:2). But Zacchaeus cannot see Jesus because he is short (19:3), so climbs a tree to catch a glimpse. Luke says that as Jesus comes to the tree, he notices Zacchaeus and commands him to hasten down, for, he says to him, "today I must stay in your house" (σήμερον γὰρ ἐν τῷ οἴκῳ σου δεῖ με μεῖναι, 19:5). Zacchaeus receives (ὑπεδέξατο) him, and after receiving him, he does something radical: he gives half of his possessions to the poor, and to whomever he cheated, he returns fourfold what he took (19:8). In response, Jesus announces that salvation has come to Zacchaeus's house; he is a son of Abraham (αὐτὸς υἱὸς Ἀβραάμ ἐστιν, 19:9).

Jesus' encounter with Zacchaeus recalls themes we encountered in the Luke 15–16. Luke concludes the story of Zacchaeus with an announcement from Jesus: "the Son of Man came to seek and to save the lost (τὸ ἀπολωλός, 19:10)." In ch. 15, Luke had told three parables, each about a lost thing (τὸ ἀπολωλός) being sought and found (15:4, 8, 32). Zacchaeus appears to be one of the found sinners Jesus spoke of. Luke also says that "all those who saw" that Jesus was about to be hosted by Zacchaeus "murmured" (διεγόγγυζον, 19:7). The only other time this verb appears is in the 15:2 where Luke says the Pharisees and Scribes were murmuring about Jesus receiving sinners (Luke 15:1–2).[45] Jesus also calls Zacchaeus a son of Abraham, which brings

---

45. The verb διαγογγύζω is used only twice in the NT (Luke 15:2, 19:7). It might be

to mind of the story of the rich man and Lazarus. A rich man has now, evidently, avoided fiery torment. And finally, Luke says that Zacchaeus received (ὑπεδέξατο) Jesus, which might bring to mind not only Jesus receiving (προσδέχεται) sinners (15:2) but also when Jesus says after the parable of the unjust manager that people should seek to be received (δέξωνται) by the friends they have made with their money (16:10).

This story has clear connections with John the Baptist's preaching as well. As the story of Lazarus recalls John the Baptist's preaching because Lazarus is received by "father" Abraham, so also does the story of Zacchaeus because he is "a son of Abraham" (cf. Luke 3:8). And Zacchaeus is called a child of Abraham for doing precisely what John the Baptist said children of Abraham should do: he gives half of his possessions to the poor (3:10–14). Zacchaeus also gives four-fold to anyone he has cheated (ἐσυκοφάντησα, 19:8). The verb συκοφαντέω ("to cheat") appears only here and in John the Baptist's preaching in the whole of the NT. John the Baptist had told the soldiers in his midst that they should not extort and cheat (συκοφαντήσητε, 3:14).[46]

Luke therefore again reveals a concern for ethics at a key point in his narrative. But what role does eschatology play in this passage? It appears that Luke wants the Zacchaeus episode to be seen in an eschatological light, for immediately after he tells Zacchaeus's story, he says those who were listening to Jesus thought that "the kingdom was immediately about to appear" (παραχρῆμα μέλλει ἡ βασιλεία τοῦ θεοῦ ἀναφαίνεσθαι) because he was drawing near to Jerusalem (19:11). Jesus then goes on to tell a parable about a man of noble birth receiving a kingdom and judging those who do not want his rule (19:11–27). In order to investigate the eschatological outlook of this passage, we must see the literary sequence in which Luke has placed both the story of Zacchaeus and the parable.

Structure

The final leg of Jesus' journey to Jerusalem begins immediately before he enters Jericho. Jesus tells his disciples, "behold we go up to Jerusalem" (ἰδοὺ

---

significant that this verb is used in the LXX almost exclusively to refer to the Israelites' grumbling in the exodus and conquest narratives (see e.g., Exod 15:24, Num 14:2). Cf. Sir 31:24 as an exception.

46. Fitzmyer notes the connections between this story and John the Baptist's preaching, 2:1222. C. Hays, *Ethics*, on the other hand, says "we should not connect Zacchaeus's promise to the instructions of John the Baptist (3:11a that those who have two tunic should share with those who have none," 177. But Hays apparently misses the other connections this story has with John the Baptist's preaching.

ἀναβαίνομεν εἰς Ἰερουσαλήμ, 18:31). Jesus also takes the occasion to remind them of what will happen to him there. He will be "handed over to the nations" (παραδοθήσεται τοῖς ἔθνεσιν). He will be killed, but on the third day he will rise again (18:32–33). The disciples, however, "do not understand" and "the saying was hidden (κεκρυμμένον) from them" (18:34). Jesus then makes his way to Jericho (18:35). The series of scenes that take place in and around Jericho (18:35—19:10) appear to parallel the scenes that take place in and around Jerusalem (19:28–19:48). In between the two sets of scenes appears Jesus' parable about receiving a kingdom. The structure therefore suggests that the two sets of scenes set in and around Jericho and Jerusalem frame and thereby shed light on the parable.[47]

The first factor that suggests that the Jericho and Jerusalem scenes are parallel is similar transitional formulas that introduce each set of scenes. After Jesus predicts his death, Luke says, "and it was that as he drew near to Jericho" (ἐγένετο δὲ ἐν τῷ ἐγγίζειν αὐτὸν εἰς Ἰεριχὼ) he met a blind man on the road (18:35). Jesus meets Zaccheaus (19:1–10) after his encounter with the blind man on the outskirts of Jericho (18:35–43). After the parable about receiving a kingdom, Luke says that Jesus "went on ahead, going up to Jerusalem" (πορεύετο ἔμπροσθεν ἀναβαίνων εἰς Ἰεροσόλυμα). He then adds, "and it was as he drew near to Bethphage and Bethany" (καὶ ἐγένετο ὡς ἤγγισεν εἰς Βηθφαγὴ καὶ Βηθανίαν, 19:29). Jesus continues to "draw near" to Jerusalem until his arrival in the coming narrative (19:37, 41). But Luke also reuses lexemes and tropes from the Jericho scenes in the Jerusalem scene, all of which again indicate that the two sets of scenes are to be seen in light of each other.[48]

As Jesus draws near (ἐν τῷ ἐγγίζειν, 18:35) to Jericho, Luke says there is a blind man who asks why a crowd is passing by him. Someone tells him that Jesus of Nazareth is passing by.[49] The blind man, evidently recogniz-

47. I owe the initial observation that the structure of this passage stretches from 18:31—19:48 to Meynet, *Rhetorical Analysis*, 32–33. Meynet generally corroborates all of my observations about the structure of the passage in his commentary, *Luc*, 707–54.

48. Why does Jesus go to Jericho after having just stated "behold we go up to Jerusalem?" (18:31). Fitzmyer, *Luke*, says, "one may wonder how the Lucan Jesus got to Jericho after what he said in 17:11 . . . in reality, we are not to ask," 2:1214. But it appears that Luke has Jesus go to Jericho before Jerusalem precisely to contrast his reception there with his reception in Jerusalem. Part of the rhetorical force of Jericho's reception in addition to its contrast with Jerusalem's might lie in the city's portrayal in the OT. Joshua proclaimed that whoever rebuilt Jericho after its destruction would be cursed (Josh 6:26).

49. This is the first time since Jesus' Nazareth sermon that Luke has said anything about Nazareth. It might be significant that it comes at the very moment that Jesus heals a blind man (cf. Luke 4:18). The miracle and its contrast with Jerusalem demonstrates that the healing of the blind is literal, but also points allegorically to Jerusalem's

ing Jesus as king, cries out (ἐβόησεν), "Son of David, have mercy on me!" (18:38). Those who were following Jesus rebuke (ἐπετίμων) him to get him to be silent (ἵνα σιγήσῃ). But he instead cries out (ἔκραζεν) all the more (18:39). He calls to the king a second time, "Son of David have mercy on me!" (18:39). Jesus then heals the man and in response the people praise God (ἔδωκεν αἶνον τῷ θεῷ, 18:43).

We have already considered some of the significant elements of the story of Zacchaeus in Jericho, but we must rehearse Luke's rhetoric in the episode to see its correlation with the events in Jerusalem. Zacchaeus, like the blind man, cannot see—though his inability to see is caused by his short stature rather than by blindness. In response to Jesus' visitation, Zacchaeus divests himself of his riches. Jesus then proclaims that salvation had come to Zacchaeus's house (τῷ οἴκῳ, 19:9) and to give reason for his actions in Zacchaeus's house, Jesus pronounces that the "Son of Man came to seek and to save the lost (ζητῆσαι καὶ σῶσαι τὸ ἀπολωλός, 19:10).

As Jesus draws near (ὡς ἤγγισεν) to Jerusalem (19:29, 37), Luke says that another crowd follows Jesus, just as a crowd followed him when he drew near to Jericho. He says, "all the multitude of the disciples began to praise God rejoicing with a loud voice for all the works of power they had seen" (ἤρξαντο ἅπαν τὸ πλῆθος τῶν μαθητῶν χαίροντες αἰνεῖν τὸν θεὸν φωνῇ μεγάλῃ περὶ πασῶν ὧν εἶδον δυνάμεων, 19:37). The people "praise" (αἰνεῖν) in response to Jesus' miracle working, just as the people had given praise (ἔδωκεν αἶνον) for the miracle of the healed blind man (18:43). The people then proclaim Jesus as king, just as the blind man had: "blessed is the one who comes, the king in the name of the Lord" (εὐλογημένος ὁ ἐρχόμενος, ὁ βασιλεὺς ἐν ὀνόματι κυρίου, 19:38).[50] In response to the crowd's praise, Luke says the Pharisees tell Jesus to rebuke (ἐπιτίμησον) his disciples (19:39). But Jesus answers: "I say to you, if these are silent (σιωπήσουσιν), the stones will cry out (κράξουσιν, 19:40). The Pharisee's reaction recalls the people's rebuke (ἐπετίμων) and attempt to silence (ἵνα σιγήσῃ) the blind man. Jesus' saying about the stones moreover recalls the blind man's persistence in "crying out" (ἔκραζεν, 18:39).

Jesus' final approach to Jerusalem then recalls the foretelling of his death just before he approached Jericho. Jesus pronounces that Jerusalem, like he, will be destroyed. Jesus foretold that he would be handed over to the "nations" (τοῖς ἔθνεσιν, 18:32); he now foretells that Jerusalem will

blindness to eschatological salvation.

50. Neither the Göttingen LXX (see Rahlfs, *Psalmi Cum Odis, ad loc.*) nor the MT of Ps 118:26 (117:26 LXX) has "the king" (ὁ βασιλεὺς), which Luke has in his quotation (εὐλογημένος ὁ ἐρχόμενος, ὁ βασιλεὺς ἐν ὀνόματι κυρίου, Luke 19:38). Luke, it appears, has added this title in order to have it recall the Jericho blind man's words.

similarly be surrounded by its "enemies" (οἱ ἐχθροί, 19:43). Jesus moreover goes into a similar level of detail about the events leading up to the city's destruction as he did when he spoke of his own destruction. Jesus will be "mocked," "insulted," "spit upon," and "flogged" (18:32–33). Jerusalem will have "barricades" set up against them; they will be "surrounded" and "hemmed in"; their enemies will "tear" them down with their children; and their enemies will not leave "one stone upon another" (19:43–44). Jesus' saying about his coming death was "hidden" (κεκρυμμένον) from his disciples (18:34); Jesus now says peace is "hidden" (ἐκρύβη) from Jerusalem's eyes (ἀπὸ ὀφθαλμῶν, 19:42).

Jesus then enters Jerusalem and goes to the temple. He enters to find it full of sellers (τοὺς πωλοῦντας, 19:45). In response, Jesus pronounces, "my house (ὁ οἶκός) is a house (οἶκός) of prayer, but you have made it a den of thieves" (19:46). Finding his own house full of cheating merchants contrasts with his reception into the house (τῷ οἴκῳ, 19:5) of Zacchaeus, a cheating tax-collector who divests himself of his ill-gotten wealth. In response to Jesus' words, the chief priests, the scribes, and the leaders of the people do the opposite of what Jesus said the Son of Man does. Whereas the Son of Man came ζητῆσαι καὶ σῶσαι τὸ ἀπολωλός, they seek to destroy the Son of Man (ἐζήτουν αὐτὸν ἀπολέσαι, 19:47). Luke plays on the semantic range of the verb ἀπόλλυμι (meaning both "to lose" and "to destroy"), connecting the two scenes via the lexeme, while at the same time contrasting the subjects' actions.[51]

Zacchaeus, Jerusalem, and Riches

The literary context in which the story of Zacchaeus appears therefore is an eschatological context. Zacchaeus receives Jesus and divests himself of his riches. Jesus therefore proclaims that "salvation" (σωτηρία) has come to his house. Jerusalem, by contrast, does not receive Jesus. The city's rejection is displayed in the way they have corrupted Jesus' own house with money. The "peace" (εἰρήνη) Jesus says Jerusalem has missed (19:42) suggests they have missed eschatological salvation.[52] The trope of eyesight in these passages likewise gives the sequence on eschatological outlook. We can recall the other passages in Luke's Gospel we have already considered where

51. Apart from Meynet, *Luc*, I have not found any other scholar who has noticed the rhetorical unity of Luke 18:31—19:48. See e.g., Bovon, *Luke 2*; Goulder, *Luke*; Bock, *Luke*; Green, *Luke*, ad loc.

52. We can again recall Zachariah's words about the people's feet being led in the way of peace (1:79; cf. 10:1–12).

eyesight also shows up in the context of eschatological announcement. The shepherds and Simeon saw the light of coming salvation (2:9, 30); all eyes were on Jesus in the Nazareth synagogue (4:20); many prophets and kings wished to see what the Seventy saw (10:23–24). The blind man's healing along with Luke's use of the trope of eyesight becomes an allegory for sight of eschatological salvation—indeed, Jesus tells the blind man that his faith has "healed" or "saved" (σέσωκέν) him (18:42),[53] which is to use the same language he will of Zacchaeus when he says "salvation" (σωτηρία) has come to his house after Zacchaeus climbs a tree to "see" (ἰδεῖν) him. But, again, peace is hidden from Jerusalem's eyes (ἀπὸ ὀφθαλμῶν, 19:42). Jerusalem, though it sees Jesus unhindered, is blind to what is before it.

The Parable of the King and the Coins

As we have already noted, in between Jesus' reception at Jericho and his rejection at Jerusalem appears a parable about a man of noble birth receiving a kingdom. Its placement in the literary structure we have identified suggests that it is simultaneously intended to be interpreted by the events surrounding it and intended to interpret those events.[54] Luke's introductory comment

53. Luke will again use the verb σῴζω in a similar way in the healing of the cripple in Acts 3–4 (see esp. 4:9).

54. Scholars have found this parable difficult to interpret. I am not denying that it is difficult; I am only suggesting that the structure I have identified strongly suggests that the parable be seen in the context of Jesus' reception at Jericho and rejection at Jerusalem. The problems of interpretation on the part of scholars mostly stem from attempting to see a genealogical relationship with Matthew's parable of the talents in Matt 25:14–30, whether directly through Matthew itself or through a common source between Matthew and Luke. Goulder, *Luke*, assumes Luke used Matthew as a source for this parable. He remarks, "sadly, Luke's last great parable from a base in Matthew is a disappointment." The allegories, according to Goulder, were not worked out properly: "the noble's return as king corresponds to Christ's return as king—but the slaughter of the unwilling citizens is likely to answer to the great massacre of 70," 682. Fitzmyer, *Luke*, assumes Q, but still compares it to Matthew. Luke's additions to the parable, he says, "create . . . the major problem in understanding the relationship between the two forms of the parable," 2:1230. He says that in Luke's form of the parable, the emphasis falls on the corrective to popular eschatological belief and focuses the Christian disciple on responsible behavior, 2:1232. The problem with both Goulder's and Fitzmyer's interpretations are that they both ignore the context in which the parable appears (cf. Bovon, *Luke 2*, who sees a hermeneutical function for the parable both for the immediate context [605] and for the Gospel as a whole [619]; see also Green, *Luke*, 674–5l; Kim, *Stewardship*, 165). By first finding historical referents to the events of the parable, they implicitly suggest Luke could have put this parable anywhere in the Gospel and it would be interpreted the same way. But it must be seen first and foremost in its literary context.

suggests that it provides a moment of reflection on the events taking place. Jesus told this parable, he says, because "they thought the kingdom of God was immediately about to appear" because he was drawing near to Jerusalem (19:11). The parable, then, ought to be understood in the context of his approach to the city. But Luke's introductory remark also suggests that the parable says something about coming eschatological events. What does it say about them? And how does Luke's attention to possessions fit into what he is saying about those eschatological events?

The parable begins by saying that a "certain man of noble birth" goes into a "far land" (χώραν μακράν) to receive for himself a kingdom and thereafter to return (19:12). Before he leaves he gives ten coins (μνᾶς) to ten servants and tells them to do business (πραγματεύσασθε) until he returns. While he is gone, the people over whom he will rule send an "ambassador" (πρεσβείαν) saying that they do not want "this one" (τοῦτον) to rule (βασιλεῦσαι) over them. The king then returns "after having received his kingdom" (λαβόντα τὴν βασιλείαν) and calls three of the ten servants to give an account of their business endeavors (19:15). The first two made ten and five more coins, respectively, and are rewarded with a number of cities to rule over equal to the number of coins they gained. The third, however, did nothing with his coin, citing the king's severity (αὐστηρός) as reason for not attempting to do business (19:21). His coin is taken away from him and given to the one who has ten (19:26). Finally, the king orders those who did not want him to rule over them to be slaughtered before him (19:27).[55]

It is not difficult to see how the parable fits thematically into the surrounding narrative. The receiving of the kingdom clearly fits with the context not only because of Luke's introductory comment about the people thinking the kingdom of God was about to appear, but also because the blind man calls Jesus the son of David (18:38) and because the Jerusalem crowd calls Jesus king (19:38). Likewise, the appearance of money in the context of receiving a kingdom appears to fit thematically since money is in view both in the Zacchaeus episode (19:8) and in Jesus' actions in the temple (19:45–46). But where is the "far off land" to which the king goes to receive his kingdom?[56] And how are we to understand the servants' money making?

55. Some scholars have suggested that the slaughter of the unwilling citizens is based on the historical events surrounding Herod Archelaus's rule. See e.g., Schultz, "Jesus as Archelaus," 105–27. But we must ask who in Luke's audience would have remembered these events if indeed they were important to understand this parable. Schultz suggests that the Archelaus motif serves as a "reminder of the seriousness of one's position vis-à-vis the Kingdom of God," 127. But does Luke need the historical referent for the slaughter of unwilling citizens to communicate the seriousness of the kingdom? I am unconvinced.

56. Scholars have frequently taken this parable as evidence that Luke was either

The fact that Luke does not identify the "far off land" is likely evidence that its location is not what is important at this point in the narrative. What is important is rather that the place where Jesus will receive the kingdom is not Jerusalem. The "far off land" thus prepares the reader to see Jesus' arrival in Jerusalem paradoxically.[57] Jesus will be proclaimed king by the crowds as he rides into the city (19:38), but his entry will not be the moment of the arrival of the kingdom. The Pharisees' attempt to silence the crowds and the sellers in the Temple confirm to the reader that Jesus' reception is double-sided. In the parable itself, it is some of the king's citizens who reject his rule and thereby incite his wrath. At the same time, the reader will still wonder where this "far

---

informing his audience of the reason for eschatological delay or responding to his audience's concern about delay. This interpretation goes back at least to Conzelmann, *Theology*, 113, 134, fn. 1; cf. 132–135. See also Fitzmyer, *Luke*, 2:1232–33. According to Carroll, *Response*, delay was a fact of history to Luke's audience. While still serving as an assurance that eschatological judgment is still coming despite the disappointment of early expectation, the parable invites Christians to be faithful stewards in their time of waiting (100). Green, *Luke*, follows Carroll on this, 674–75. Similarly, Bock, *Luke*, says "Jesus wants the disciples to understand that Jerusalem is about to be the place of passion, not parousia," and Luke is thus saying "Jesus will be gone for some time . . . there is an interim period" to demonstrate faithfulness with God's gifts, 2:1531, 1543–44. The problem with these interpretations is (again) that they all remove the parable from its literary context and thereby interpret the parable not on the terms set by the narrative, but on what is presumed to be the historical situation to which Luke writes. Some of Luke's audience may have had questions about delay, but that is not at all clear from what Luke has said. Jesus is about to enter Jerusalem. All that Luke says it that the people thought the kingdom was immediately about to appear upon his entry into the city. He only suggests that the arrival of the kingdom will not come at that precise moment. Bovon, *Luke 2*, suggests that it is "reading too much into the text to think that Luke made a distinction between the time of narration (at the time imminence was out of the question) and the time of the narrator (at the time of writing imminence was an appropriate category)," 611. But why is it to read too much into the text to make this distinction? Bovon does not say. If we were to apply Bovon's interpretive method elsewhere, we would have to conclude that Luke wants Christians to continue to announce that "the kingdom of God has drawn near" just as the Seventy did (Luke 10:9, 11). But that would contradict Bovon's assertion that for Luke "the parousia is delayed" (*Luke 2*, 611). I am not saying Bovon is correct about Luke's eschatological outlook. The example of the Seventy simply demonstrates that we must make a distinction between the time of the narrative and the time of the author's actual historical situation—otherwise we end up saying that Luke contradicts himself when he might not be.

57. Johnson, "Lukan Kingship Parable," 139–59, argues that Jesus' reception in Jerusalem is evidence that Luke actually wants to confirm the people's expectation in 19:11: "Jesus *is* proclaimed as King and does exercise rule through his apostles in the restored Israel," 159. While Johnson is in my opinion correct not first to seek the interpretive key for this parable in the delay of the parousia in Luke's own day (140; cf. Tiede, *Prophecy and History*, "this is not a story of eschatological delay," 79), he does not give sufficient weight to the fact that Jesus must go to a foreign land to receive his kingdom. Again, Luke does not say where this foreign land is, but it seems clear that it is not Jerusalem.

off land" is. We should recall that the entire literary sequence is overshadowed by Jesus' foretelling of his death just before his entry into Jericho (18:31–34). Luke does not say explicitly that the "far off land" is his death, but the reader has at the very least been given a clue that his death and resurrection have something to do with the receiving of the kingdom.

When the king goes to the "far off land" to receive his kingdom, he tells his servants, as we have noted, to "do business" (πραγματεύσασθε, 19:13). The king's command appears to contrast with the previous scene. Zacchaeus had just divested himself of his wealth, seemingly suggesting that the wealth itself was problematic. The servants, on the other hand, have been encouraged to make as much money as possible—indeed, the king's reward correlates to the amount they gained. Zacchaeus's wealth was, of course, apparently ill-gotten, at least in part, since he admits to having "cheated" (ἐσυκοφάντησα), and there is nothing to suggest that the servants in the parable are to use any unethical means to gain as much money as possible. But Zacchaeus also gives away half of what he owns, which seems to suggest that his divesting himself of wealth is a good thing in and of itself.

Yet, for contrasting with the Zacchaeus episode, there is one point of common ground between the two stories. That common ground is that the characters are both expected to do something with their possessions. There is, in other words, no room to suggest that one's possessions have nothing to do with the kingdom. On the contrary, one's relationship to the kingdom is determined by what one does with possessions. The third servant in particular appears to suggest this: he is called "evil" (πονηρὲ) for doing nothing with what he had been given (19:22). Each of the servant's experiences also appears to suggest this.

The king praises the first servant who made ten more coins and calls him "good" (ἀγαθὲ), and then says "because you have been faithful in the least, have authority over ten citites" (ὅτι ἐν ἐλαχίστῳ πιστὸς ἐγένου, ἴσθι ἐξουσίαν ἔχων ἐπάνω δέκα πόλεων, 19:17). Luke appears to be playing here with language he has already used in his Gospel. The phrase "faithful in the least" (ἐν ἐλαχίστῳ πιστὸς) recalls Jesus' sayings after the parable of the unjust manager. Immediately after Jesus speaks of making friends with money in Luke 16:9, he says "the one who is faithful in the least" (ὁ πιστὸς ἐν ἐλαχίστῳ) is also faithful in much (16:10). He goes on to say that "if you are not faithful with another's who will give to you what is yours?" (εἰ ἐν τῷ ἀλλοτρίῳ πιστοὶ οὐκ ἐγένεσθε, τὸ ὑμέτερον τίς ὑμῖν δώσει; 16:12).[58] In the parable of the king and the coins, the first and second servant have done just that: they have

---

58. Green, *Luke*, thinks the phrase is a "deliberate echo" of Luke 16:10, 679; cf. Fitzmyer, *Luke*, 2:1236; Wolter, *Lukasevangelium*, 621.

been faithful with another's, so they have been given cities which will be their own. It is perhaps significant that Jesus recalls a phrase in the parable of the king and the coins from a context in which he had told another story about being shrewd with one's access to another's possessions.

The king's response to the third servant likewise recalls one of Jesus' sayings after the telling of a parable. The king takes the singular coin of the third servant away because he had hidden it away in a handkerchief rather than following the king's command. The king explains his actions by saying that "to all who have it will be given, but from the one who does not have even that which he has will be taken away" (παντὶ τῷ ἔχοντι δοθήσεται, ἀπὸ δὲ τοῦ μὴ ἔχοντος καὶ ὃ ἔχει ἀρθήσεται, 19:26). The aphorism recalls Jesus' words after the parable of the sower. There he had told the story of the various ways in which people "hear the word of God" (8:11). Various soils represent the various ways in which people "hear" (8:12–14). Jesus concludes his sayings after the parable by challenging his audience: "see therefore how you hear, for he who has, it will be given to him, but he who does not have, even that which he thinks he has will be taken up from him" (βλέπετε οὖν πῶς ἀκούετε· ὃς ἂν γὰρ ἔχῃ, δοθήσεται αὐτῷ· καὶ ὃς ἂν μὴ ἔχῃ, καὶ ὃ δοκεῖ ἔχειν ἀρθήσεται ἀπ᾽ αὐτοῦ, 8:18). Luke may be playing with the language and imagery of the parable of the sower since Jesus uses the language of sowing and reaping in the parable of the king and the coins.[59] The evil servant tells the king that he did nothing with his coin because, "you are a severe man, taking up that which you did not deposit and reaping what you do not sow" (ὅτι ἄνθρωπος αὐστηρὸς εἶ, αἴρεις ὃ οὐκ ἔθηκας καὶ θερίζεις ὃ οὐκ ἔσπειρας, 19:21).[60]

It thus appears that Luke plays with the language and imagery of earlier parables and the sayings of Jesus' associated with them in the parable of the king and the coins. The experience of the first two servants confirms yet again the correlation of one's use of possessions in the present with eschatological reward. In this light, Zacchaeus appears to be guaranteed such a reward precisely because he did what the future king expects one to do with one's possessions. He was faithful in least, which indicates he will be faithful with much. The example of the third servant suggests something similar. Whereas in the parable of the sower it was seeds that represent the word of God that are sown and reaped, in this instance it is coins. Yet in this instance the coins do not appear to have an allegorical meaning, not only because Luke does not give one explicitly, but also because the

59. Green, *Luke*, again suggests Luke is deliberately echoing Luke 8:18 here, 680; cf. Fitzmyer, *Luke*, 2:1238; Bock, *Luke*, 2:1541; Wolter, *Lukasevangelium*, 624.

60. The king agrees with the third servant that he is severe, 19:22.

episodes of Zacchaeus and Jesus' entry in the temple are themselves about money. But the similar language and imagery both of sowing and reaping, and of taking up from the one who has ties one's use of possession closely with how one encounters the announcement of the coming kingdom. To be ready for the kingdom one must, like good soil, produce many fold from what one is given (cf. 8:15).

All of this, again, is said in an eschatological context. The kingdom will not appear immediately when Jesus enters Jerusalem, but judgment is coming. Those who rejected the king's rule will be slaughtered before him (19:27). It is perhaps significant that it is before the king actually receives his kingdom that he is rejected by some of his citizens. This element of the story may—like the servants' use of their king's coins—shed light on the coming events in Jerusalem. Judgment will not take place immediately, but those who will be judged unfaithful are those who reject now.

Conclusion

Luke continues to emphasize eschatology and ethics in Jesus' ministry. The Seventy look for hospitality as they announce the nearness of the kingdom. Jesus tells his hearers that if they make friends with their money, those friends will welcome them into eternal dwellings. Jesus announces salvation to Zacchaeus's house after he shares his possessions. Those who do not hospitably receive Jesus and his messengers, those who do not make friends with their possessions, will be destroyed. Their enemies will surround them; it will be worse for them in that day than it will be for Sodom.

We have appreciated Luke's emphasis on eschatology by tracking the way in which he reuses various tropes, lexemes, and themes from earlier passages in his Gospel. The most significant reuses for our question are the reused elements from John the Baptist's preaching. John the Baptist preached eschatology and ethics, and by repeatedly recalling John the Baptist's preaching throughout Jesus' ministry, Luke continues to emphasize those two related matters. The Christ's eschatological harvest begins in the sending of the Seventy. Since John the Baptist, the kingdom is announced. Lazarus and Zacchaeus are both children of Abraham.

In addition to John the Baptist's preaching about eschatology and ethics, Luke has continued to use the tropes of hearing and seeing which he used in the infancy narrative, in John the Baptist's preaching, and in Jesus' Nazareth announcement. These tropes emphasize the eschatological nature of what he narrates. Simeon, we will recall, proclaims that he sees salvation in Jesus. John the Baptist is the voice that people hear in the wilderness, and his ministry enables all flesh to see the coming eschatological salvation. All eyes are on Jesus in the Nazareth synagogue. We have now seen that Jesus is the prophet like Moses who the people must hear. Many kings and prophets wished to see and hear what the Seventy did, but did not. Father Abraham tells the rich man that his relatives ought to listen to Moses and the prophets. And, finally, while a blind man and a vertically-challenged sinner see salvation in Jesus, Jerusalem—despite no disability—remains blind.

As we saw in Chapter Two of this study, Luke's ethics appears to continue to have the formation of a people in view. This is most clear in Jesus' pronouncement in Luke 16:9 that his hearers must make friends with their money. God and his Christ execute judgment, but one's neighbors also appear to have the prerogative either to receive people into or to reject people from their eternal dwellings. Calling both Lazarus and Zacchaeus children of Abraham also appears to emphasize the formation of a people. Children of Abraham are what John the Baptist says God is looking for when he begins his ministry to prepare a people for the Lord. Finally, it appears that the formation of a people is what is in view in the sending of the Seventy and in Jesus' entry into Jerusalem. It is as cities that "all the places that Jesus was about to go" (9:52) either receive or reject his messengers. Jericho receives; Jerusalem rejects. It is, of course, only the citizens who reject the king who are slaughtered before him in the parable of the king and the coins, and the king's servants—like Zacchaeus—are judged on their individual merit. But the good servants will nevertheless rule over cities, and Jesus will be king over them all.

Israel will be ruled by Jesus, but it is clear that Israel will not have the same make-up after Jesus receives his kingdom in the far off land to which he travels. In order to be eschatological Israel, the people must be Abraham's children. And in order to be Abraham's children, they must share their possessions.

4

Sharing in the Last Days

The Jerusalem Church

Introduction

J ohn the Baptist preaches eschatology and ethics. Jesus likewise preaches eschatology and ethics in his Nazareth sermon. As I argued in Chapter Three, Luke continues to emphasize these two apparently related matters in Jesus' ministry. The kingdom of God is now proclaimed, so Jesus and his messengers ought to be hospitably received. In this chapter, we come to the portion of Luke's narrative that in part occasioned the present investigation. As we saw in the previous chapter, Luke reuses tropes, themes, and lexemes from John the Baptist's preaching in Jesus' ministry where an emphasis on eschatology and ethics also appears. At the beginning of Acts, Luke again reuses such material from John the Baptist's preaching. Peter, like John the Baptist, announces coming eschatological events (Act 2:17, cf. 3:20–21). An emphasis on ethics emerges in this context: the members of the new community formed on the day of Pentecost share their possessions with one another (2:42–47; cf. 4:32–35).[1]

The first task of this chapter is simply to demonstrate that Luke continues to emphasize eschatology and ethics at the beginning of his second volume. Eschatology has been a much-debated issue among Acts scholars. Scholars have often suggested that Acts was written, like Luke's Gospel, in response to the problem of eschatological delay. Or, if not in response to delay, they suggest that Luke at the very least assumes such a situation. Conzelmann's work on Lukan theology, which assumes Luke wrote in response to

---

1. On the unity of Luke–Acts, see chapter 1, n9.

eschatological delay, mentions Acts 1:6–7 in this respect. He claims that the disciples' question about the timing of eschatological events is "dismissed on grounds of principle."[2] More recently, Pervo has said, "eschatology, long a burning issue in the study of the Gospel, is not a prominent topic in Acts. Judgment and parousia remain on the calendar, without an explicit assertion of imminence or concern about the subject. Hints of the tendency to individualize eschatology, one mark of the absence of imminence, are present."[3] I cannot settle the question of imminence in Luke's works. But I suggest in this chapter that Luke at the very least begins his second volume with an outlook to eschatological events.[4] Beginning his narrative this way sets the terms for the rest of the book.

By contrast, most scholars recognize the centrality of ethics at the beginning of Acts. The summary statements (2:42–47; 4:32–35)—for which the sharing of possessions is central—have generated much discussion in both commentaries and monographs on Lukan ethics. Pervo, however, doubts that ethics—like eschatology—is central to Luke's concerns in the book. He suggests that the "two principal themes of Jesus' message, eschatology and ethics, receive limited coverage in Acts, which focuses on the means of salvation, an assumed need not related to an imminent end."[5] Such a sweeping statement of Acts is not easy to disprove, though this chapter and the next will seek at the very least to suggest that Pervo's assessment may miss the mark. For now, it is worth saying simply that sheer bulk of material is not necessarily the measure of how important a topic is to Luke. It seems to me that since Luke twice focuses on shared possessions when he describes the converted community formed after both of Peter's public sermons in Acts 1–4, we should take this as an indication that ethics

2. Conzelmann, *Theology*, 121 (cf. Conzelmann, *Acts of the Apostles*, xlv). See also Haenchen, *Acts*, 94–96; Maddox, *Purpose*, 129–30; and Wilson, *The Gentiles*, 59–87. Carroll, *Response*, says that there is a "soft-pedaling of imminent future hope"—though that eschatological outlook corresponds only to the narrative situation. Luke wanted to encourage his own audience to expect an imminent eschaton, 121–22.

3. Pervo, *Acts*, 25. Keener, *Acts,* though he does not necessarily assume that Luke wrote in response to eschatological delay, asserts that "eschatology is not a major emphasis in Acts," and that "Luke does not emphasize imminent future eschatology the way Mark or Matthew does," 1:518–19.

4. In contrast to most Lukan scholars, Haacker, "Der Geist," suggests that Luke has not abandoned imminent expectation. He points to passages such as Acts 14:22 where Paul says "we must go through many tribulations to enter the kingdom of God." He suggests that "Die Wir-Form dieser Aussage ist wie in 1 Thess 4.15 (,wir, die wir leben und übrigbleiben bis zur Ankunft des Herrn') ein Ausdruck der Naherwartung, so dass von einer 'complete absence of imminent expectation' in der Apostelgeschichte (Wilson) eben doch nicht geredet werden kann!" (345).

5. Pervo, *Acts,*" 19

continues to be an important theme for Luke. Likewise, eschatology does not receive attention in long discourses, but it is nevertheless central to both of Peter's sermons.

The second task of this chapter is to demonstrate how Luke's emphasis on eschatology and ethics fits within his broader rhetorical purposes. This chapter considers roughly the first five chapters of Acts. As we saw throughout his Gospel, Luke organizes his narrative into digestible literary sequences. Luke appears to organize his narrative of Acts 1:1—5:16 into two sequences: Acts 1–2 and Acts 3:1—5:16. These two sequences parallel each other by emphasizing—among other things—eschatology and ethics. In both literary sequences, Peter warns of coming eschatological events (Act 2:17; 3:20–21). Both sequences conclude with a summary of the Jerusalem community's life together that emphasizes in particular the sharing of possessions (2:42–47; 4:32–35). As we shall see, Luke also relates these two digestible literary sequences together by reusing various tropes, themes, and lexemes from Acts 1–2 in Acts 3:1—5:16.

Structure

The two literary sequences of Acts 1–2 and 3:1—5:16 parallel each other in general form.[6] In both sequences a miracle occasions a public sermon from Peter. Many are saved as a result of Peter's public sermon in each instance, and Luke concludes the sequences with a summary of the Jerusalem community's life together. In the first sequence, the Holy Spirit is poured out (2:1–4). Peter explains to the crowds who have seen this that the miracle of Pentecost is a result of Jesus' resurrection from the dead (2:32). Jesus' resurrection and the out-pouring of the Holy Spirit are moreover evidence that it is the "last days" (ταῖς ἐσχάταις ἡμέραις, 2:17). Three thousand people are added to the community as a result of Peter's announcement (2:41). Luke then describes the Jerusalem community's life together: they have "all things common" (ἅπαντα κοινά, 2:44).

---

6. Scholars almost all agree that Acts 1–2 forms a literary unit and that a new literary unit begins at 3:1. Few, however, agree about where the second unit should end. Pervo, *Acts*, identifies Acts 3–7 as a unit, 97–98; Parsons, *Acts*, notes that the story of the lame man in Acts 3:1—4:31 is "clearly set off from the rest of Acts by narrative summaries on either side (2:41–47; 4:32–37); Spencer, *Acts*, suggests that Acts 3–5 forms a literary unit (cf. Marguerat, *First Christian Historian,* 158–61). Cf. the "narrative blocks" of Baker, *Identity,* 71–76. These scholars, however, do not generally note the structural and thematic similarities between Acts 1–2 and 4—5:16. Zehnle, *Peter's Pentecost,* on the other hand, at least notices the similar content in Peter's two sermons in the two sequences, 19–26.

In the second sequence, a cripple is healed (3:1–10). Peter explains to the crowd who have seen this take place that the cripple has been healed through the name of Jesus "whom God raised from the dead" (ὃν ὁ θεὸς ἤγειρεν ἐκ νεκρῶν, 3:15). Jesus' resurrection and the cripple's healing are evidence that "times of refreshing" (καιροὶ ἀναψύξεως, 3:20) are coming. Five thousand people believe as a result of Peter's proclamation. Luke then concludes the sequence by again speaking of the Jerusalem community having "all things common" (ἅπαντα κοινά, 4:32).

The second literary sequence as I have identified it extends beyond the second summary statement (4:32–35) to include the story of Ananias and Sapphira and Luke's account of the apostles' continued healing activities. As I have argued before, no literary structure should necessarily be totalizing, not only because he may not have given his narrative a totalizing literary structure, but also because Luke may have intended multiple configurations of his narrative.[7] The reason the story of Ananias and Sapphira and the account of the apostles' continued healing activities have been included is because they both appear to be an extension of the second summary statement. The story of Ananias and Sapphira concerns one couple's deceit in laying their possessions at the feet of the apostles (5:2), which recalls the summary statement's description of the members of the community laying the proceeds of their possessions at the apostles' feet (4:35). The account of the apostles' continued healing activities (5:12–16) is included because it recalls the first summary statement of Acts 2:42–47. In Acts 5:12, Luke says the apostles continued to perform many "signs and wonders" (διὰ δὲ τῶν χειρῶν τῶν ἀποστόλων ἐγίνετο σημεῖα καὶ τέρατα πολλὰ ἐν τῷ λαῷ). Luke had similarly said in the first summary statement that the apostles were performing many "wonders and signs" (πολλά τε τέρατα καὶ σημεῖα διὰ τῶν ἀποστόλων ἐγίνετο, 2:43).

In addition to the parallel forms of the two literary sequences, Luke re-uses—as I have already mentioned—numerous tropes, themes, and lexemes from the first sequence in the second. These will be detailed in the exegesis below, but the most prominent tropes should be mentioned here because they are central to both sequences and because they are tropes Luke has already used in his Gospel in the context of eschatological announcement. Jesus tells the apostles that they will be his witnesses (μάρτυρες, 1:8). In both of Peter's sermons he claims that he and the other apostles are that very thing—witnesses of the risen Jesus (2:32; 3:15). In the context of claiming

7. See p. 29 above. We should note in this respect that the some portions of the first sequence (e.g., the selection of the twelfth, 1:15–26) and some portions of the second sequence (e.g., the arrest and trial of Peter and John, 4:1–22) do not have counterparts in their correlating sequences.

to be witnesses of the risen Jesus, Peter also appeals to the crowds' status as witnesses of the miracles that have occasioned his preaching. On the day of Pentecost, Peter tells them that they "see and hear" (βλέπετε καὶ ἀκούετε) the outpouring of the Holy Spirit (2:33). On the occasion of the healed cripple, Peter reminds the crowd that they "see and know" (θεωρεῖτε καὶ οἴδατε) the cripple who has been healed (3:16). These tropes of hearing and eyesight are key in Peter's public proclamation. The people are eyewitnesses of the miracles, and Peter and the apostles are eyewitnesses of the raised Jesus. Like Simeon (Luke 2:30), and like the Seventy (Luke 10:24), the apostles and the crowds are eyewitnesses of eschatological events.

Pentecost: Acts 1–2

The Restoration Question

Immediately before Jesus ascends into heaven, the disciples ask him, "will you at this time restore (ἀποκαθιστάνεις) the kingdom to Israel?" (1:6). Jesus responds that it is not for them "to know the times or the seasons (χρόνους ἢ καιρους) which the Father has set in his own authority" (1:7). He goes on to tell them that the Holy Spirit will come upon them and they will be his witnesses (μάρτυρες) to the end of the earth (1:8). Does the Lukan Jesus attempt here to temper the disciples' hope for an imminent eschaton?[8] Jesus' redirection to focus them on a mission to be his witnesses to the ends of the earth might suggest so. At the same time, Jesus at the very least affirms the disciples' hope for "times and seasons" to come. And he does not say in his response that the kingdom is not imminent—he merely says that its timing is not for them to know. But regardless of what Lukan Jesus is or is not saying about the timing of the eschaton, it seems clear that Luke wishes to begin his second volume—just as he did his first—with an outlook to eschatological events.[9]

8. Haenchen, *Acts*, says that Luke has here "decisively renounced all expectation of an imminent end," 143. Cf. Conzelmann, *Theology*, 121; and Fitzmyer, *Acts*, 201. Parsons, *Acts*, suggests that Jesus' answer is a "reproof" of the apostles' question; "the burning issue is not 'When will the kingdom be restored to Israel?' Rather, it is 'Who is commissioned to spread the good news on worldwide missions?'" (28). Cf. Barrett, *Commentary*, 78; Carroll, *Repsonse*,123–28; Marshall, *Luke: Historian and Theologian*, 157–58; Jervell, *Theology*, 1, 107. Eckey, *Die Apostelgeschichte*, however, points out that the negative aspect of Jesus' response looks very similar to Jesus' saying in Mark13:32— i.e., that only the Father knows the day or the hour (48). This may suggest that Jesus' response in Acts 1:7–8 cannot be used to say that Luke has rejected the expectation of an imminent end any more than Mark has.

9. As Brawley, *Centering on God*, suggests, "although [Jesus] refuses to provide a

The disciples' eschatological question clearly makes sense at this point in Luke's double-work. Resurrection is, according to Luke, an eschatological event (cf. Luke 20:27–40), and Jesus has just been raised from the dead. Jesus has moreover been "saying things concerning the kingdom of God (τῆς βασιλείας τοῦ θεοῦ, 1:3) in his post-resurrection appearances to the disciples. Furthermore, Jesus has just promised the baptism in the Holy Spirit: "John baptized in water, but you will be baptized in the Holy Spirit" (1:5). John the Baptist had said that in addition to baptizing in the Holy Spirit, the Christ would be the eschatological judge (cf. Luke 3:15–17). It therefore makes perfect sense for the disciples to wonder about the timing of the "kingdom" (τὴν βασιλείαν, 1:6).

It also makes sense for the disciples to ask if the kingdom at this time will be restored "to Israel" (τῷ Ἰσραήλ). Luke's Gospel began and ended on this matter. Simeon and Anna, we will recall, wait for "the comfort of Israel" (Luke 2:25) and the "redemption of Jerusalem" (2:38), respectively. At the end of the Gospel, the two disciples on the road to Emmaus say they had hoped that Jesus of Nazareth was the one who was "about to redeem Israel" (ὁ μέλλων λυτροῦσθαι τὸν Ἰσραήλ, 24:21). Acts will moreover close on the same question. Paul will speak of the "hope of Israel" (τῆς ἐλπίδος τοῦ Ἰσραήλ, 28:20) and "the kingdom of God" (τὴν βασιλείαν τοῦ θεοῦ, 28:23) to the Judean leaders of Rome.[10]

Jesus' promise of the coming baptism in the Holy Spirit might also have occasioned the "to Israel" part of the disciples' question. Some of the OT

---

time table, he affirms a divine plan (1:7). That leaves the question of the restoration of the kingdom to Israel open," 43. Salmeier, *Restoring the Kingdom*, suggests that Jesus' response causes more narrative questions to arise for the reader—"when will the kingdom be restored? What is that kingdom (is it the same thing as the kingdom of God)? Will the narrative describe the restoration?" (11). On the centrality of the divine plan in Acts, see Squires, *Plan of God*.

10. Maddox, *Purpose*, suggests that Jesus does not reject the disciples question because they were expecting an imminent eschaton, but because of the "to Israel" part of their question. Jesus disapproves of "the traditional, nationalistic sense" of their question. He continues that the kingdom according to Luke is "not Israel's private prerogative," 106–8. Maddox may be right that Luke does not see the kingdom as "Israel's private prerogative," but it seems unlikely to me that Luke intends the reader to understand Jesus' response as a rejection of the "to Israel" part of their question precisely because Luke consistently raises the matter of God's promises to Israel. Contrary to Maddox, numerous scholars have suggested that Luke wants to keep Israel's hopes in view here. Bauckham, "Restoration" in Scott, *Restoration*, suggests that Luke "relates the 'witnessing' task of the twelve apostles to the restoration of Israel and to the conversion of nations," 475. Keener likewise suggests that the disciples' question "presupposes a theology of Israel's restoration that is indeed affirmed in some of the texts in the Gospel," 1:683. Cf. Pao, *New Exodus*, 95–96; Salmeier, *Restoring the Kingdom*, 79–90; Eckey, *Die Apostelgeschichte*, 47–48.

prophets looked forward to the outpouring of the Holy Spirit as the time of Israel's eschatological restoration. The oracles in Ezekiel 36–37 are illustrative. God says to Israel, "I will take you out of the nations and will gather you out of every country and I will lead you into your land" (36:24 LXX). At the time of the gathering, God continues, "I will give my spirit to you (τὸ πνεῦμά μου δώσω ἐν ὑμῖν) and I will do it so that you will walk in all my commandments and you will keep and do my decrees" (36:27 LXX). This oracle comes right before the vision of dry bones, which narrates the resurrection of Israel and reasserts that God will give his Spirit to them (37:14).

Isaiah looked forward to something similar. Israel will remain in ruins, Isaiah says, "until the Spirit comes from on high" (32:14–15). It is possible that Jesus' promise of the outpouring in Acts 1:8 reuses some of the language from Isa 32:15:

ἕως ἂν ἐπέλθῃ ἐφ᾽ ὑμᾶς πνεῦμα ἀφ᾽ ὑψηλου Isa 32:15

ἀλλὰ λήμψεσθε δύναμιν ἐπελθόντος τοῦ ἁγίου πνεύματος ἐφ᾽ ὑμᾶς Acts 1:8

Acts 1:8 does not speak of the Spirit coming from "on high" (ἀφ᾽ ὑψηλου). But Luke's parallel scene at the end of his Gospel does:[11]

καθίσατε ἐν τῇ πόλει ἕως οὗ ἐνδύσησθε ἐξ ὕψους δύναμιν Luke 24:49[12]

Luke does not mention any prophet by name at this point in his narrative, nor does he appeal explicitly to any OT passage. Would anyone in Luke's audience have been able to see a connection between Jesus' promise of the Holy Spirit and the disciples' question? Luke will shortly quote the prophet Joel explicitly in reference to the outpouring of the Holy Spirit (Acts 2:17–21), so even if they were not aware of Ezekiel and Isaiah, his audience will soon know that the out-pouring of the Spirit was foretold in the OT.[13]

---

11. Pao, *New Exodus*, 92. Pao suggests that the whole of Acts 1:8 is reused material from Isaiah. The phrase ἕως ἐσχάτου τῆς γῆς he says is sourced from Isa 49:6 (ἰδοὺ τέθεικά σε εἰς διαθήκην γένους εἰς φῶς ἐθνῶν τοῦ εἶναί σε εἰς σωτηρίαν ἕως ἐσχάτου τῆς γῆς). And the title μάρτυρες he says comes from Isa 43:10–12 (γένεσθέ μοι μάρτυρες, κἀγὼ μάρτυς, λέγει κύριος ὁ θεός, καὶ ὁ παῖς, ὃν ἐξελεξάμην, ἵνα γνῶτε καὶ πιστεύσητε καὶ συνῆτε ὅτι ἐγώ εἰμι, ἔμπροσθέν μου οὐκ ἐγένετο ἄλλος θεὸς καὶ μετ᾽ ἐμὲ οὐκ ἔσται· ἐγὼ ὁ θεός, καὶ οὐκ ἔστιν πάρεξ ἐμοῦ σῴζων. ἀνήγγειλα καὶ ἔσωσα, ὠνείδισα καὶ οὐκ ἦν ἐν ὑμῖν ἀλλότριος· ὑμεῖς ἐμοὶ μάρτυρες κἀγὼ μάρτυς, λέγει κύριος ὁ θεός), *New Exodus*, 91–96. Bauckham, "Restoration" in Scott, *Restoration*, suggests the same, 475.

12. Cf. Luke 1:35.

13. Keener, *Acts*, says: "the prophets had regularly linked God's pouring out his Spirit with the time of Israel's restoration, and so any talk about the Spirit's outpouring

Whether or not Luke is drawing on the OT prophets in this instance, what follows Jesus' final promise of the Holy Spirit (1:8) again seems to set an eschatological stage for the rest of the narrative.[14] Jesus' final words to the apostles, as we have already noted, commission them as his "witnesses" (μάρτυρες) to the ends of the earth. In Jesus' ascension, Luke emphasizes the apostles' status as witnesses:

> And after saying these things he was lifted up while they were watching (βλεπόντων αὐτῶν) and a cloud took him from their eyes (ἀπὸ τῶν ὀφθαλμῶν αὐτῶν). And as they were looking intently (ἀτενίζοντες ἦσαν) into heaven where he went, behold (ἰδοὺ) two men appeared (παρειστήκεισαν) to them in white clothing and they said, 'Galilean men, why do you stand staring (ἐμβλέποντες) into heaven? This Jesus who was taken up from you into heaven will come in the way that you saw (ἐθεάσασθε) him going into heaven. Acts 1:9–11

The repeated references to the apostles' eyesight suggests that to be Jesus' witnesses (μάρτυρες) is to be his eyewitnesses.[15] The angels' final words to the apostles inform them that their mission as eyewitnesses is a task of eschatological nature. They will claim to the world that Jesus will return because they saw him ascend. Luke says that they will be able to claim this precisely because they saw Jesus ascend with their own eyes: he will come in same way they saw him go (1:11).[16]

---

was de facto eschatological in character," 1:682. Numerous other scholars have suggested more generally that Israel's restoration is in view in Luke's double-work. Fuller, *Restoration*, says "it is clear that Israel's restoration lies at the center of Luke's eschatology," 268, cf. 257–69; Pao, *New Exodus*; Bauckham, "Restoration" in Scott, *Restoration*, 435–88; Ravens, *Restoration*. Turner, *Power*, 267–317, 428–31. Jervell, *People*, 41–74; Denova, *Things Accomplished*, 155–77.

14. Pervo's claim that the disciples question exemplifies the practice in literary tradition that permitted pupils to ask "dull or inappropriate questions so that teachers could promulgate the correct view" (*Acts*, 41) seems to miss the mark. The disciples question seems to me to be both logical and appropriate. Jesus, as we have noted, has been speaking of the kingdom, which would naturally cause the disciples to ask the question that they did.

15. Luke has moreover already mentioned that the resurrected Jesus "presented himself living with many proofs after he suffered" (1:3).

16. The ascension is clearly one of the most important (if not the most important) events of the narrative since it is what makes the rest of the narrative possible. As Sleeman, *Geography*, says, the ascension "exercises an unceasing influence over the whole narrative and its theology." Sleeman points to the "trailing off of οὐρανός references within Acts 11:18" which "coincides with the climactic labeling of believers as 'Christians' in 11:26," as evidence of the influence the ascension excercises in the narrative, 257. But the ascension's importance is clear even apart from the use of the term οὐρανός:

Immediately after Jesus ascends into heaven, the apostles go to Jerusalem to await the Spirit as per Jesus' instructions (1:12, cf. 1:4). But before the Spirit is poured out, they must become twelve again. A twelfth is necessary because Judas has died in the very field he bought with the money he gained from betraying Jesus (1:18). Whereas Luke has not yet appealed explicitly to the OT Scriptures, in this instance he does. Peter says "it is necessary to fulfill the scriptures" (ἔδει πληρωθῆναι τὴν γραφὴν, 1:16). Ps. 69:26 (68 LXX) foretold Judas's death, and Ps 109:8 (108 LXX) counsels that another should take his place (Act 1:20). The twelfth, Luke goes on to say, must have been with Jesus since the baptism of John until the day Jesus ascended, and he must be a witness (μάρτυρα) of his resurrection (1:22). The twelfth apostle will have the same eschatological mission as the other eleven: he will be an eyewitness, a μάρτυς, proclaiming Jesus' resurrection and return to the ends of the earth.

The fact that Peter insists that they must fulfill the scriptures by selecting a twelfth apostle might indicate that Luke has Israel's restoration in view.[17] Luke did say in his Gospel that the apostles would "sit on thrones judging the twelve tribes of Israel" (Luke 22:30).[18] Selecting the twelfth before the Holy Spirit is poured out might moreover indicate that Luke has such passages as Ezek 36–37 and Isa 32:15 in view. But, again, whether he does or does not have these passages in view, it is clear that Luke has begun to set an eschatological stage for the rest of his narrative. Resurrection will be proclaimed by Jesus' eyewitnesses. And Jesus will return in the same way they saw him go.

---

it is what makes possible the outpouring of the Holy Spirit (2:33), which itself creates the conditions for the rest of the narrative. Since Jesus' return is in view in his ascension, this likely indicates that Jesus' return exercises a similar influence. Indeed, the very next time after Pentecost that Luke mentions Jesus' ascension is in the context of promising his return (Acts 3:19–21).

17. Though Pervo, *Acts*, does not suggest Israel's restoration is in view, he puts the oddity of the scene well: "why tell this story describing a method not employed thereafter to select a person who has no role in the narrative," 48. Other scholars, however, suggest that Israel's restoration is probably in view. See e.g., Keener, *Acts*, 1:752; Pao, *New Exodus*, 123–29; Fuller, *Restoration*, 260–61; Denova, *Things Accomplished*, 169. Parsons, *Acts*, notes that it might be significant that Luke also notes that there were one hundred and twenty others present (Acts 1:15). Later rabbinic literature says that one hundred and twenty men are necessary to form constitute a local Sanhedrin (*Sanhedrin*, 1.6), 32.

18. This saying comes in the context of Judas' betrayal (22:3), the final Passover meal (22:7–20), his counsel to be servant leaders (22:24–27), and the giving of a new covenant (22:29).

What Might this Mean?

Luke describes coming of the Spirit in terms similar to OT theophanies.[19] Luke says that there was a roar (ἦχος) out of heaven (ἐκ τοῦ οὐρανοῦ) that bore a "mighty wind" (πνοῆς βιαίας) and filled the whole house (ἐπλήρωσεν ὅλον τὸν οἶκον) where they were staying. Tongues of fire (γλῶσσαι ὡσεὶ πυρός) sit on each one of them (2:2–3), and they all speak in tongues as the Spirit gives utterance. All those outside who had gathered in Jerusalem for the festival are astounded (ἐξίσταντο, vv. 7, 12). At Sinai, a trumpet roared (ἤχει), and there was fire and smoke on top of the mountain. All the people were amazed (ἐξέστη, Exod 19:16–19). Elijah calls fire "out of heaven" (ἐκ τοῦ οὐρανοῦ) when the whole burnt offerings are set ablaze on Mt. Carmel (1 Kgs 18:38–39). At Horeb, he experiences a mighty wind (πνεῦμα μέγα κραταιὸν), an earthquake, and fire before hearing the voice of the Lord in a small whisper (1 Kgs 19:11–12). When Solomon dedicates the Temple, fire comes out of heaven (ἐκ τοῦ οὐρανοῦ) and the glory of the Lord fills the house (δόξα κυρίου ἔπλησεν τὸν οἶκον, 2 Chron 7:1–2). In Ezekiel's vision of the future temple, the glory of the Lord comes with "the voice of an encampment, as a voice doubled many times" (φωνὴ τῆς παρεμβολῆς ὡς φωνὴ διπλασιαζόντων πολλῶν, Ezek 43:2). Fire, wind, and a loud noise are all characteristic of the arrival of God's presence. Luke's description of the coming of the Spirit does not necessarily indicate that the event is an eschatological one, but it does at the very least put the event on par with other seminal moments in Israel's history.

In addition to using language similar to OT theophanies, Luke appears to reuse language from John the Baptist's preaching. John the Baptist said that the Christ would baptize in Spirit and in fire (ἐν πνεύματι ἁγίῳ καὶ πυρί, Luke 3:16). On the day of Pentecost there is a "mighty wind" (πνοῆς βιαίας) and "tongues as of fire" (γλῶσσαι ὡσεὶ πυρὸς) appear on the apostles (Act 2:3). Luke likely describes the coming of the πνεῦμα ἁγίου as a πνοή since the term πνεῦμα can mean both "wind" and "spirit." At that moment all those present were filled with the Holy Spirit and, Luke adds, they all "began to speak in other tongues (γλώσσαις) as the Spirit (πνεῦμα) gave them to utter (2:4). Calling the fire γλῶσσαι πυρὸς suggests a correlation between the uttered γλώσσαις and the tongues of fire.[20]

---

19. Scholars have generally recognized that Luke is here drawing on language from OT theophanies. See Spencer, *Acts*, 32; Pervo, *Acts*, 61; Fitzmyer, *Acts*, 234, Keener, *Acts*, 1:784–87; Wenk, *Community-Forming Power*, 247–51.

20. It is not unlikely that Luke would have wanted the reader to see that he was reusing imagery from John the Baptist's preaching since he has already twice explicitly reminded the reader of John the Baptist (1:5, 22).

Yet, the fire for John the Baptist seems to have been only the fire of judgment: "every tree that does not bear good fruit will be cut down and thrown into the fire (πῦρ)" (Luke 3:9). And speaking of the Christ, he said that "the winnowing fork is in his hand to clean out his threshing floor; he will gather the grain into his barn, but the chaff he will burn up with unquenchable fire (πυρί, Luke 3:17). The fire therefore appears to be reserved for the wicked. But John the Baptist at the same time says that the very people he had baptized (i.e., those who had repented, cf. 3:3) were going to be baptized both in Spirit and in fire. The pronouns indicate he is addressing the same audience: "I baptize ὑμᾶς . . . but he will baptize ὑμᾶς in the Spirit and in fire (3:16). The fire in John the Baptist's preaching thus appears to be at once for all his hearers and for only those who do not bear good fruit. This ambiguity in John the Baptist's preaching is perhaps what can allow Luke to suggest that Jesus' followers are baptized both in the Spirit and in fire on the day of Pentecost.[21]

As there was at John the Baptist's assembly in the wilderness, a crowd of Abraham's descendants is gathered (Acts 2:5–13; cf. Luke 3:7–8). Luke says that the crowd is formed of "Judeans, reverent men from all nations under heaven" (Ιουδαῖοι, ἄνδρες εὐλαβεῖς ἀπὸ παντὸς ἔθνους τῶν ὑπὸ τὸν οὐρανόν, 2:5). "All nations" is hyperbolic, and Luke likely wants it to be recognized as such.[22] Here again we can see that Luke appears to have Israel specifically

21. Keener suggests that "Luke's informed audience would quickly connect the fire with Luke 3:16, which was originally a promise of end-time judgment." He suggests that the fire in Luke's writing "may function proleptically for purification (Luke 12:49–50)" and asserts that the fire "symbolizes the eschatological judgment that is the converse of baptism in the Spirit (3:16)," 1:804. Barrett, *Acts*, says "it is very probable that Luke saw in it a fulfillment of the Baptist's prophecy," 1:114. Fitzmyer, *Acts*, by contrast, claims the fire "has nothing to do with the fire of judgment or of everlasting punishment often used for the "Holy Spirit and fire" of Luke 3:16, 238.

22. Some scholars have suggested that Luke attempts to demonstrate that "all nations" are indeed there representationally in his list of the different places people have come from in 2:9–11. Bauckham, "James and the Jerusalem Church" in Bauckham, *Palestinian Setting*, claims that Luke lists the nations "in four groups corresponding to the four points of the compass" if plotted on the map of Strabo, the first century geographer. Parthians, Medes, Elamites, residents of Mesopotamia stretches to the east (v. 9a). Cappadocia, Pontus, Asia, Phrygia, Pamphylia are north of Judea (v. 9b–10a). Egypt, the parts of Libya belonging to Cyrene, visitors from Rome, Cretans are to the west (v. 10b–11a). And, finally, Luke mentions Arabs, who would have been from the south of Jerusalem, 417–27. Cf. Spencer, *Acts*, 34; Parsons, *Acts*, 40. See also James M. Scott, "Acts 2:9–11 As an Anticipation of the Mission to the Nations" in Ådna and Kvalbein, *Mission*, 87–124. It is not clear that Strabo had a map, but we hardly need to plot the different locales on a map or find a pattern in that plotting to see that Luke thinks his list of nations is a representation of the "all nations" he has said are there on the day of Pentecost.

in mind. Twelve apostles have been chosen off the cusp of a question about God restoring the kingdom "to Israel" (1:6). And now the Spirit is poured out at the precise moment that Judeans from all over the world are gathered in Jerusalem. The reader who already knows the rest of the story might also see in the gathering of Judeans from all nations under the heavens a foreshadowing of the witnessing to the ends of the earth that the apostles will do. All the languages the Judeans from various parts of the world hear those filled with the Spirit speaking might in particular foreshadow this (2:8, 11). But up until this point in the narrative only Israel is in view. Peter's repeated address to his audience as Ἰουδαῖοι (2:14), Ἰσραηλῖται (2:22), and ἀδελφοί (2:29) in his speech that follows indicates Luke wants the crowd's Judean make-up to be kept in view (cf. 2:39).

Is the outpouring of the Holy Spirit an eschatological event? Luke does not yet say, but the ways in which the event recalls John the Baptist's preaching at least raises the question. Indeed, Luke may want the reader to ask with the crowds in Jerusalem, "what might this mean?" (τί θέλει τοῦτο εἶναι, 2:12).

These Are the Last Days

Peter proclaims Jesus' resurrection to the crowd. Jesus has been raised from the dead, so the Spirit is poured out, and the prophet Joel foretold this event. Peter addresses them, "Judeans . . . pay attention to my words" (ἄνδρες Ἰουδαῖοι . . . ἐνωτίσασθε τὰ ῥήματά μου, 2:14). Peter, it appears, engages in his first act as a witness (μάρτυς, cf. 1:8) to Jesus.[23] Peter stands "with the eleven" (ἕνδεκα, 2:14), a detail that is likely meant to bring to mind the role that he and the other eleven have been commissioned to fulfill (cf. 1:22, 26). Peter moreover "utters" (ἀπεφθέγξατο, 2:14) his words to the crowd, just as he and the eleven had "uttered" (ἀποφθέγγεσθαι, 2:4) the words given to them by the Spirit. The reuse of the verb suggests that they the twelve have now received the power to be Jesus' witnesses, just as Jesus said they would (cf. 1:8).

Peter says that Joel foretold this event, and Joel identified it as an event of the last days: "and it will be in the last days (ἐν ταῖς ἐσχάταις ἡμέραις), God says, I will pour out my Spirit" (2:17). Peter goes on to quote the prophet, who speaks of the coming "great and manifest day of the Lord" (ἡμέραν κυρίου τὴν μεγάλην καὶ ἐπιφανῆ, 2:20). The words "in the last days" (ἐν ταῖς ἐσχάταις ἡμέραις) do not appear in the extant versions of the LXX.[24]

---

23. On the Spirit's empowerment for witness in Acts, see Haya-Prats, *Empowered Believers*, 97–233.

24. See Ziegler, *Duodecim Prophetae*, ad loc.

Joel's words in the Greek versions say that it will be "after these things" (μετὰ ταῦτα) that the Holy Spirit will be poured out. Some manuscripts of Acts are consistent with the Greek versions.[25] But it is nevertheless likely that Luke inserted these words himself to emphasize the eschatological nature of the event.[26]

The reason it appears Luke likely inserted the words ἐν ταῖς ἐσχάταις ἡμέραις himself is that other parts of his quotation of Joel are inconsistent with Greek versions. These changes moreover are likely his own because he reuses the adjusted portions of the quotation in the coming narrative. The Greek versions of Joel 3:3 read "and I will give wonders in the heavens and on the earth" (καὶ δώσω τέρατα ἐν τῷ οὐρανῷ καὶ ἐπὶ τῆς γῆς).[27] Luke's version, however, reads "I will give wonders in the heavens above and signs on the earth below" (καὶ δώσω τέρατα ἐν τῷ οὐρανῷ ἄνω καὶ σημεῖα ἐπὶ τῆς γῆς κάτω, Acts 2:19). Luke makes three adjustments to this phrase: he adds the noun σημεῖα and he adds two prepositions ἄνω and κάτω. Luke will use the words σημεῖον and τέρας together several times in the narrative that follows, including immediately after the Joel quotation. Peter says that Jesus was shown to the people "in powers and wonders and signs" (δυνάμεσι καὶ τέρασι καὶ σημείοις, 2:22; cf. 4:30, 5:12, 6:8, 7:36, 14:3, 15:12).[28]

25. B, 076, (C pc) sa^mss are consistent with the Greek verisons of Joel. The LXX μετὰ ταῦτα moreover is consistent with the MT וְהָיָה אַחֲרֵי־כֵן (Joel 3:1).

26. Metzger, *Textual Commentary*, claims that "it was probably the author himself who substituted ἐν ταῖς ἐσχάταις ἡμέραις . . . for μετὰ ταῦτα of the Septuagint . . . which is inappropriate for the context of the narrative in Acts." He suggests that the words faithful to the extant Greek versions in later manuscripts should be taken as the work of an Alexandrian corrector who brought the text into conformity with the prevailing text of the Septuagint, 257. Pervo, *Acts*, on the other hand, argues that the LXX's μετὰ ταῦτα should be maintained as the original text of Acts. He claims it fits on theological and textual grounds. He suggests that μετὰ ταῦτα would have been understood as "following the passion, death, resurrection and ascension of Jesus" (79). He suggests that ἐν ταῖς ἐσχάταις ἡμέραις may have been introduced because μετὰ ταῦτα may have seemed like a "dangling prepositional phrase" (77). He moreover agrees with Haenchen (*Acts*, 179) and Conzelmann (*Acts*, 19) that the phrase ἐν ταῖς ἐσχάταις ἡμέραις simply does not seem very Lukan, 76–79.

27. See Ziegler, *Duodecim Prophetae, ad loc.* All verse numbers from Joel follow the numbering of the LXX.

28. Luke also reuses two other parts of the quotation in the coming narrative. The verb "to pour out" (ἐκχέω, 2:17, 18) is used when, after proclaiming Jesus' resurrection and ascension (2:22–32), Peter says Jesus "poured out" (ἐξέχεεν) the Holy Spirit. Luke moreover reuses the final line of the quotation of Joel, "each person who calls upon the name of the Lord will be saved" (ἔσται πᾶς ὃς ἂν ἐπικαλέσηται τὸ ὄνομα κυρίου σωθήσεται, 2:21). Luke appears to have ended the quotation here so the read⟨ easily recall it when Luke reuses it as the final words of Peter's sermon. The pr⟨ the Holy Spirit, Peter says, will be given to "as many as call upon the name of our God" (ὅσους ἂν προσκαλέσηται κύριος ὁ θεὸς ἡμῶν, 2:39). These two porti⟨

If Luke changed Joel's "after these things" (μετὰ ταῦτα) to "in the last days" (ἐν ταῖς ἐσχάταις ἡμέραις), then we can make sense of the change since, as we have already noted, the Joel quotation goes on to speak of the "great and manifest day of the Lord" (ἡμέραν κυρίου τὴν μεγάλην καὶ ἐπιφανῆ, 2:20). The phrase ἐν ταῖς ἐσχάταις ἡμέραις merely foreshadows the mention of the "day of the Lord" at the end of the quotation.

But it appears that Luke did not add these word himself simply because he thought that the outpouring of the Holy Spirit meant that it was the last days (though, if these are his words, he obviously did think that). Luke appears to have selected the phrase from a passage in another OT prophet that is similar to the Joel quotation. We should recall that Luke has done this before: he inserted Isa 58:6 into a quotation of Isa 61:1–2 in Jesus' Nazareth sermon (Luke 4:18–19).[29]

Two other OT prophets, Isaiah and Micah, foretold events similar to the events Joel foretold with similar language and imagery. In the context of foretelling the future outpouring of the Holy Spirit (Joel 3:1–5), Joel prophesies that God will judge from Jerusalem. God's judgment will come from the city: he will "cry out from Zion and out of Jerusalem he will utter his voice" (ὁ δὲ κύριος ἐκ Σιων ἀνακεκράξεται καὶ ἐξ Ιερουσαλημ δώσει φωνὴν αὐτοῦ, Joel 4:16). The judgment will take place when the nations gather in Jerusalem: "gather and come all surrounding nations!" (συναθροίζεσθε καὶ εἰσπορεύεσθε, πάντα τὰ ἔθνη κυκλόθεν, 4:11; cf. 4:2). And the nations' gathering will be for war: their plowshares will be turned into swords and pruning hooks into spears (συγκόψατε τὰ ἄροτρα ὑμῶν εἰς ῥομφαίας καὶ τὰ δρέπανα ὑμῶν εἰς σειρομάστας, 4:10).

Isaiah 2:1–5 and Micah 4:1–4 have very similar elements in their prophecies. Both speak of the exaltation of the mountain of the Lord to the highest place:

> The mountain of the Lord will be visible and the house of God will be on the highest mountain.

> ἐμφανὲς τὸ ὄρος κυρίου καὶ ὁ οἶκος τοῦ θεοῦ ἐπ᾽ ἄκρων τῶν ὀρέων
> Isa 2:2

> The mountain of the Lord will be visible, ready on the summit of mountains

---

quotation are not adjusted by Luke as Joel 3:3 is, but their appearance in the narrative that follows indicates at the very least that Luke is paying attention to the details of his Joel quotation.

29. See p. 58 above.

ἐμφανὲς τὸ ὄρος τοῦ κυρίου, ἕτοιμον ἐπὶ τὰς κορυφὰς τῶν ὀρέων
Mic 4:2

Both speak of God judging between nations:

And he will judge between the nations

καὶ κρινεῖ ἀνὰ μέσον τῶν ἐθνῶν Isa 2:4

And he will judge between many people

καὶ κρινεῖ ἀνὰ μέσον λαῶν πολλῶν Mic 4:3

Both speak of swords and spears being turned into plowshares and pruning hooks:

They shall beat their swords into plowshares and their spears into sickles

συγκόψουσιν τὰς μαχαίρας αὐτῶν εἰς ἄροτρα καὶ τὰς ζιβύνας αὐτῶν εἰς δρέπανα Isa 2:4

They shall beat their swords into plowshares and their spears into sickles

κατακόψουσιν τὰς ῥομφαίας αὐτῶν εἰς ἄροτρα καὶ τὰ δόρατα αὐτῶν εἰς δρέπανα Mic 4:3

And finally, both claim that these things take place in the last days:

Because it will be in the last days

Ὅτι ἔσται ἐν ταῖς ἐσχάταις ἡμέραις Isa 2:2

And it will be in the last days

Καὶ ἔσται ἐπ' ἐσχάτων τῶν ἡμερῶν Mic 4:1

The similarities among all three prophets make it likely that Luke changed Joel's μετὰ ταῦτα to ἐν ταῖς ἐσχάταις ἡμέραις.[30] There is, of course, the discrepancy between Joel's turning of farm tools into weapons and Isaiah's and Micah's turning of weapons into farm tools, but it is clear they are all drawing on common imagery and all agree that farm tools and weapons will in one form or another be present on the day of judgment. It moreover appears that Luke is drawing the phrase from Isaiah in particular since the dative

30. The correlations Acts 2:17 has with these OT prophets gives good reason to reject Pervo's claim that ἐν ταῖς ἐσχάταις ἡμέραις was added simply to make up for the "dangling prepositional phrase" that would have been there had μετὰ ταῦτα been preserved (Pervo, *Acts*, 77).

ταῖς ἐσχάταις ἡμέραις following the preposition ἐν appears in the LXX only in Isa 2:2, whereas the genitive ἐσχάτων τῶν ἡμερῶν following the preposition ἐπί—as it does in Micah—appears sixteen times.[31]

The prophecies in Isaiah 2:1–5, Micah 1:1–4, and Joel 3:1–5 all have the national establishment of Israel in view. The supremacy of Zion is central to each prophet. Moreover, the restoration of Israel is foretold on either side of the verses from Joel quoted in Acts:

> I will restore to you the years which the grasshopper and the locust and the mildew and the caterpillar ate . . . and you will know that I myself am in the midst of Israel and I myself am the Lord your God. Joel 2:25, 27

> Therefore behold I—in those days and at that time—when I bring back the captives of Judah and Jerusalem . . . And I will gather all the nations and Iwill lead them into the valley of Jehosephat and I will judge there against those who scattered them into the nations and divided up my land and I will judge on behalf of my people, my inheritance, Israel. Joel 4:1–2

It is not clear how much of the context of Joel's prophecy Luke has in mind. If Luke himself inserted ἐν ταῖς ἐσχάταις ἡμέραις, as it appears that he did, then at least some of the context of Joel 3:1–5 is. Luke has nowhere said that Israel's restoration has occurred. But the disciples question about the restoration of the kingdom to Israel, the formation of the twelve, the Judeans gathered from all nations under the heavens, the quotation of Joel 3:1–5, and the fact that all of this takes place in Jerusalem suggest that Luke may have Israel's restoration in view. If Israel's restoration is in view, then this at the very least again indicates that Luke has the formation of a people in view in his double work. Are the twelve and their companions perhaps the prepared people of God whom the narrative has been anticipating since the annunciation of John the Baptist?

31. Gen 49:1; Num 24:24; Deut 4:30, 8:16; Josh 24:27; Hos 3:5; Mic 4:1; Jer 23:20, 25:19, 37:24; Ezek 38:8, 16; Dan 2:28, 29, 45, 10:14. Strazicich, *Joel's Use of Scripture*, suggests that Luke has made "a conscious alteration of the LXX Joel 3:1." It is "a deliberate re-interpretation in order to bring Joel's message into alignment with an *eschatological* emphasis." He moreover suggests that "the substituted phrase stems from Isa 2:2"—though he does not speculate why Luke thought this was an appropriate context from which to select the phrase, 277.

Resurrection

Luke notes the crowd's amazement upon hearing Galileans speak in the various crowd members' own languages twice: they "were amazed and marveled" (ἐξίσταντο δὲ καὶ ἐθαύμαζον, 2:7), and they "were amazed and perplexed" (ἐξίσταντο δὲ πάντες καὶ διηπόρουν, 2:12). As we have already noted, this leads them to ask "what might this mean?" (τί θέλει τοῦτο εἶναι; 2:12). Peter claims that the Spirit has been poured out and that this means that it is the last days (2:17). But Peter has yet to explain what has made this event possible. To this matter Peter turns next in his sermon: Jesus has been raised from the dead, and it is he who has poured out the Spirit.[32] In order to substantiate Peter's claim that Jesus has been raised from the dead, Luke again uses the tropes of hearing and seeing, which we have seen him use repeatedly throughout his Gospel. Peter appeals to what the crowd has seen and heard in order to corroborate what he and the apostles claim to have seen and heard.

Peter begins his proclamation of Jesus' resurrection by telling the crowd to "listen to these words" (ἀκούσατε τοὺς λόγους τούτους, 2:22). As he had at the beginning of the sermon, Luke again draws attention to Peter's spoken words and the crowds' listening ears (cf. ἐνωτίσασθε τὰ ῥήματά μου, 2:14). He says that "Jesus of Nazareth, a man shown by God to you in power and wonders and signs (δυνάμεσι καὶ τέρασι καὶ σημείοις) which God did through him in your midst, just as you know (καθὼς αὐτοὶ οἴδατε)," was raised from the dead (2:22). The mention of τέρασι καὶ σημείοις connects Jesus' wonder-working with the Joel citation, which promised τέρατα and σημεῖα before the great and manifest day of the Lord. But to τέρατα and σημεῖα Luke also adds δυνάμεσι. This is likely to signify that Jesus' σημεῖα and τέρατα were done through the Holy Spirit, since Jesus had said just before his ascension, "you will receive power (δύναμιν) when the Holy Spirit comes upon you" (1:8). But none of this is news to the crowds: all of this, Peter says to them, is "just as you know" (καθὼς αὐτοὶ οἴδατε, 2:22). The people, in other words, are witnesses of Jesus' τέρατα and σημεῖα.

Peter claims that the Scriptures foretold Jesus' death and resurrection. He quotes David to demonstrate this:

> I saw the Lord always before me because he is at my right hand
> . . . because you will not forsake my life in hades (ἐγκαταλείψεις

---

32. On the centrality of resurrection in Lukan theology, see Anderson, "God Raised," and Horton, *Death and Resurrection.*

τὴν ψυχήν μου εἰς ᾅδην), neither will you give your holy one to
see corruption (διαφθοράν) Acts 2:25, 27; Cf. Ps 15:8–11[33]

Peter's logic is clear: if David wrote this, and David died and saw corruption,
then the Scripture must not be about David. And if Scripture is always true,
then it must be about someone else. That someone else, Peter claims, is Jesus. David therefore announced "the resurrection of Jesus (τῆς ἀναστάσεως
τοῦ Χριστουν) because [Jesus] neither was forsaken in Hades (ἐγκατελείφθη
εἰς ᾅδην) nor did his flesh see corruption (ἡ σὰρξ αὐτοῦ εἶδεν διαφθοράν),"
(2:31). Luke reuses terminology from the Psalm he just quoted to make the
connection explicit.[34]

But David does not mention Jesus of Nazareth by name. If the Scripture is fulfilled, then there must be evidence that Jesus is the one who ful-
fills it. To address this possible discrepancy, Peter asserts that God raised
Jesus from the dead and, speaking for himself and the twelve, says "we are
witnesses" (ἡμεῖς ἐσμεν μάρτυρες, 2:32). Peter and the eleven can claim
that the Psalm is now a prophecy fulfilled because they are witnesses of
the raised Jesus.

Peter then connects Jesus' resurrection with the outpouring of the
Holy Spirit. Jesus is "exalted to the right hand (τῇ δεξιᾷ) of God, and having received the promise of the Holy Spirit from the Father, he poured out
(ἐξέχεεν) this which you see and hear (βλέπετε καὶ ἀκούετε)" (2:33). The
mention of the "right hand" connects the Psalm with the Joel citation. Since
Jesus is at the right hand of the Father (ἐκ δεξιῶν μού, 2:25),"[35] the Spirit is
poured out (ἐξέχεεν, cf. 2:17, 18). With mention of the outpoured Holy Spirit,
Peter again identifies the crowds as witnesses of Jesus' actions: they "see and
hear" (βλέπετε καὶ ἀκούετε) the Spirit being poured out (2:33).

The apostles and the crowds are both witnesses. The crowds are witnesses of the τέρατα and σημεῖα Jesus performed (2:22) and they are eyewitnesses of the Pentecost event. Peter claims that he and the eleven are
witnesses of the event that connects the two events of which the crowds are
witnesses. They are witnesses of the raised Jesus and of his ascension to the

33. Ps 16:8–11 (MT).

34. We should note that Peter's interpretation is in fact an interpretation. In its
original context, the author of the Psalm's assertion that God would not let his flesh
see corruption probably meant merely that God would not let his enemies kill him at
that time.

35. There is the discrepancy, however, whether Jesus is at the right hand of the
Father or the Father is at the right hand of Jesus. If they are both at each other's right
hand then we have to imagine that they are facing opposite directions. But the right
hand more likely signifies proximity to God and place of prominence, not the literal
right hand that opposes the left.

right hand of the Father. The crowds obviously trust their own eyes and ears, but do they trust the eyes and ears of the apostles?

Sharing Possessions

The crowd heeds Peter's exhortation to listen to him (cf. 2:14, 22). Luke says that "after hearing (ἀκούσαντες) these things they were stabbed in the heart,"[36] and they ask "what shall we do?" (τί ποιήσωμεν, 2:37). Peter promises that if they repent and are baptized, they too will receive the gift of the Holy Spirit, for, despite the fact that they killed Jesus, the promise (ἡ ἐπαγγελία) is to them and to their children and to all those who are far off, "as many as call upon the name of the Lord" (ὑμῖν . . . καὶ τοῖς τέκνοις ὑμῶν καὶ πᾶσιν τοῖς εἰς μακράν, ὅσους ἂν προσκαλέσηται κύριος ὁ θεὸς ἡμῶν, 2:39). Peter closes his remarks by bringing his audience back to his opening Scripture. To say that the promise is "to all" says in prose what Joel put in verse: the Spirit is poured out on sons and daughters, young men and old men, male servants and female servants (2:17–18). Peter moreover concludes by recalling the final line of the Joel passage, which promises "each one who calls upon the name of the Lord will be saved," (2:21). To be saved according to Joel, we should recall, is to be saved on "the great and manifest day of the Lord" (2:20). The outpouring of the Spirit means the judgment is near, so Peter's audience engages in repentance. Three thousand are baptized.

After Peter concludes his announcement of Jesus' resurrection, the out-pouring of the Holy Spirit, and the coming day of judgment, the Jerusalem believers form a community around shared possessions. Their community appears to be an outflow of Peter's announcement of eschatological events. Luke says that they were all "persevering" (προσκαρτεροῦντες 2:42) in the teaching of the apostles and that they were all "together" (ἐπὶ τὸ αὐτό, 2:47). The use of the verb προσκαρτερέω and the phrase ἐπὶ τὸ αὐτό recall the pre-Pentecost gathering of Jesus' witnesses in Jerusalem. Luke also mentions that many wonders and signs (τέρατα καὶ σημεῖα) were done by the Apostles (2:43). This recalls not only the Joel quotation (2:19), but also that Jesus had done many τέρατα καὶ σημεῖα (2:22).

Shared possessions appear to be the central ingredient in the Jerusalem community's existence.[37] Not only does Luke say in the first clause of

36. For the crowd to hear is for the crowd to heed Peter's exhortation to "hear" his words, 2:14, 22.

37. Scholars have noted the affinities that Acts 2:42–47 (and the corresponding summary statement in 4:32–35) has both with the ideals of the Qumran community and the ideals of some Greco-Roman philosophical sects. On the parallels with Qumran,

the summary that they were "persevering . . . in fellowship (τῇ κοινωνίᾳ, 2:42)"—a fellowship that is seen most clearly in common (κοινά) possessions (2:44)—he also appears to demonstrate it structurally. Luke describes the community's shared possessions at the center of his account of the community, and the attributes of the community on either side of his account of their shared possessions appear parallel. Both begin by saying they were all "persevering" (προσκαρτεροῦντες) together and end by saying they were all "together" (ἐπὶ τὸ αὐτό).[38]

Ἦσαν δὲ προσκαρτεροῦντες τῇ διδαχῇ τῶν ἀποστόλων καὶ τῇ κοινωνίᾳ, τῇ κλάσει τοῦ ἄρτου καὶ ταῖς προσευχαῖς. ἐγίνετο δὲ πάσῃ ψυχῇ φόβος, πολλά τε τέρατα καὶ σημεῖα διὰ τῶν ἀποστόλων ἐγίνετο. πάντες δὲ οἱ πιστεύοντες ἦσαν ἐπὶ τὸ αὐτὸ   2:42–44a

καὶ εἶχον ἅπαντα κοινὰ καὶ τὰ κτήματα καὶ τὰς ὑπάρξεις ἐπίπρασκον

καὶ διεμέριζον αὐτὰ πᾶσιν καθότι ἄν τις χρείαν εἶχεν·   2:44b–45

καθ' ἡμέραν τε προσκαρτεροῦντες ὁμοθυμαδὸν ἐν τῷ ἱερῷ, κλῶντές τε κατ' οἶκον ἄρτον, μετελάμβανον τροφῆς ἐν ἀγαλλιάσει καὶ ἀφελότητι καρδίας αἱ νοῦντες τὸν θεὸν καὶ ἔχοντες χάριν πρὸς ὅλον τὸν λαόν. ὁ δὲ κύριος προσετίθει τοὺς σῳζομένους καθ' ἡμέραν ἐπὶ τὸ αὐτο   2:46–47

see esp. Brian Capper, "The Palestinian Cultural Context of Earliest Christian Community of Goods" in Bauckham, *Palestinian Setting*, who argues for the direct influence of Qumran on the Jerusalem community (323–56). Cf. Brooke, "Luke–Acts"; Johnson, *Acts of the Apostles*, 62; Fitzmyer, *Acts*, 270; Keener, *Acts*, 1:1019–21; C. Hays, *Ethics*, 195–200. The example of Qumran is interesting to the extant that it shows that an ethics of shared possessions shows up in other literature of the time in the context of eschatological expectation. But even if we could argue convincingly that Luke was drawing on the example of Qumran, we would need to ask what effect—if any—Luke intended Qumran's example to have on his audience. It is not at all clear either that Luke's audience would have known of Qumran or, if they did, that that knowledge would have had any effect on how they understood Luke's work. On Greco-Roman philosophical ideals see esp. Sterling, "'Athletes of Virtue,'" 679–96, who argues that the summary statements functioned apologetically: they show that Christians, like other people, have their "athletes of virtue." The problem with Sterling's account is that Luke seems to suggest that everyone, not an elite few, share possessions in the Jerusalem community. Luke says "all . . . had all things common" (2:44). This issue with Sterling's account, however, does not preclude the possibility that at least some of Luke's Greek educated audience would have seen some general parallels between the Christian community and some Greco-Roman philosophical sects. Cf. Dupont, *The Salvation of the Gentiles*, 88; Pervo, *Acts*, 90–91; Johnson, *Acts*, 62; Keener, *Acts*, 1:1013–19; Hays, *Ethics*, 200–209; Seccombe, *Possessions*, 200–209.

38. Keener, *Acts*, also thinks 2:42–47 is structured chiastically, 1:991–92.

In addition, the two sections that frame the central description of their shared possessions have corresponding elements. Both describe the breaking of bread (2:42, 46). Persevering in the temple (2:46) recalls the community's persevering in prayer (2:42). Luke says they had grace towards all the people (2:47), which might recall the many signs and wonders done by the apostles (2:43). To say they had joy and singleness of heart (2:46) might likewise loosely recall the fear that was upon them all (2:43). Finally, Luke says in both sections that many were continually being saved (2:44, 47).

At the center of the summary Luke says they had all things "common" (κοινά, 2:44). They sold their belongings and possessions (τὰ κτήματα καὶ τὰς ὑπάρξεις) and divided them to all just as any had need (2:45). Sharing possessions thus appears to be the core community action around which everything else revolves.

Ethics thus follows eschatology just as it did in John the Baptist's preaching.[39] John the Baptist said the wrath is "about to be" (Luke 3:7) immediately before he tells his hearers to share their possessions (Luke 3:10–14). Peter says "these are the last days" (Act 2:17) and the Pentecost converts share their possessions (Act 2:42–47). Indeed, not only does Luke revisit the themes of eschatology and ethics together at the beginning of both of his works, but it also appears that he plays on material from John the Baptist's preaching in Peter's.

Following the warning of judgment, Peter's crowd asks "what shall we do?" (τί ποιήσωμεν, 2:37). This is the same question the crowds asked John the Baptist when he warned them of the coming judgment (τί οὖν ποιήσωμεν, Luke 3:10). Peter tells the crowd to repent and be baptized for the forgiveness of their sins (μετανοήσατε, φησίν, καὶ βαπτισθήτω . . . εἰς ἄφεσιν

---

39. Pervo, *Acts*, says "Luke not only foreshadowed the glorious future but also depicted the formation of Christian community as an eschatological event, a miracle," 95. Seccombe, *Possessions*, suggests that though Acts "does not yield anything direct to confirm" his interpretation, he thinks there is "a strong eschatological factor, a partial 'realization' of the Kingdom" in the first five chapters of Acts. There is moreover "an ethical anticipation of [the Kingdom's] social values and conditions," 220. Keener, *Acts*, suggests "the Spirit's empowerment for eschatological living, though less explicit in the text" appears to motivate at least some of what Luke describes in the summary statement, 1:1038. Barrett, *Acts*, on the other hands, suggests that why the Christians shared possessions "cannot be inferred from the text." He speculates that historically, eschatology may have had something to do with it: "their practice may have been the result of their eschatological beliefs: if the world was to end shortly an immediate pooling and common charitable use of all resources might well seem prudent. There was no need to take thought for the morrow since there would not be one." But, he adds, "Luke himself did not hold this view of the [eschatological] future and this may account for the absence from his text of this reason for a practice of which he retains account," 168. Barrett, it seems to me, does not pay sufficient attention to the narrative flow of Acts: eschatological proclamation leads directly into the summary statement.

τῶν ἁμαρτιῶν ὑμῶν, v. 38), just as John the Baptist proclaimed a "baptism of repentance for the forgiveness of sins," (βάπτισμα μετανοίας εἰς ἄφεσιν ἁμαρτιῶν, Luke 3:3). Peter, like John the Baptist, says that this is offered to the "children" (τέκνα) of Israel, the descendents of Abraham (Act 2:39, Luke 3:8). Finally, Peter urges the crowds to "be saved from this crooked generation" (σώθητε ἀπὸ τῆς γενεᾶς τῆς σκολιᾶς ταύτης, 2:40), which might recall the Isaiah quotation Luke applied to John the Baptist: "the crooked ways will be straight," (καὶ ἔσται τὰ σκολιὰ εἰς εὐθείαν, Luke 3:5) so that all flesh will see the salvation (τὸ σωτήριον) of God (Luke 3:6).

Pentecost: Conclusion

The thematic and lexical correlations Peter's preaching has with John the Baptist's preaching might suggest that Luke sees the Jerusalem community as the people prepared for the coming of the Lord. Luke does not continue to speak explicitly of a prepared people or a prepared way in Acts as he does in his Gospel (Luke 1:17, 9:52). But Luke nevertheless does have the formation of a people in mind. The summary of the community's life alone demonstrates this. But does Luke see the newly formed community as an eschatological Israel? The apostles' eschatological question (Act 1:6), the selection of the twelfth apostle, the gathered Judeans on the day of Pentecost, and the outpouring of the Holy Spirit suggest that he does.

Whether or not Luke sees the Jerusalem community as an eschatological Israel, it is clear that he brings eschatology and ethics together in the opening proclamation of Acts, just as he did in the opening proclamations of his Gospel. Luke, as we have seen, has Peter declare through the prophet Joel that it is the last days. He calls the crowd to repent, and they form a community around shared possessions. For Luke the appropriate question in response to a warning of divine judgment evidently is "what shall we do?" The answer in both John the Baptist's preaching and in Peter's is repentance—and sharing possessions is evidently a major part of what it means to repent.

The Healed Cripple: Acts 2:1—5:16

Introduction

Eschatology and ethics again appear together in the second literary sequence of Acts (3:1—5:16). Peter announces the coming "times of restoration" (καιροὶ ἀναψύξεως) which will occur when God sends "the Christ appointed for you,

Jesus" (τὸν προκεχειρισμένον ὑμῖν χριστὸν Ἰησοῦν). The sequence then ends with another summary statement about the Jerusalem community in which Luke says they had "all things common" (ἅπαντα κοινά, 4:32).

The healing of a cripple occupies the center stage of the second sequence. As a result of the man's healing, a crowd gathers and Peter again proclaims Jesus' resurrection and that this Jesus now offers the forgiveness of sins to the people. The commotion in the temple catches the attention of the Sadduccees who detain and question the apostles. But because the Sadduccees cannot deny the miracle of the healed cripple, they must release the disciples. After their release, Peter and John return to the other disciples and pray. During their prayer, Luke says they are all again filled with the Holy Spirit, and immediately thereafter Luke writes a second summary about the life of the Jerusalem community.

The healing of the cripple appears to be a resurrection-like miracle: the man's disability puts him in a death-like posture, and it is out of this posture that Peter raises him. As a resurrection-like miracle, the event is symbolic.[40] To be sure, Luke claims a miracle did in fact happen, which means Luke does not want it to be seen as a mere literary creation. But Luke still thinks that the cripple's healing points beyond itself, and does so in two ways. First, it points to Jesus' resurrection. By using the same language and imagery for the cripple's healing as he does for Jesus' resurrection, Luke draws the parallel. Second, it points to the possibility of others' resurrection.[41] By pointing to Jesus' resurrection, the miracle points to Jesus' return, and when Jesus returns, Peter says the times of restoration will come, "which God spoke through the mouths of his prophets long ago" (ὧν ἐλάλησεν ὁ θεὸς διὰ στόματος τῶν ἁγίων ἀπ᾽ αἰῶνος αὐτοῦ προφητῶν (3:21). The key rhetorical move Luke makes is to identify the crowds and the Sadducees as eyewitnesses—the same move he made in the first sequence. They cannot deny that the cripple was raised because they have seen him with their own eyes.

40. An early indication that this miracle is likely to be understood symbolically is that Luke says that *many* wonders and signs were done by the apostles (2:43)—yet Luke only narrates one. Luke evidently thinks this miracle is a good representative of the apostles' wonder working and as such likely demonstrates what the apostles' miracle working was all about.

41. Both Pervo and Parsons suggest that the healing of the cripple is symbolic. They both point to Luke's apparent reuse of Isa 35:6 in Acts 3:8 and to Luke's concluding remark that the man had been crippled for forty years (4:22). But neither of them note how these details cohere with the cripple's healing being resurrection-like, how Luke situates this in a defense of the apostles' status as eyewitnesses of Jesus' resurrection, or how all of this coheres with Acts 1–2. See Pervo, *Acts*, 101; Parsons, *Body and Character*, 118–19; Cf. Spencer, *Acts*, 52. Horton, *Death and Resurrection*, on the other hand, notes as I have how Luke's rhetoric characterizes the cripple's healing as a resurrection-like miracle, 69–71.

If they cannot deny what their own eyes have seen, this problematizes their denial of what the apostles' eyes have seen.

The Raised Cripple

As he did at Jesus' ascension, Luke emphasizes eyesight in the story of the healed cripple. At the beginning of Acts 3, Peter and John go up to the temple, and as they approach they meet a cripple stationed at the Beautiful Gate (3:2). Luke says that the cripple, "seeing (ἰδὼν) Peter and John about to go into the temple, asked to receive alms. And after looking intently (ἀτενίσας) at him, Peter with John said, 'look (βλέψον) at us!'" (3:3–4). After he is healed, Luke says that the crowd saw (εἶδεν) him and recognized him as the one who used to sit at the Beautiful Gate and ask for alms (3:9–10). Through repetition of words that emphasize eyesight, Luke builds a case for the reliability of eyewitness accounts. The cripple knows who healed him, the apostles know who they healed, and the crowd can testify that the former Beautiful Gate beggar now walks.[42]

Peter tells the cripple that he has no silver or gold, but that which he does have he gives to him. He then commands the cripple "rise and walk!" (ἔγειρε καὶ περιπάτει, 3:6).[43] Luke uses the verb ἐγείρω, a synonym for the verb ἀνίστημι. Luke has already used the verb ἀνίστημι twice to refer to Jesus' resurrection (2:24, 32).[44] The verb ἐγείρω could simply mean "to stand

---

42. The reason Luke mentions at which gate the cripple begged is so the cripple can be identified. The actual historical location of the Beautiful Gate is irrelevant. Scholars have failed to locate it anyway, see e.g., Fitzmyer, *Acts*, 277–78; Pervo, *Acts*, 99; Keener, *Acts*, 2:1047–50.

43. א B D sa all support the shorter reading of Peter's command which omits the first imperative ἔγειρε. Metzger, *A Textual Commentary*, says "it is difficult to decide whether the words ἔγειρε καὶ are a gloss, introduced by copyists who were influenced by such well-known passages as Mt 9.5; Mark 2.9; Luke 5.23; Jn 5.8, or were omitted in several witnesses as superfluous, since it is Peter himself who raises up the lame man (ver. 7)" (267). The incongruity of Peter's command and action makes the presence of the first imperative the more difficult reading. Moreover, as I note, this incongruity is what seems (in part) to characterize the miracle as resurrection-like. From a form-critical perspective, Pervo, *Acts*, notes "there are no examples of healings [in the NT] with the bare imperative 'walk,'" which would suggest that the first imperative is part of the original reading, 100. Barrett, *Acts*, on the other hand, favors the shorter reading, suggesting that the first imperative was added precisely to make the command follow the more common formula, 1:183. The verb ἔγειρε, however, is but one of the several ways (which I detail below) that Luke characterizes the healing as resurrection-like. The internal evidence therefore suggests that the first imperative is original.

44. Luke also uses ἀνίστημι in 1:15 when Peter "stands up" in the midst of the disciples.

up,"[45] but this is the first time Luke has used the verb in Acts, and Luke will use ἐγείρω to speak of Jesus' resurrection in what follows (3:15). Apart from the meaning of the verb, two other factors suggest that Luke intends to evoke resurrection in Peter's command. First, there is the discrepancy between Peter's words and actions. Peter commands the cripple to rise and walk (ἔγειρε καὶ περιπάτει, 3:6). Both verbs are in the imperative. Yet, Luke says, Peter "raised" (ἤγειρεν) the cripple in the indicative. Peter, not the cripple, is the active agent in the healing. This is remarkably similar to how Luke has twice described Jesus' resurrection in the first sequence. In both 2:24 and 2:32, Luke says that "God raised" (ὁ θεὸς ἀνέστησεν) Jesus from the dead. God, not Jesus, is the active agent in Jesus' resurrection. The second factor is that Luke says Peter seized the cripple by the right hand (τῆς δεξιᾶς χειρὸς, 3:7). Luke may be playing with the imagery in a way that recalls Jesus' ascension to the right hand (τῇ δεξιᾷ τοῦ θεοῦ) of the Father. Luke moreover mentions Jesus' exaltation to God's right hand twice in the first sequence, and both instances come immediately after saying that God raised Jesus from the dead (2:25 and 2:33, 34).

Luke says that "leaping [the cripple] stood and he was walking and he went with them into the temple, walking and leaping and praising God" (ἐξαλλόμενος ἔστη καὶ περιεπάτει καὶ εἰσῆλθεν σὺν αὐτοῖς εἰς τὸ ἱερὸν περιπατῶν καὶ ἁλλόμενος καὶ αἰνῶν τὸν θεόν, 3:8). The repetition of the verbs περιπατέω and ἅλλομαι and the parallel of "going into the temple"/ "praising" might draw attention to the cripple's celebration for a good reason. Luke might be describing the cripple's healing in the terms that Isa 35:6 describes Israel's restoration.[46] Isaiah says that the time of God's judgment and recompense God "will come and save (σώσει) us . . . then the cripple (ὁ χωλός) will leap (ἁλεῖται) as a deer," (Isa 35:4–6). The question, however, is—as always—who in Luke's audience would have understood the reference. But if at least some in Luke's audience would have been able to note the parallels, this might indicate that Luke is concerned with Israel's restoration.

Resurrection (Again)

Luke continues to emphasize eyesight as Peter begins his second public announcement of Jesus' resurrection. Luke says that Peter, "seeing (ἰδὼν) the people said to them . . . Israelites, why do you marvel upon this thing or look intently (ἀτενίζετε) upon us . . . ?" (3:12). The triangle of eyewitnesses is now

45. BDAG, 271.

46. Pervo, *Acts*, 101; Parsons, *Body*, 118–19; Spencer, *Acts*, 52; Keener, *Acts*, 1:1073; Fitzmyer, *Acts*, 279.

complete. The cripple knows who healed him, Peter knows who he and John healed and to what crowd they speak, and now the crowd knows not only who was healed, but also who performed the healing.

The miracle is the grounds for Peter's challenge to his hearers. Peter addresses them, "Israelites . . . the God of Abraham, the God of Isaac, and God of Jacob—the God of our fathers—glorified his servant Jesus." God glorified him, but, Peter says, the crowd handed him over and denied (ἠρνήσασθε) him before Pilate (3:13). And Peter repeats the charge in the next verse: "you denied (ἠρνήσασθε) the holy one and asked for a murderer to be given to you." The sin of the crowd was that they denied Jesus. Luke will return to the matter of denial later, but for now the point is that Israel's sin was absolute—by choosing a murderer and killing the "founder of life" (3:15), they chose death over life.

Nevertheless, God raised (ἤγειρεν) Jesus from the dead, and, Peter says, "of this we ourselves are witnesses (μάρτυρες), (3:15). Luke now brings to the forefront the matter of eyewitness that he has been subtly building in the narrative. He does this in three ways. First, he uses the verb ἐγείρω to refer to Jesus' resurrection for the first time in Acts, which recalls Luke's first use of the verb to refer to the cripple's healing just moments earlier. And Luke again describes Jesus as the passive agent in his resurrection: God raised (ὁ θεὸς ἤγειρεν) Jesus from the dead, just as Peter raised (ἤγειρεν) the cripple. Second, Peter calls himself and John μάρτυρες, which recalls both Jesus' commission on the day of ascension and the apostles' claim on the day of Pentecost (1:8–11; 2:32). As is evident in both those instances, to be a μάρτυς is to be an eyewitness. Third, immediately after asserting that he and John are μάρτυρες of the resurrection, Peter switches back to talking about the cripple: "upon faith in [Jesus'] name, this one whom you see and know (θεωρεῖτε καὶ οἴδατε)" was healed (v. 16). Peter identifies the crowd as eyewitnesses, just as he and John are. The use of the paired verbs "see and know" recalls Peter's use of the paired verbs "see and hear" (βλέπετε καὶ ἀκούετε) in 2:33. There, Peter had made the same argument: he asserted on the day of Pentecost that he and the apostles are witnesses of the resurrection (2:32) and then identified the crowd as eyewitnesses of the Pentecost event. The question is therefore the same as it was on the day of Pentecost: does the crowd trust Peter and John's eyes as much as they trust their own?[47]

The crowd killed Jesus in ignorance (κατὰ ἄγνοιαν), which seems to suggest why they still have the chance to repent. Peter's exhortation to repent

---

47. Soards, *Speeches*, suggests that Luke uses speeches in Acts "to create the overall unity of the account," 182. This appears to be the case both in Peter's Pentecost address and in his sermon after the healing of the cripple: the meaning of the events is exposed by Peter's announcement of Jesus' resurrection from the dead.

parallels his exhortation to repentance on the day of Pentecost. In both instances, Peter commands, "repent!" (μετανοήσατε, 2:38; 3:19) so that their sins (τῶν ἁμαρτιῶν [2:38] / τὰς ἁμαρτίας [3:19]) might be forgiven. And in both instances, Peter commands that this be done so that something in addition to the forgiveness of sins might come about. In the first instance, it is so that they might receive the gift of the Holy Spirit (τὴν δωρεὰν τοῦ ἁγίου πνεύματος, 2:38). In the second, it is so that seasons of refreshing (καιροὶ ἀναψύξεως, 3:20) might come.[48] The people's repentance will thus evidently result in the coming of eschatological events. The relationship between their repentance and the coming of eschatological events is clear in the "so that" (ὅπως) between Peter's command and the promise of Christ's return.

Luke appears to be reusing material from the opening of Acts in Peter's announcement of coming eschatological events. Peter's words, "so that seasons of refreshing might come" (ὅπως ἂν ἔλθωσιν καιροὶ ἀναψύξεως) parallel a second statement, "and so that he might send his chosen one to us, Christ Jesus" (ἀποστείλῃ τὸν προκεχειρισμένον ὑμῖν χριστὸν Ἰησοῦν). After saying that Jesus will return, he adds that heaven must receive Jesus "until the times of restoration (χρόνων ἀποκαταστάσεως) of all things" (3:21). The promise of restoration (ἀποκατάστασις) might recall the apostles' question to Jesus just before his ascension: "will you at this time restore (ἀποκαθιστάνεις) the kingdom to Israel?" (1:6). Peter moreover says that it is necessary for heaven (οὐρανὸν) to receive Jesus until the times of restoration. To speak of Jesus' reception in heaven recalls his ascension into heaven (εἰς τὸν οὐρανὸν, 1:11). Peter also parallels καιροὶ ἀναψύξεως with χρόνων ἀποκαταστάσεως. Speaking of καιροὶ and χρόνων might also recall Jesus' answer to the disciples' question: "it is not for you to know the χρόνους ἢ καιροὺς which the Father has established in his own authority" (1:7).[49]

---

48. Pao, *New Exodus*, notes the correlations between Acts 3:19–21 and Acts 2:38/ Acts 1:6–8. But he see "seasons of refreshing" as synonymous with the gift of the Holy Spirit. He suggests that Luke is therefore suggesting that the restoration of Israel (which coincides with the coming of the Spirit) is not something that takes place in an instant, but over a period of time. His interpretation relies on translating the preposition ἄχρι as "after" instead of "until" (which is how he says the word must be translated in Acts 20:6), 134–35. The problem with this translation is that it renders the Acts 3:21 unintelligible. On Pao's account the verse would read "whom heaven must receive after the restoration of all things." But heaven has already received Jesus—what is awaited is his return.

49. Pervo, *Acts*, notes that Luke's use of the terms καιροὶ and χρόνων along with the concepts of "refreshing" and "restoration" in Acts 3:19–21 are "atypical," and suggests that Luke may have used some traditional material in writing this section of his narrative, 107–8. Luke may be using tradition, but Luke's language in Acts 3:19–21 is not entirely "atypical" as Acts 1:6–7 demonstrates.

The parallels Peter's words have with the opening scenes of Acts might again suggest that Jesus does not deny that the apostles should continue to expect and hope for "the times and seasons which God has put in his own authority" (1:7).[50] Jesus did not give them a time-table, but a mission. Yet in giving them a mission, it appears Jesus at least gave them the ordering of events that will result in the coming of the "times and seasons." Peter has now said that the people must repent "so that" (ὅπως) those times and seasons might come, which suggests that he and the other apostles are witnesses "so that" (ὅπως) the times and seasons will come.

But with restoration will come the judgment, as Peter also made clear on the day of Pentecost (cf. 2:20). The noun ἀποκατάστασις appears to function as a catch-word for the Scripture passage Peter quotes next. Peter says that Moses told the people of Israel that God would "raise (ἀναστήσει) a prophet ... like me; listen to him!" (3:22; cf. Deut 18:15). The terms ἀποκατάστασις and ἀνίστημι share a common root (στάσις). In its original context in Deuteronomy, ἀνίστημι refers only to the vocational commissioning of a prophet. But in the context of Peter's sermon—and indeed in the context of the broader narrative—Luke appears to have given it a secondary meaning. Jesus was not only "raised" as a prophet when the Spirit anointed him (Luke 3:22; 4:18–19), he was also raised from the dead.[51]

After identifying Jesus as the prophet like Moses, Peter adds, "each person (ψυχὴ) who does not listen to that prophet will be cast out (ἐξολεθρευθήσεται) of the people (ἐκ τοῦ λαοῦ)" (3:23). The second half of the quotation does not come from Deut 18, but appears to be a stock phrase in Pentateuchal writings that warn that a ψυχὴ will be cast out of the λαός for various violations (see e.g., Exod 31:14, Lev 23:29, Num 9:13, Deut 9:6).[52] Regardless of how Luke has put this quotation together, the message is clear. In order to enter eschatological restoration the people must repent. If they do not, they will be judged and cast out.

Peter concludes by saying that not only Moses, but all the Prophets (πάντες οἱ προφῆται) from Samuel onward spoke of these days (τὰς ἡμέρας

50. Keener, Acts, suggests that Acts 3:19–21 "reflects an expectation of at least a potentially imminent end, an ideology Luke apparently connects with the earliest church," 2:1105. Again, we cannot settle the question of imminence in Luke's double-work, but Acts 3:19–21 might suggest that Luke, like Mark, thinks the end will come when the Christian announcement has been heard and heeded (cf. Mark 13:10).

51. On the centrality of Deut 18:15 in Lukan theology, see p. 73 above.

52. The future ἔσται following the future ἀναστήσει of the previous verse suggests that 3:23 is a continuation of the quote from Deut 18:15, and thus flows well. The Nestle-Aland suggests Lev 23:29 (cf. Pervo, Acts, 109; Eckey, Die Apostelgeschichte, 1:110; Keener, Acts, 2:1116–17), but Bauckham, "Restoration," in Scott, Restoration, suggests it is a conflation with Num 15:31.

ταύτας, 3:24). Peter then reminds them, "you are the sons of the covenant which God made with your fathers, saying to Abraham, 'in your seed all nations of the earth will be blessed.'[53] To you first God sent his son after raising (ἀναστήσας) him (3:25–26)." The prepositional phrase ἐκ νεκρῶν is not attached to ἀναστήσας in this instance, and thereby carries the same ambiguity that it did in the citation from Deut 18. God has raised the prophet like Moses. He was raised as a prophet and he was raised from the dead. And Jesus' raising signifies again that the people stand at an eschatological crossroads. If they listen, they can be raised like the cripple. If they do not listen, they will be judged and cast out.

Trial

The Sadduccees become irritated that Peter and John are proclaiming "the resurrection (τὴν ἀνάστασιν) of the dead in Jesus" (4:2), so they put them in prison until they can try them the next day before the Sanhedrin. They seek to silence the apostles. But it is they who Luke says are silenced by the miracle of the raised cripple.

The Sadduccees' only question to the apostles is "by what power (δυνάμει) and in what name did you do this?" (4:7). Luke's answer is that it was by the power of the Holy Spirit (cf. 1:8) and in the name of Jesus. Peter responds "full of the Holy Spirit" (4:8) saying, "if today we are examined about the good deed done for the crippled man, in whom this one was healed (σέσωται), let it be known that [it was] ... in the name of Jesus of Nazareth," (4:9–10). Curiously, Luke uses the verb σώζω, "to save," to speak of the crippled man's healing—though the verb can also commonly mean "to heal."[54] Luke's use of the verb is noteworthy because of what follows. Peter asserts to the leaders that they crucified Jesus, but that God raised (ἤγειρεν) him from the dead. For the second time in this sequence Luke uses ἐγείρω to refer to Jesus' resurrection, the same verb he used to describe the "raising" of the cripple by Peter. And, once again, Jesus, like the cripple, is the passive agent: God raised Jesus. Because Jesus was raised from the dead, Peter announces that there is salvation (ἡ σωτηρία) in no other, "for there is no other name under heaven that is given among men in which it is necessary for us to be saved (σωθῆναι, 4:12). By using the noun σωτηρία and the verb σώζω Peter makes the cripple's healing or "salvation" the paradigm for what must happen for everyone. Just as the savior saved the cripple, so must all of people also be saved by him.

53. Cf. Gen 12:3
54. BDAG, 982–83.

Thus Peter again challenges the people to repent, and the leaders are left silent, Luke says, "without answer" (οὐδὲν εἶχον ἀντειπεῖν, 4:12). But Luke makes clear that it is not his words that impact his interrogators. On the contrary, it is what they see with their eyes that leaves them without answer. They see (θεωροῦντες) that Peter and John are illiterate and uneducated (ἀγράμματοί καὶ ἰδιῶται). They also recognize (ἐπεγίνωσκον) that Peter and John had been with Jesus (4:13). But most importantly, they see (βλέποντες) the man who had been healed standing before them (4:14). The emphasis on eyesight again brings to the fore the theme of witness. The Sanhedrin have themselves become eyewitnesses.

With words reminiscent of the crowd's on the day of Pentecost, the Sanhedrin ask themselves, "What shall we do (τί ποιήσωμεν) with these men?" (4:16; cf. 2:37). The reason they must deliberate is because they are without options: "all those dwelling in Jerusalem (πᾶσιν τοῖς κατοικοῦσιν Ἰερουσαλὴμ)" know that the cripple has been healed and, the Sanhedrin say, "we are not able to deny (οὐ δυνάμεθα ἀρνεῖσθαι) it." The Sanhedrin are about to commit an error similar the one the crowd had committed. The crowd denied (ἠρνήσασθε) Jesus (3:13, 14). Luke has the Sanhedrin's own words condemn them: if they cannot deny that the cripple was raised, how can they deny that Jesus was?

Despite having no response, they still forbid Peter and John from speaking or teaching (μὴ φθέγγεσθαι μηδὲ διδάσκειν, 4:18). But Peter and John respond, "we are not able (οὐ δυνάμεθα) not to speak of that which we have seen and heard (εἴδαμεν καὶ ἠκούσαμεν, v. 20). The Sanhedrin were "not able (οὐ δυνάμεθα) to deny"; the apostles are "not able (οὐ δυνάμεθα)" to be silent. The paired verbs "seen and heard" once again remind the readers of the apostles' status as witnesses and echo again the paired verb Peter used when speaking to the crowd in the last scene. Referring to the cripple, Peter had said "this one whom you see and know (θεωρεῖτε καὶ οἴδατε, 3:16)."

Regrouping

Even though it was the miracle that convinced the Sadducees, and even though the Sadducees know that the apostles are ἀγράμματοί and ἰδιῶται, it is the fact that the apostles continue to speak that concerns them. This is why Luke says the Sadducees were irritated that the apostles were "teaching (διδάσκειν) the people and announcing (καταγγέλλειν)" Jesus' resurrection (4:2). It is why they forbid the apostles from "speaking or teaching" (μὴ φθέγγεσθαι μηδὲ διδάσκειν, 4:14). And it is why the apostles say they must continue to speak (λαλεῖν) about Jesus (4:20). To be a witness is not only to see, but also to hear.

The miracle allowed others to see the power of the Holy Spirit, but they also needed to hear what the apostles had to say about the event for the truth to be fully disclosed. It is because of this need for spoken witnesses that the apostles regroup with the believing community and ask God to give them boldness to continue to speak the word of God (4:29).

The community's prayer for boldness is simultaneously a critique of the Sanhedrin. Just as David foretold Jesus' resurrection, so David also foretold the turning of Israel against Jesus. They quote Ps 2:1–2 (Act 4:25–26):

> Why do the nations (ἔθνη) rage and the people (λαοὶ) plot in vain? The kings of the earth (οἱ βασιλεῖς τῆς γῆς) present themselves, and the rulers (οἱ ἄρχοντες) together with them.

The community identifies two groups in David's poetic parallelisms. The "nations" (ἔθνη) are the Gentiles and "people" (λαοὶ) are the people of Israel.[55] Similarly, the "kings of the earth" are Gentile kings, while "rulers" (οἱ ἄρχοντες) are the rulers Jerusalem and its Temple (cf. 4:5). This interpretive move becomes clear as the prayer continues, "Herod and Pontius Pilate with the nations (ἔθνεσιν) and with the people of Israel (λαοῖς Ἰσραήλ)" gathered against Jesus, God's anointed (4:27). Israel, according to the believers, has aligned itself with the enemies of God. As the last Psalm Luke quoted indicates, God's enemies will be put under Jesus' feet (Act 2:34–35; Cf. Ps 109.1).

Because Israel killed Jesus, the apostles and their companions know Israel might kill them too—as their recent arrest demonstrates—which is why they seek boldness. Their prayer is that they might continue to be witnesses as they are commissioned by Jesus to be. Again we see that for the apostles to be a witness is to be a witness in word and in deed—i.e., to witness with things that can be heard and things that can be seen. First they ask that they might continue to speak (λαλεῖν) with all boldness (μετὰ παρρησίας πάσης) and, second, they ask that God would continue to stretch out his hand to heal and that there might continue to be signs and wonders (σημεῖα καὶ τέρατα). The people will hear as the apostles speak with boldness, and the people will see with signs and wonders performed. Luke says that they were all filled with the Holy Spirit and "were speaking the word of God with all boldness" (ἐλάλουν τὸν λόγον τοῦ θεοῦ μετὰ παρρησίας). In other words, they again receive power to be Jesus' witnesses (cf. 1:8).[56]

---

55. The plural λαοὶ makes Luke's interpretation of the passage a little bit awkward (and perhaps forced) since it seems odd to apply the term "peoples" to the one people Israel. But this is evidently what he wants to do since, as I note, he applies the term again in the plural to the people of Israel in 4:27 (λαοῖς).

56. Luke characterizes the second outpouring of the Holy Spirit as a mini-Pentecost not only by mentioning another theophanic element (the place shakes), but also

Sharing Possessions (Again)

As in Acts 1–2, ethics follows eschatological proclamation. The whole series of scenes beginning at Acts 3:1 has revolved around the healing of the cripple. The healing is what occasions Peter's sermon. Peter's sermon occasions his and John's arrest, and their arrest is what leads them to seek the Scriptures to understand what has taken place as they pray for boldness to continue witnessing. Luke then again describes the life of the Jerusalem community: they had "all things common" (ἅπαντα κοινά, 4:32).

Luke appears to structure his second summary of the Jerusalem community's life chiastically, just as he does the first. But whereas Luke had put the sharing of possession at the center of the first summary statement (2:42–47), in the second summary Luke puts witness to the resurrection in the central position. Luke begins by saying that they were all "one heart and soul (καρδία καὶ ψυχὴ μία)" and that "there was no one who called his possessions his own, but all things were common (κοινά) among them," (4:32). He then says that the apostles were witnessing (ἀπεδίδουν τὸ μαρτύριον) with great power (δυνάμει μεγάλῃ) to the resurrection of the Lord Jesus (4:33). He concludes by repeating that the community had common possessions: no one had any "lack" (ἐνδεής) because everyone sold their possessions and put the proceeds at the feet of the apostles (4:34–35):

> Τοῦ δὲ πλήθους τῶν πιστευσάντων ἦν καρδία καὶ ψυχὴ μία, καὶ οὐδὲ εἷς τι τῶν ὑπαρχόντων αὐτῷ ἔλεγεν ἴδιον εἶναι ἀλλ᾽ ἦν αὐτοῖς ἅπαντα κοινά (4:32)

> καὶ δυνάμει μεγάλῃ ἀπεδίδουν τὸ μαρτύριον οἱ ἀπόστολοι τῆς ἀναστάσεως τοῦ κυρίου Ἰησοῦ, χάρις τε μεγάλη ἦν ἐπὶ πάντας αὐτούς (4:33)

> οὐδὲ γὰρ ἐνδεής τις ἦν ἐν αὐτοῖς· ὅσοι γὰρ κτήτορες χωρίων ἢ οἰκιῶν ὑπῆρχον, πωλοῦντες ἔφερον τὰς τιμὰς τῶν πιπρασκομένων καὶ ἐτίθουν παρὰ τοὺς πόδας τῶν ἀποστόλων, διεδίδετο δὲ ἑκάστῳ καθότι ἄν τις χρείαν εἶχεν (4:34–35)

To say that the apostles were witnessing to Jesus' resurrection is a fitting summary of the preceding narrative. The apostles have been witnessing in word and deed to Jesus' resurrection through the healing of a cripple and public proclamation. Moreover, for Luke to say that they were witnessing "in great power" (δυνάμει μεγάλῃ) is likely again to refer to the empowerment

---

by suggesting that the Holy Spirit again comes upon them for the precise task that Jesus said he would come in the first place: so that they would have power to be his witnesses (cf. 1:8). Placing a mini-Pentecost at this point in the narrative suggests that another literary sequence is coming to a conclusion.

of the Holy Spirit, since power is what Jesus said they would receive for their witnessing (cf. 1:8). The structure of the summary statement might moreover indicate that Luke sees the sharing of possessions as the proper context in which the apostles' proclamation of the resurrection ought to be seen. And since the proclamation of Jesus' resurrection appears to imply everything else Peter said in his sermon—including the need to repent so that Jesus might return from heaven and bring times of refreshing—then this strongly suggests that Luke sees a connection between eschatological proclamation and sharing possessions.

But why is it fitting to proclaim Jesus' resurrection in the context of shared possessions? But Luke may have passages from Deuteronomy in mind here. Luke has quoted Deuteronomy explicitly in Peter's sermon when he claimed that Jesus is the prophet like Moses foretold in Deut 18:15. I suggested that Luke intends a double meaning in the verb ἀνίστημι. God both "raised" Jesus as a prophet and "raised" him from the dead. Luke's language in two instances in the second summary statement might also be drawn from Deuteronomy. Luke says that all those in the nation were καρδία καὶ ψυχὴ μία (4:32), which might be language from the Shema: "love the Lord your God with all you heart and all your soul and all your strength (ἐξ ὅλης τῆς καρδίας σου καὶ ἐξ ὅλης τῆς ψυχῆς σου καὶ ἐξ ὅλης τῆς δυνάμεώς σου, Deut 6:5).[57] Deut 6:6 adds that "these words" should be in their hearts and souls (ἐν τῇ καρδίᾳ σου καὶ ἐν τῇ ψυχῇ σου).[58] We should note that the Shema begins with "hear!"—a trope that we have seen is very important to Luke's purposes.

---

57. C. Hays, *Ethics*, notes that Luke's language looks similar to the Deuteronomic phrase, but thinks it is better to see Luke's language as an adoption of Aristotle's truism that friends are "one soul," (192; cf. 201–10). He says this because Deuteronomy's use of "heart and soul" refers to the individual, not to the heart and soul of the community. We cannot exclude the possibility that at least some of Luke's audience would have noted that Luke's language is similar to the language used by some philosophical sects. But Luke does not have to use a phrase in the exact way it was in its original context either, which may mean he has Deut 6:4–6 in mind. Haenchen, *Acts*, also notes the connection Acts 4:32 has with Deut 4:5–6, but insists that Luke has only "fused his OT heritage, transmitted via LXX, with Greek material" (also referencing the common philosophic principle that friends have all things common), 230–31; cf. Pervo, *Acts*, 126–27. Keener, *Acts*, discusses the similarities the language has with Greek philosophical writings about friendship, but nevertheless suggests that "'heart and soul' reflects Luke's biblical idiom, presumably from LXX passages about wholehearted devotion to the Lord, perhaps most familiarly from the passage that would be recited with the Shema (Deut 6:5–6)," 2:1176–77. Cf. Marguerat's discussion, *Historian*, 74.

58. Deut 6:6 might make sense of Luke's omission of ἐξ ὅλης τῆς δυνάμεώς from his summary. Moreover, the phrase καρδία καὶ ψυχη is a common refrain in Deuteronomy, see 4:29; 10:12; 11:13, 18; 13:4; 26:16; 30:2, 6, 10.

Luke also says that there was no one who had "lack" (ἐνδεής, 4:34). The term ἐνδεής is a *hapax legomenon* in the NT. It is used only twenty-four times in the LXX, three of which are in Deut 15. There, God declared that there were to be no poor in Israel (15:4).[59] The words in Deuteronomy are addressed to Israel as a nation: there were to be no poor in the land God was giving them as an inheritance. Deut 15:4 comes in the context of the author of Deuteronomy saying that to care for the poor in the land is to "listen with listening to the voice of the Lord" their God (ἀκοῇ εἰσακούσῃτε τῆς φωνῆς κυρίου τοῦ θεοῦ ὑμῶν). If Luke is drawing on Deuteronomy in composing his second summary statement, the trope of listening, which also appears in Deut 18:15 (when Moses says that the people should "listen" to the prophet like him who God will raise) and in the Shema, might have motivated Luke's selection of the term ἐνδεής.

If Luke is drawing on Deuteronomy in the second summary statement, then this might again indicate Luke sees the Jerusalem community as an eschatological Israel. But whether or not Luke is drawing on Deuteronomy several matters remain clear. First, the apostles' proclamation in Acts 3:1–5:16 is eschatological: Jesus has been raised and he will return from heaven to bring times of refreshing. Second, Luke's summary of the Jerusalem community's life, which has the sharing of the possessions as the most prominent feature, flows directly out of the series of scenes that concern the apostles' proclamation. Third, according to Luke's summary statement, the apostles' eschatological proclamation about Jesus' resurrection continues to be the same. And finally, that eschatological proclamation continues to come in the evidently important context of shared possessions.

Ananias and Sapphira

Luke's second summary statement appears to end at 4:35, since from 4:36–5:16 Luke speaks of Barnabas, and Ananias and Sapphira. At the same time, the stories of Barnabas, and Ananias and Sapphira concern the same matters as the summary: the laying of possessions at the apostles' feet (cf. 4:35). The story of Ananias and Sapphira is thus likely an extension of the summary statement in 4:32–35.[60] Indeed, it appears that the summary statement continues to 5:16, as I noted above, since 5:12–16 speak in summary fashion of the apostles' doing "signs and wonders" (σημεῖα καὶ

---

59. The allusion to Deut 15:4 is commonly noted. See e.g., Pervo, *Acts*, 127; Fitzmyer, *Acts*, 314; Parsons, *Acts*, 73; Keener, *Acts*, 2:1177–78; Eckey, *Apostelgeschichte*, 128.

60. Pervo, *Acts*, puts 5:1–16 in a structural unit with 4:32–37 as I do, 125–37. But he does not note the lexical correlations 5:1–16 has with 2:42–47.

τέρατα), which the first summary had also spoken of (2:43). After both the death of Ananias (5:5) and the death of Sapphira (5:11), Luke moreover says that fear (φόβος) came upon all those who heard, which might also recall the fear spoken of in the first summary statement (5:11; cf. 2:43). This of course means that the second summary statement is much longer than the first and is not strictly parallel to it. But this may simply be one instance that demonstrates that Luke's narrative is not reducible to a strict structure and is capable of multiple configurations.

Ananias and Sapphira sell a field and Ananias (with the knowledge of his wife, 5:2) holds back a portion of the proceeds before placing the remaining sum of money at the apostles' feet. Ananias dies for his sin. Subsequently, Sapphira appears before the apostles and, after lying as her husband did, dies for her sin as well. Luke is careful to note that by all appearances they gave to the community just as everyone else had. They brought (ἐνέγκας) the proceeds (τῆς τιμῆς) of their sale and put (ἔθηκεν) them at the feet of the apostles (τοὺς πόδας τῶν ἀποστόλων). Their actions parallel what Luke said was generally true of those who owned property (4:34–35)[61] and was true in particular of Barnabas (4:36–37).[62]

The issue with Ananias and Sapphira's actions appears not to be that they did not give all of their possessions, but that they lied.[63] Indeed, Peter reminds Ananias that his possessions were his own and that they were

61. οὐδὲ γὰρ ἐνδεής τις ἦν ἐν αὐτοῖς· ὅσοι γὰρ κτήτορες χωρίων ἢ οἰκιῶν ὑπῆρχον, πωλοῦντες ἔφερον τὰς τιμὰς[τῶν πιπρασκομένων καὶ ἐτίθουν παρὰ τοὺς πόδας τῶν ἀποστόλων, διεδίδετο δὲ ἑκάστῳ καθότι ἄν τις χρείαν εἶχεν.

62. Ἰωσὴφ δὲ ὁ ἐπικληθεὶς Βαρναβᾶς ἀπὸ τῶν ἀποστόλων, ὅ ἐστιν μεθερμηνευόμενον υἱὸς παρακλήσεως, Λευίτης, Κύπριος τῷ γένει, ὑπάρχοντος αὐτῷ ἀγροῦ πωλήσας ἤνεγκεν τὸ χρῆμα καὶ ἔθηκεν πρὸς τοὺς πόδας τῶν ἀποστόλων.

63. Interpreters, both ancient and modern, have found this story theologically troubling. For a short history of interpretations, see Pervo, *Acts*, 131–32. Marguerat, *Historian*, puts modern interpreters' puzzling well: "how can one justify the tragic disproportion between Ananias and Sapphira's crime and the sanction that strikes them?" (155); cf. Fitzmyer, *Acts*, 317; Spencer, *Acts*, 57; Parsons, *Acts*, 75–76. See also McCabe, *Ananias and Sapphira*. Marguerat, *Historian*, also gives a helpful summary of five interpretive approaches scholars have generally taken: (a) an aetiological reading: the story is a response to early Christians' anxiety about the destiny of those who died before the parousia; (b) Qumran reading: Luke seeks to mimic the Qumranian expulsion from the community for rule violations; (c) Typological reading: there are intertextual connections with the story of Aachan in Joshua 7; (d) Institutional reading: this is an early story that vindicates excommunication from the church; (e) Salvation-history reading: Ananias and Sapphira block the actions of the Spirit, so they must be removed (157). Marguerat himself offers another typological analysis, suggesting that Luke has here told a sort of new Adam and Eve story (174–76 [cf. Phillips, *Diverse Frames*, 130–43]). While Marguerat's analysis offers some important observations, there does not appear to me to be enough evidence to sustain his typological reading.

in his power to keep or donate (5:4).[64] Peter moreover asserts twice that Ananias lied, once on either side of reminding Ananias that his possessions were his own. By identifying their sin as lying, Luke might intend to contrast their actions with the witness of the Jerusalem community. As we noted, the Jerusalem community witnesses in word and deed to the risen Jesus. The Sadduccees tried to silence the apostles, but they said they would speak anyway and then prayed for boldness to continue doing so. And, we should remember, they spoke with boldness as they were empowered by the Spirit to do so (4:31). But whereas the believing community witnesses in word by the power of the Holy Spirit, Luke says Ananias and Sapphira lie to the Holy Spirit (5:3, 4).[65]

The emphasis Luke gives to speech and hearing in the passage might add to the suggestion that their sin contrasts with the true witness of the community. Luke says that it was specifically while Ananias heard Peter's words that he died (ἀκούων δὲ ὁ Ἀνανίας τοὺς λόγους τούτους πεσὼν ἐξέψυξεν, 5:5). When Peter interrogates Sapphira, he says that she and her husband "agreed," or "spoke with" one another (συνεφωνήθη, 5:9). And Luke adds that after both the death of Ananias and of Sapphira fear came "upon all those who heard" (ἐπὶ πάντας τοὺς ἀκούοντας ταῦτα, 5:5, 11).[66] Ananias and Sapphira lied, but Peter speaks and they die. Now, it appears, "all those who heard" have witnessed the power of the community's speech.[67]

---

64. The Greek is a little difficult to translate, but the meaning is clear: οὐχὶ μένον σοὶ ἔμενεν καὶ πραθὲν ἐν τῇ σῇ ἐξουσίᾳ ὑπῆρχεν; Marguerat's wooden translation is helpful: "your possession remaining does it not remain yours and what has been sold, was it not in your possession?" (Historian, 169).

65. Marguerat, Historian, points out how the use of the verbs πίμπλημι (4:31) and πληρόω (5:3) help make a rhetorical contrast: the believers were "filled" with the Spirit; Ananias is "filled" with Satan, 170.

66. Marguerat, Historian, 171.

67. Scholars have often missed the rhetorical connections the story of Ananias and Sapphira has with the preceding narrative. Scholars are rightly concerned foremost to explain the logic of divine punishment. But instead of looking for rhetorical connections with the surrounding material (beyond the theme of shared possessions), scholars have instead searched outside the immediate context for answers. Hays, Ethics, seeks to place the punishment within the general bounds of Lukan theology: he gives a catalogue of material from Luke's Gospel and simply asserts that the punishment is "in keeping with the teaching of Luke and Acts," (222–25). Capper, "Goods" in Bauckham, Palestinian Setting, suggests that the Qumran community provides the interpretive key (337–41). Harrill, "Divine Judgement," 351–69, suggests that the Greco-Roman cultural context of "oaths, vows, and promises" provides the interpretive key (351–69). I am not suggesting that by placing the story in its rhetorical context the theological problems disappear. Rather, I am suggesting that the theological problem must begin to be addressed within the rhetorical confines Luke has provided in his narrative.

But it does not appear that Luke is here suggesting that just any lie would have resulted in Ananias's and Sapphira's deaths. Luke is clear that it was the particular lie about the sum of their donation to the community that was the issue. Again, Luke parallels their actions with what he had said was true generally of the community: they brought (ἐνέγκας) the proceeds (τῆς τιμῆς) of their sale and put (ἔθηκεν) them at the feet of the apostles (τοὺς πόδας τῶν ἀποστόλων, 5:2; cf. 4:34–35). Luke moreover describes their deaths similarly to how he described the giving of possessions to the community. Luke says that Ananias "fell" (πεσὼν) and was "carried out" (ἐξενέγκαντες). Sapphira likewise fell at Peter's feet (ἔπεσεν . . . πρὸς τοὺς πόδας αὐτοῦ) and was "carried out" (ἐξενέγκαντες). Describing their deaths in this way again makes clear how central shared possessions are to the Jerusalem community.

Does Luke intend Ananias and Sapphira's deaths to be seen in an eschatological light? It is not clear whether he does, but one element of the story might point in this direction. Luke appears to play with the language of "one heart and soul" (καρδία καὶ ψυχὴ) that he had used in at the beginning of the second summary statement (4:32). In both of Peter's assertions that Ananias lied, he says that it was Ananias's heart that was first corrupted: "why has Satan filled you heart . . . ?" (διὰ τί ἐπλήρωσεν ὁ σατανᾶς τὴν καρδίαν σου, 5:3); "why did you put this thing in your heart?" (τί ὅτι ἔθου ἐν τῇ καρδίᾳ σου τὸ πρᾶγμα τοῦτο, 5:4). And to describe their deaths, Luke says that Ananias and Sapphira both ἐξέψυξεν (5:5, 10). Luke might be playing on the root of the verb to suggest that a heart (καρδία) that is not one with the community is a soul (ψυχὴ) not one with the community, so that soul (ψυχὴ) must die (ἐξέψυξεν).

If the Jerusalem community is supposed to be composed of those who will be saved on the day of the Lord (cf. Act 2:21), then for Luke to suggest that Ananias and Sapphira are not one heart and one soul with the community suggests that they are not part of those who will be saved on the last day. Peter, we should also recall, warned that that all those who do not listen to the prophet like Moses will be "cast out of the people" (ἐξολεθρευθήσεται ἐκ τοῦ λαοῦ, 3:23). The ἐξ- prefixes on the verbs describing Ananias and Sapphira's deaths (ἐξέψυξεν, ἐξενέγκαντες) along with the emphasis on speech and hearing in the passage might suggest theirs is an eschatological expulsion from "the people."

Conclusion

Luke sets an eschatological stage for the narrative of Acts. In the first moments of his second volume, the resurrected Jesus speaks of the kingdom of God to his disciples (1:3). This occasions an eschatological question from the disciples: "will you at this time restore the kingdom to Israel?" (1:6). Jesus does not give them a direct answer, but tells them that they will be his witnesses. In the next moment of the narrative, Luke emphasizes the disciples' eyesight as Jesus is taken into heaven. The angel then tells them that the things of which they are eyewitnesses sets them on an eschatological mission: they will proclaim to the world that Jesus will come back in the same way they saw him go.

Both of Peter's sermons in Acts 1–2 and 3:1—5:16 have an outlook to eschatological events. When the Spirit is poured out, Peter says this is evidence that it is the "last days" (2:17) and that the "day of the Lord" (2:20) is coming. The people must therefore repent. The healing of the cripple itself is a miracle that implies an eschatological outlook since it is a resurrection-like miracle. Peter moreover announces after the cripple has been raised that if the people repent, God will send Jesus from heaven who will bring "seasons of refreshing" and "times of restoration" (3:19–21).

Ethics follows eschatology at the beginning of Acts. Both of Peter's eschatological announcements result in the conversion of thousands (2:41; 4:4). And those who convert, Luke says, share their possessions with one another. The placement of the two summary statements (2:42–47; 4:32–35) at the conclusion of the two opening literary sequences of the book suggests that the community's shared life is a result of Peter's eschatological announcements.

Both the structures of the summary statements and the example of Ananias and Sapphira demonstrate that the sharing of possessions is the central ingredient to the Jerusalem community. In the first summary statement, the sharing of possessions appears at the center of the summary, with the beginning and ending portions mirroring each other. In the second summary statement, the sharing of possessions frames the witnessing of the community (4:32–35). Luke says that they shared the possessions on either side of saying that they continued to witness to the resurrection of the Lord Jesus. The example of Ananias and Sapphira confirms the importance of shared possessions: when they lie about the sum of their donation, they fall dead at the feet of the apostles—the very place those in the community had been placing their possessions. The manner of their deaths might suggest that to donate all one's possessions was to donate one's life. When

Ananias and Sapphira lied about giving all of their possessions, their lives were demanded of them.

In addition to demonstrating a relationship between eschatology and ethics at the beginning of Acts, we have also demonstrated in part how Luke's concern for these two related matters fits within his larger rhetorical purposes. The apostles' eschatological task is to be witnesses of the resurrected Jesus. Peter and the apostles claim to be precisely that on the day of Pentecost and on the occasion of the cripple's healing. Luke reuses the tropes of seeing and hearing that we have seen him use repeatedly in his Gospel in the context of eschatological announcement to identify Peter and apostles as witnesses. Luke moreover identifies the crowds at Peter's sermons as witnesses of the miraculous events by using these tropes. The crowds both see and hear the event of Pentecost, and the crowds see and know the healed cripple. They cannot deny their own eyes and ears, so, Luke proposes, they should not deny the apostles'.

But what is the relationship between eschatology and ethics? The summary statements at the very least suggest that—as we saw in Luke's Gospel—Luke envisions the formation of an eschatological people. The sharing of possessions is evidently one of the key elements in the eschatological peoples' formation. Beginning his second volume on the matter of a people being formed around eschatological announcement and the sharing of possessions suggests that these matters will continue to be important in the rest of Luke's second volume.

5

Received and Rejected in Acts

Hospitable Gentiles

Introduction

The opening of Acts focuses strictly on Israel. It is Ἰουδαῖοι "from every nation under heaven" who see and hear the Pentecost event (2:5). Their identity as such is emphasized in Peter's repeated address to them as "Judeans" (2:14), "Israelites" (2:22), and "brothers" (2:29, 37).[1] The Spirit is poured out in the last days on Judeans and they form a community around shared possessions. But the Spirit blows where it wishes, which results in the question of the Gentiles. What must they do to be saved?[2] This chapter considers the continued relationship of eschatology and ethics in Luke's narrative of Gentile inclusion.

I consider three passages in this chapter: the Cornelius episode (9:32—10:48), Paul and Silas in Philippi (16:1–40), and Paul's shipwreck at Malta and arrival in Rome (27:1—28:31). The unifying feature of these three passages is the hospitality of Gentiles. In Luke's program to justify the Gentile mission, he consistently characterizes the Gentiles who receive the gospel as those who receive the apostles. Gentiles receive the apostles by sharing their possessions. For Luke, salvation is a social event. We saw something similar to this in Luke's Gospel. To receive the Seventy with food and shelter, Jesus said, was to receive him and the one who sent him (Luke 10:1–16).[3]

1. Cf. Acts 3:12, 17; 4:10.

2. Cf. Acts 15:1, καί τινες κατελθόντες ἀπὸ τῆς Ἰουδαίας ἐδίδασκον τοὺς ἀδελφοὺς ὅτι, ἐὰν μὴ περιτμηθῆτε τῷ ἔθει τῷ Μωϋσέως, οὐ δύνασθε σωθῆναι.

3. The continued rhetorical influence of the sending of the Seventy in Luke's thought is evidenced, among other things, in Paul and Barnabas's shaking off of the

Apart from the trope of hospitality, these particular passages are chosen because they come at pivotal points in the narrative. Cornelius is the first major convert in the Gentile mission, and his conversion is the necessary precursor to the Jerusalem council in Acts 15.[4] Philippi is the first Gentile mission after the Jerusalem council decides that Gentiles can be part of the rebuilt tent of David (cf. Acts 15:16) without needing to be circumcised.[5] And, finally, the shipwreck in Malta is the culminating encounter with Gentiles. That fact, combined with the sheer length of the narrative, indicates that it is an important passage for Luke's purposes.

As in previous chapters, I will attempt to place each passage in the literary structure in which it appears. Placing passages in their literary contexts will illuminate the role eschatology and ethics have within Luke's broader rhetorical purposes. As we shall see, the trope of eyesight again emerges in Luke's second volume. This trope not only unifies the final literary sequence of Luke's second volume, but also suggests that Luke wishes to end his second volume with an emphasis on coming eschatological events since, as we have seen, this trope repeatedly appears in the context of eschatological proclamation.

Eschatology after Acts 3

The eschatological outlook of each passage will be addressed below, but because of the common view that Luke places little emphasis on eschatological expectation in Acts as a whole and that whatever Luke has to say about eschatology ends after Acts 3, a few remarks on Lukan eschatology in Acts after Ch. 3 are in order.[6]

---

dust of Antioch of Pisidia from their feet in response to the city's rejection (Acts 13:51). This recalls Jesus' command to the Seventy to do this very thing should they encounter rejection (Luke 10:11).

4. I say "major" because Philip's encounter with the Ethiopian eunuch (Acts 8:26–40) is also an encounter with the Gentile world, but Luke does not place as much weight on that event as he does on Cornelius's conversion.

5. Two other passages in Acts would be worth exploring on the themes of eschatology and ethics. First, there is Paul's missionary sojourn in Ephesus where (just as in Philippi) the local economy is upset by his proclamation (18:23—21:14; esp. 19:13–40). Second, there is the Luke's account of the aid sent from Antioch to Jerusalem in the famine, which appears to be Luke's way of demonstrating the relationship between the Antioch and Jerusalem churches (11:27—12:25).

6. Pervo, *Acts*, states that eschatology "is not a prominent topic in Acts," 25. Carroll, *Response*, notes the apparent eclipsing of eschatology after Acts 3 and admits that Acts is not "as rich in explicitly eschatological material as the gospel [sic]." He claims that though imminent hope was still relevant to his audience, "hope for an imminent

First, even if Luke said nothing more about eschatological expectation after his third chapter, one could not claim that it was not important to Luke. This is not only because that is not how narratives in general work (i.e., an audience should not and most likely will not forget the beginning of a story),[7] but also—and most importantly—because that is not how Luke writes. One example will suffice. In Luke 2:32, Simeon embraces the child Jesus and blesses God because now "a light of revelation for the nations and the glory of [his] people Israel" has come.[8] Simeon's words speak of a light (φῶς) shining on the Gentiles (ἐθνῶν), yet there is nothing of this in his Gospel narrative. It is not until Acts 8 that there is a Gentile (the Ethiopian eunuch) who truly sees the light. Should a reader be expected to forget that Luke put these words on Simeon's lips at the beginning of his Gospel narrative simply because Luke says nothing of a light shining for the Gentiles in his Gospel? By no means. Not only should a reader not forget, but how is it possible for an attentive reader not to remember Simeon's words when she begins to read of the Gentile mission in Acts, especially when Paul says that the Lord has made him "a light to the nations" (φῶς ἐθνῶν, Acts 13:47)? Similarly, Luke says at the beginning of Acts that it is the "last days" (2:17),[9] and that cannot be forgotten.

Second, Luke continues to reuse material from John the Baptist's eschatological proclamation throughout his narrative. The reuse of John the Baptist's preaching is significant because this has been the anchor that has grounded the discussion of eschatology in Luke and Acts in this study so far. Most significantly, at the beginning of each of Paul's three missionary journeys, Luke speaks of the "way" (ὁδός), which refers to the proclamation made by Paul and his missionary compatriots. Paul says to the Judean false prophet Bar-Jesus, "son of the devil . . . why do you not cease from perverting the straight paths of the Lord?" (υἱὲ διαβόλου . . . οὐ παύσῃ διαστρέφων τὰς ὁδοὺς τοῦ κυρίου τὰς εὐθείας; 13:10). In Philippi, the fortune-telling slave girl follows Paul and Silas crying out that they proclaim "the way of salvation" (ὁδὸν σωτηρίας, 16:17). And in Ephesus, Priscilla and Aquila accurately explain to Apollos "the way of God" (τὴν ὁδὸν τοῦ θεοῦ)[10] since he knew

---

parousia is never appropriate" for the narrative itself, 122. Keener, *Acts*, says that "Luke does not emphasize imminent future eschatology the way that Mark or Matthew does," 1:518. See also Haenchen, *Acts*, 94–103; Maddox, *Purpose*, 130; Wilson, *Gentiles*, 78. Cf. Mount, *Pauline Christianity*, 59–104, and pp. 6 and 101 of this study.

7. I am grateful to Prof. Steve Mason for making this point to me.

8. φῶς εἰς ἀποκάλυψιν ἐθνῶν καὶ δόξαν λαοῦ σου Ἰσραήλ.

9. For a discussion of this passage and the textual variants associated with the phrase "in the last days," see p. 112 above.

10. Cf. τὴν ὁδὸν τοῦ κυρίου, 18:25.

only of the baptism of John (18:24–26). Speaking of the "way" in conjunction with other language that either recalls John the Baptist's preaching ("crooked/straight," "salvation") or by invoking John the Baptist by name suggests that Luke is reusing language that recalls John the Baptist's eschatological proclamation (Luke 3:2–17). That these instances come in structurally significant passages in the narrative is even more suggestive. It appears that Luke wants the reader to see Christians as following a continuous line from John the Baptist.

Third, in a similar vein, it is noteworthy that where Luke does mention eschatological events explicitly, he uses language that may recall John the Baptist's preaching. Eschatological events are "about to be" (μέλλω, cf. Luke 3:7). At the Areopagus, Paul tells his Gentile audience of the about-to-be judgment of the whole world (μέλλει κρίνειν τὴν οἰκουμένην, 17:31). Paul speaks to Felix both of the about-to-be resurrection (ἀνάστασιν μέλλειν ἔσεσθαι) and of the about-to-be judgment (τοῦ κρίματος τοῦ μέλλοντος, 24:15, 25). To Agrippa and Festus Paul speaks of all the things the Prophets said are about to be (οἱ προφῆται ἐλάλησαν μελλόντων γίνεσθαι καὶ Μωϋσῆς, 26:22). The case of Felix is particularly significant because it suggests that Luke is again anchoring himself in the language of John the Baptist's eschatological proclamation, for it comes in the context of Paul's defense of the "way" (ὁδός, 24:14, 22).

Finally, Luke sets the reader's eyes toward eschatological hope at the end of his narrative.[11] The word ἐλπίς, though hardly used before Paul's arrest in Jerusalem,[12] appears after his arrest in each of the five successive scenes. Paul proclaims that it is on account of the hope of Israel, the hope of resurrection, that he is arrested and on trial in each of his appearances before authorities in Jerusalem (the Sanhedrin, Felix, Agrippa/Festus).[13] And upon his arrival in Rome, he tells the Judean leaders that it is on account of "the hope of Israel" (τῆς ἐλπίδος τοῦ Ἰσραὴλ, 28:20) that he is in chains. The term is also used once in between Jerusalem and Rome, the significance of which is discussed below.[14] As Paul tells Felix, this hope is "about to be"

11. Mason, "Speech-Making II," says that the use of the word "hope" toward the end of Acts reflects the "growing optimism that comes from the spread of the faith," see: 147–71, esp. 155. Mason may be correct that it expresses optimism, but the optimism is met with an equal perplexity over Judean rejection and the question of whether the hope is well-founded. See p. 175 below.

12. The term is used in the quotation of Ps 16 in Acts 2:26, and in Acts 16:19 when Luke speaks of the loss of the "hope of gain" to the slave owners whose servant girl Paul had just liberated from a spirit.

13. 23:6, 24:15, 26:6–7, respectively.

14. See p. 168 below.

(24:15). Eschatological proclamation is not eclipsed from the narrative. On the contrary, it appears that this is the very matter with which Luke concludes his second volume.[15]

Raising Gentiles: Acts 9:32—10:48

Introduction

The miracle of Cornelius's conversion, like that of the healed cripple in Acts 3, appears to be a resurrection-like miracle. Peter commands Cornelius, who lies prostrate on the ground, to "rise" (ἀνάστηθι, 10:26). If Luke intends Cornelius's conversion to be resurrection-like, then the miracle would seem to have an eschatological character, pointing beyond itself to coming eschatological events.[16] Luke moreover says that Cornelius is known for, among other things, his charity toward the people (10:2). Eschatology and ethics are again linked in the first major foray of the Christian message into the Gentile world.

Structure

Luke signals a new stage of the narrative with a brief summary statement in 9:31—"and the churches . . . had peace." A transition is also signaled by a return to Peter's character, who, except for a brief appearance in Samaria (8:20–24), has faded into the background since 5:42. Saul (soon to be called Paul, 13:9) has just converted and appeared in Jerusalem, and Luke will rotate stories from here on between the characters of Peter and Paul until the council in Ch. 15. Luke moreover appears to signal that the switch to Peter in 9:32 to the end of Paul's first missionary journey in 14:28 is a structured sequence in the narrative by beginning and ending the sequence with a miracle of a healed cripple. Peter heals Aeneas (9:32–35); Paul heals an unnamed cripple in Lystra (14:8–10). Luke may intend both miracles to be

---

15. For recent studies that present a challenge to those who suggest that eschatology is not important to the whole of Acts, see e.g., Salmeier, *Restoring the Kingdom*; Horton, *Death and Resurrection*; Anderson, *"God Raised"*; and Haacker, "Der Geist."

16. Pervo, *Acts*, also suggests that Peter's raising of Cornelius is resurrection-like and even goes one step further to suggest that "all wonders [in Acts] have an eschatological dimension, as signs, synecdoches, foretastes, and so forth, of God's promises," 254. Horton, *Death and Resurrection*, sees most miracles in Acts as signs of resurrection. Horton says that the Cornelius episode functions "to reveal the crucial role of the messianic pattern within the conversion process," 75. He also points the command ἀνάστηθι as evidence that Luke intends the miracle to symbolize resurrection, 76.

resurrection-like: both apostles command cripples to "rise" (ἀνάστηθι, 9:34; 14:10).[17] Having both performed these wonders in the name of the risen Lord among the Gentiles, Peter and Paul can be a double witness to the conversion of the Gentiles (15:3–12).

The Cornelius episode is composed of three consecutive miracles that all appear to be resurrection-like. The scenes are connected most noticeably by the identical imperative Peter speaks to Aeneas, Tabitha, and Cornelius: ἀνάστηθι (9:34, 40; 10:26).[18] But the scenes are also brought into literary relationship by how they begin and end. They all begin by naming "a certain" (τις) person who lives in a certain city (Lydda, Joppa, Caesarea, 9:32–33, 36; 10:1), and all three episodes end with conversions (9:35, 42; 10:47–48).

Aeneas

The first scene in Lydda is striking for its brevity and oddity. Why narrate so briefly the healing of cripple at this point in the narrative?[19] The interpretive key might lie in that the scene is familiar: it recalls Peter's first miracle in the book of Acts, the healing of the cripple at the Beautiful Gate (3:6–7). Here, as at the Temple, Peter meets a man lying on the ground who has been crippled for a certain number of years,[20] and invoking the name of Jesus Christ, he

---

17. On Aeneas, see p. 145. The healing of the cripple in Lystra recalls the resurrection-like healing of the cripple in Acts 3 because he "leapt and was walking" (ἥλατο καὶ περιεπάτει), just as the cripple did at the Beautiful Gate (cf. περιπατῶν καὶ ἁλλόμενος, 3:8). Horton, *Death and Resurrection*, also suggests that the healing of the cripple in Lystra is resurrection-like. He points, as I do, to the ways in which the healing recalls the two previous healings of cripples in Acts (the beggar at the Beautiful Gate and Aeneas), 73–74.

18. Pervo, *Acts*, also notices this, 253, 274. Horton, *Death and Resurrection*, also suggests that miracles of Aeneas (72–73) and Tabitha (63–65) are resurrection-like miracles, but misses the fact that Peter gives the identical command to Aeneas, Tabitha, and Cornelius. He therefore misses the way in which the miracles of Aeneas and Tabitha prepare for and enlighten the Cornelius episode.

19. Bock, *Acts*, 377, suggests that the healing "lays the ground work for conversions to the Lord in Lydda and the Sharon region." But Bock does not suggest why it is important for Luke's purposes that these as opposed to other conversions are noteworthy enough to include in Luke's narrative. Spencer, *Acts*, suggests the story functions at least in part to demonstrate "Peter's continuing partnership with Jesus." He points both to the fact that the healing act "mirrors one of Jesus' mighty works (Luke 5:17–26), and to Peter's words, which put Jesus in focus: "Jesus Christ heals you (9:34)," 106. Parsons, *Acts*, notes the similarities between the Aeneas and Tabitha episodes and suggests that the spotlight is on Tabitha. He suggests that Peter's healing of Aeneas is simply a stop on Peter's "'inspection tour' among some of the churches," 137.

20. Eight in this instance, 9:33; forty in 4:22.

commands the cripple to "rise" (ἀνάστηθι, 9:34).[21] The people of Lydda see (εἶδαν) and, as a result, believe (9:35), just as the people saw and believed at the Beautiful Gate (cf. 3:9).[22] The parallels with Peter's first miracle raises the question whether this, like Peter's first healing of a cripple, is also a resurrection-like miracle.[23] It is possible that Luke intends no symbolic meaning to the command. Indeed, what other command would Peter give to a cripple in order to heal him? But both the similarities this scene has with Peter's first miracle and the rhetorical connections it has with what follows suggest that Luke has characterized this as a resurrection-like miracle.

Tabitha

Luke's description of Tabitha is both similar and dissimilar to Luke's previous description of characters. Like the Seven and Stephen, Luke says Tabitha is πλήρης of two characteristics.[24] But whereas the Seven and Stephen are πλήρης of "the Holy Spirit and wisdom" (6:3) and "grace and power" (6:8),[25] Tabitha is πλήρης of "good works and of almsgiving she used to practice." Tabitha's notability is that she is charitable.[26]

The plot moves quickly after Tabitha's introduction: she becomes sick and dies (9:37). Upon hearing that Peter is in Lydda, two men are sent to retrieve him, evidently because they assume that he can do something about Tabitha's death. "Rising" (ἀναστὰς), Luke says, Peter went with them" (9:39). Upon Peter's arrival, Luke elaborates on what he meant by Tabitha's good works. In an upper room where Tabitha's body lays, there is a multitude of

---

21. The verb is ἔγειρε in 3:6. See p. 125 above.

22. As Spencer, *Acts*, notes, "such a miracle [in Lydda] is impressive but not overwhelming at this juncture, given Peter's earlier healing of another lame man who had been disabled from birth for forty years," 102. Cf. Parsons, *Acts*, 137.

23. Those who speculate about the Christian or non-Christian status of Aeneas ask a question not raised by the narrative. See, e.g., Fitzmyer, *Acts*, 444; Barrett, *Acts*, 1:480; Bock, *Acts*, 376.

24. Up until this point in the narrative, the only characters described as being πλήρης of something are the Seven and Stephen.

25. Cf. 6:3; 7:55.

26. Parsons, *Acts*, pointing to the example of Tob 1:16–18, suggests that Tabitha's "kind deeds" functions "as a kind of umbrella for specific acts of Jewish piety, which included giving 'clothing to the naked.'" He suggests that Tabitha's kind deeds were not, however, limited to acts of charity, 139. This is undoubtedly correct, but it is nevertheless clear that Luke thinks her giving of clothes to widows is what is most important about her character. Cf. Reimer, *Women*, 31–70.

widows (αἱ χῆραι) weeping and showing Peter the clothes Tabitha had made for them while she was still alive (9:39).[27] Tabitha had clothed the poor.

After dismissing everyone from the room, Peter says to Tabitha's corpse, "Tabitha, ἀνάστηθι" (9:40), and she miraculously comes back from the dead. Peter gives her his hand, raises her up (ἀνέστησεν αὐτήν), and then presents her "living" (παρέστησεν αὐτὴν ζῶσαν) to those who are present (9:41). Luke's words might be intended to recall the beginning of his narrative, when Jesus "presented himself living" (παρέστησεν ἑαυτὸν ζῶντα) after his resurrection (1:3). Unlike Aeneas's rising, Tabitha's healing not merely able to resemble, but in fact is a resurrection. She is living after having been dead.

Placing a resurrection miracle immediately after the raising of Aeneas might be intended to retrospectively shed light on that miracle. The command that Peter whispers to Tabitha (ἀνάστηθι) is the very same command Peter had spoken to Aeneas. This again suggests that Aeneas's healing, like the cripple's at the Beautiful Gate, is symbolic—a miracle that mimics resurrection. Peter has now raised two people. Many believe and Peter, Luke says, remains (μεῖναι) in Joppa with a man named Simon (9:42–43).

The narration of Peter's second raising is slightly longer than the first, and all of the extra details Luke includes appear to set up for what follows. The most significant details are Luke's characterization of Tabitha. She is "full of good works and of almsgiving she used to practice," and she made clothes for the vulnerable of society. At this point in Acts, one gets the impression that Luke is describing the model Christian, and that if anyone should be raised from her deathbed, it is she.[28] Indeed, it seems that even the other characters in the story assume this. Why else would two men be sent for Peter, and why else would Peter come? Moreover, precisely because it is a resurrection miracle, the story can pose the question, "if this is the kind of person who is raised back to the present life, then what type of person will be raised on the last day?" The answer is obvious.

27. It is worth noting here that Tabitha performs one of the acts of charity that John the Baptist looked for among the true children of Abraham. He counseled the one with two cloaks to give to the one with none (Luke 3:11).

28. This appears to be Peter's logic in the Cornelius episode. Peter points to Cornelius's fear of God and acts of righteousness as evidence that Cornelius is acceptable to God (10:35). C. Hays, *Ethics*, 233–34, suggests that Tabitha might have been raised for this reason as well. Referring to her care for widows, he asks, "Is such a banal act of charity plausibly the reason for which she is resurrected?" His discussion of other widows in the OT and in Lukan writings suggests an answer in the affirmative.

Cornelius

Cornelius is a Gentile among Gentiles: he resides in a city named to honor the emperor (Καισάρεια), is a centurion, and is in a cohort from Italy—the land of imperial headquarters (10:1).[29] But despite being the ultimate Gentile in a narrative that, up until this point, has focused largely on Israel, Luke immediately casts him in a favorable light.[30] He is devout, fears God,[31] gives "many alms to the people" (ποιῶν ἐλεημοσύνας πολλὰς τῷ λαῷ), and prays ceaselessly to God (10:2). The mention of charity recalls the last episode. The last person in the narrative to give alms was raised from the dead.

An angel visits Cornelius who tells him that his prayers and charity have "gone up into remembrance before God" (ἀνέβησαν εἰς μνημόσυνον ἔμπροσθεν τοῦ θεοῦ, 10:4).[32] The second mention of Cornelius's charity both reminds the reader again of Tabitha and signifies that this is a defining characteristic of Cornelius. The angel tells Cornelius to send men to find Simon who is called Peter, who is staying as a guest (ξενίζεται) in a tanner named Simon's house in Joppa. The sending of two men[33] and a soldier to seek out Peter in nearby town on behalf of a godly and charitable man might lead to certain expectations. Again, the last time that happened, someone was raised from the dead.[34]

29. It is historically problematic that Luke says there was a cohort in Caesaea at this time. According to the evidence, there "only auxiliary troops were stationed in peace time in Judaea," Schurer, *History*, 1.365 and n. 54.

30. This is not the first time that Luke has cast a centurion in a favorable light. See Luke 7:1–10.

31. On the meaning of "godly" and whether there was a class of god-fearers at the time of the events Luke records, see Keener, *Acts*, 2:1751–53 and Barrett, *Acts*, 1:499–501,

32. Luke may be playing with cultic imagery here. Sacrifices in the OT are at times described as a μνημόσυνον that goes up in the smoke (see e.g., Lev 2:2, 9; Num 5:26). Cf. C. Hays, *Ethics*, 235; Pervo, *Acts*, 268

33. Luke is careful to say that it was "two" (δύo), 10:7, which seems to suggest he wants to recall the sending of two people on Tabitha's behalf (9:38).

34. Flessen, *Exemplary Man*, argues that Cornelius "is a model man for Luke's audience" in the respect that his key qualities are "submission, piety, and generosity," 157. She also examines how these qualities contrast with the characterizations of Graeco-Roman military men in other ancient literature, 114–156. C. Hays, *Ethics*, argues that the importance of almsgiving in God's response to Cornelius should not be downplayed: "Acts 10.31–32 allocates an instrumental role to Cornelius's almsgiving. 'Your prayer has been heard and your alms have been remembered before God. Send *therefore* (οὖν) to Joppa and ask for Simon,'" 235.

Hospitality noticeably emerges as a theme in this literary sequence.[35] The healing of Tabitha concludes with Peter's "remaining" (μεῖναι) with Simon, who is a tanner (9:34). And in the angel's instructions to Cornelius, he mentions that he is being "entertained as guest" (ξενίζεται) by the same Simon. Nothing about this is shocking. Simon Peter, a Judean, is being given food and shelter by another Judean. What is shocking is the vision Peter has while Cornelius's emissaries are en route.

Peter goes to the rooftop of Simon the tanner's house to pray (10:9). He becomes hungry, and so those below begin to prepare a meal. Peter falls into a trance and sees a vision (10:10). The heavens are opened and a giant cloth comes down filled with all sorts of "four-footed animals, reptiles of the earth, and birds of the air" (10:12).[36] A voice from the sky commands Peter to eat, but he refuses.[37] Never, he says, has he eaten anything "common and unclean" (κοινὸν καὶ ἀκάθαρτον, 10:14). This all happens a second time, after which the Lord responds to Peter, "that which God has made clean (ἐκαθάρισεν) you should not call common (μὴ κοίνου, 10:15). After a third time, the cloth recedes into heaven (10:16).

The discomfort Peter would have felt cannot be overestimated. Food was, in part, what made Israel Israel. The "do not defile yourselves" which comes at the end of a detailed list of what not to eat in Lev 11 is followed immediately by, "I am the Lord who brought you up out of the land of Egypt" (Lev 11:44–45). One can moreover see the symbolic nature of sharing of food in Luke's own narrative. Not only does the risen Jesus eat with the disciples (1:4),[38] but food is also part of what Luke mentions

35. Cf. Jipp, *Hospitality*, 204–18; and C. Hays's discussion of hospitality after Acts 6, *Ethics*, 248–54.

36. Pervo, *Acts*, notes that the way in which this verse might recall Gen 1:24–25 and may be an indication of Christian apologetic to circumvent Mosaic law by appealing to the original goodness of all creation, 269–70. Cf. Parsons, *Acts*, 145.

37. The command is "kill and eat!" (θῦσον καὶ φάγε). Parsons, *Acts*, suggests that Luke may be playing on the semantic range of the verb θύω, which can mean both "kill" and "sacrifice." The verb is used elsewhere in Luke–Acts to refer to religious or cultic sacrifice (Luke 22:7; Acts 14:13, 18). The (likely) play on this word correlates with the play on cultic sacrifice when Luke speaks of Cornelius's good deeds going up as a μνημόσυνον before God (cf. Lev 2:2, 9; Num 5:26).

38. The verb συναλίζω in Acts 1:4 can also mean simply "to bring together" or to "stay with." But it does not appear to mean only that Jesus brought the disciples together in this instance, for one verse earlier Luke says Jesus spent forty days with them. The NRSV, therefore, simply translates it as "staying with" in an apparent attempt not to constrict the meaning of the verb only to sharing food. However, sharing food obviously was part of what they did in those forty days if Jesus was indeed "staying with" them, which is why Acts 10:41 can be seen as a deliberate echo of 1:4. The BDAG itself suggests this, 964. Luke's Gospel also ends with Jesus twice eating food with disciples:

the community shares in his first community summary (2:42–46).[39] "All things," including food, were "common" (κοινά) among Christians, to be sure (2:44)—but only things that themselves were not "common" and "unclean" (κοινὸν καὶ ἀκάθαρτον, 10:14).

Peter is confused, but not for long. Cornelius's agents knock on the front door wondering if they have found the house where Peter is "entertained as guest" (ξενίζεται, 10:18). One can never be sure of the significance of numbers in ancient narrative, but in this case perhaps Luke intends there to be proportion between the vision and the men who arrive. Just at the moment that Peter is puzzling over the vision that came in three movements, the Spirit says, "behold three men are seeking you" (10:19). Immediately after hearing their mission in brief, Peter invites them in—he "entertains them as guests" (αὐτοὺς ἐξένισεν, 10:23).[40] Luke does not explain what it means for Peter to entertain someone as guest while being himself a guest, but that is beside the point.[41] Whatever it looked like in practical terms, the point is that Peter shares food and shelter with them.

The beginning of the next scene again recalls the Tabitha episode. After the two men asked Peter to come to Tabitha's abode, Luke says that he "getting up went with them" (ἀναστὰς ... συνῆλθεν αὐτοῖς, 9:39). Similarly, Luke now says that Peter "getting up, went with" Cornelius's messengers (ἀναστὰς ἐξῆλθεν σὺν αὐτοῖς, 10:23). Some of the Judean brothers go with him and, upon arrival, Peter and the others find not only Cornelius, but also his relatives and close friends. Cornelius collapses at Peter's feet and begins to worship him (10:25).

The ways in which this episode has been recalling the events around Tabitha all appear to prepare for what happens next. Peter, just as he had commanded Tabitha, and just as he had commanded Aeneas before her, says

once in a village on the road to Emmaus (Luke 24:30), and once when he appears in the disciples' midst and eats a piece of broiled fish (24:41). Luke obviously thinks it was important that Jesus ate with the disciples, which is why he undoubtedly chose a verb in Acts 1:4 that can mean both to "stay with" and to "eat with."

39. In addition to the summary statements, the distribution to the widows in Acts 6 and Antioch's charity in the famine can be mentioned (11:27–29). Food is the issue over which the community of local Judeans and Hellenists are either be divided or united. The sharing of food is the means by which the Antioch church identifies itself with Jerusalem Christians.

40. Luke says that God says to go down from the rooftop to meet the messengers "without hesitation" (μηδὲν διακρινόμενος, 10:20). Parsons, *Acts*, suggests that Luke may be playing on the semantic range of the verb which can mean both "without hesitation" and "without discrimination," 147. Cf. BDAG, 231.

41. Parsons, *Acts*, notes that it does not appear to have been as much of a problem for Judeans to entertain Gentiles as it was the other way around, 148. Cf. Keener's discussion, *Acts*, 2:1777–8.

to Cornelius, ἀνάστηθι (10:26). And just as he had taken Tabitha by the hand and raised her (ἀνέστησεν αὐτήν, 9.41), so now Peter raises Cornelius (ἤγειρεν αὐτὸν, 10:26). Cripples can be raised; the dead can be raised; now, evidently, Gentiles can be raised too.[42] The command might moreover suggest an eschatological significance just as it perhaps did in the Tabitha episode: if Gentiles can be raised now, then it appears they can also be raised on the last day. We must reiterate here, as we did in reference to Aeneas's healing, that Peter's command may have no symbolic meaning to it. Again, what other command would Peter give to Cornelius lying prostrate before him? People moreover routinely "rise" both in Luke's narrative and in the NT generally.[43] But the question here is not what the word does or does not do generally in Luke's writing or in other NT writings, but how in functions in this context. Peter has given the same command to three different people lying before him in a clearly demarcated literary sequence suggests that Luke intends a symbolic meaning in Peter's command to Cornelius.[44]

Still, there is one significant difference between this command and the previous ones. Peter is the one who gives the command, but it appears as if he knows not what he says, for Peter did not give the command to Cornelius to heal him or to raise him from the dead, but to prevent him from worshipping him. "I am only a man," he says (10:26). Peter's character, it appears, does not know the significance of his own command.

Peter's next words address the crowd to explain his and the other Judeans' presence. "You know," he says, "that it is unlawful for a Judean man to become close to or come to a foreigner" (ὑμεῖς ἐπίστασθε ὡς ἀθέμιτόν

42. Obeisance may also be an issue here since it is an issue later in Acts, both when Herod fails to give glory to God (12:23) and when Paul and Barnabas are incorrectly identified as deities at Lystra (14:11–15). To be sure, Peter does not want Cornelius to worship him, which is why he says "I am only a man." But it appears something more is going on here precisely because Cornelius has already been identified as a God fearer and no further mention is made of his mistake. It is rather his fear of God and his righteousness—and therefore his acceptance by God—that continues to be the matter in focus. Cf. Parsons, Acts, 148; Keener, Acts, 2:1780–86.

43. See e.g., Luke 4:16, 38, 39; Matt 9:9.

44. The verb ἀνίστημι appears in the aorist second person singular only in Acts in the NT. In Acts, the verb appears in this form seven times, three of which are in the Aeneas, Tabitha, and Cornelius episodes. The other four instances themselves would require fuller investigations to see whether they carry a similar double meaning. The first instance of the verb appears when the angel of the Lord tells Philip to "rise" and go south (8:26). This instance does not appear to carry any further meaning. But the remaining 3 instances might. The verb appears in this form in Paul's conversion story (9:6), in the healing of the cripple at Lystra (14:10), and in Paul's final recounting of his conversion before Festus and Agrippa (26:16). I have already suggested that Luke might intend the healing at Lystra to be resurrection-like, and as I detail below, Paul's final recounting of his conversion is full of symbolism (see p. 167).

ἐστιν ἀνδρὶ Ἰουδαίῳ κολλᾶσθαι ἢ προσέρχεσθαι ἀλλοφύλῳ). But he has realized that "no person is to be said to be common or unclean" (μηδένα κοινὸν
ἢ ἀκάθαρτον λέγειν ἄνθρωπον, 10:28). Here Peter indicates that he has made
the connection between the appearance of the three men at Simon the tanner's doorstep and the vision. If no food is κοινὸν ἢ ἀκάθαρτον then he has
concluded that neither are any humans. This is why, Peter says, he has come
"without objection" (ἀναντιρρήτως, 10:29). If no food is unclean, then Peter
can eat Cornelius's food. If he can eat Cornelius's food, he can eat it with
him. And if he can eat it with him, then it would stand to reason that they
could have "all things common" (ἄπαντα κοινὰ; cf. 2:44).

After Cornelius explains that an angel instructed him to send for Peter
so that he could hear what God would say, Peter tells him of the things that
happened in Judea: John baptized, Jesus was anointed; Jesus healed, was
killed, but was raised from the dead (10:37–40).[45] And of all these things,
Peter says, "we are witnesses" (ἡμεῖς μάρτυρες, 10:39). The form of proclamation and the claim to be a witness both recall the opening of Acts. As
was said in connection with the selection of Matthias (1:21–26), an apostle
must have been with Jesus since the baptism of John (10:37), and he must
be a witness (μάρτυς, 10:39) of his resurrection (10:40). John's proclamation
and the apostles' status as eyewitnesses moreover are central to Peter's two
sermons in Jerusalem in Acts 1–4. But Peter adds one detail here that he has
not been mentioned since the very opening of Acts. They—the witnesses—
ate and drank with the risen Jesus (συνεφάγομεν καὶ συνεπίομεν αὐτῷ, 10:41;
cf. 1:4). Why this is important to remark upon here is not entirely clear. But
perhaps Luke intends proportion between Jesus' resurrection and the present situation: Peter ate and drank with the risen Lord; now, he is going to eat
and drink with a risen Gentile.

Peter's homily then appropriately moves from Jesus' resurrection to
the last day: the resurrected one is he "who is promised by God to be judge
of the living and the dead" (10:42). "To this," Peter says, "all the Prophets
witness that all (πάντα) who believe in him will receive the forgiveness of
sins through his name" (10:43). At the beginning of Acts, Peter announced
the last days (2:17). The reader now gets the feeling that a new stage in the
story is afoot, for Peter is again announcing the coming end.

---

45. Luke says that Jesus healed "all those oppressed by the devil" (τοὺς
καταδυναστευομένους ὑπὸ τοῦ διαβόλου). Parsons, *Acts*, notes that the verb
καταδυναστεύω appears only here and in Jas 2:6 in the NT. In Jas 2:6, the verb is used
in an economic sense. Parsons suggests that Luke here "employs the economic terminology of the Greco-Roman patronage system and also of the Jewish Scriptures to
interpret Jesus' minister as engaged in fulfilling the Isaianic vision," 153. As Keener,
Acts, notes, it is more likely that Luke has sickness or infirmity in view, 2:1802–4.

Luke then says that "while Peter was still speaking these words, the Holy Spirit fell upon all those who heard the word" (ἔτι λαλοῦντος τοῦ Πέτρου τὰ ῥήματα ταῦτα ἐπέπεσεν τὸ πνεῦμα τὸ ἅγιον ἐπὶ πάντας τοὺς ἀκούοντας τὸν λόγον).[46] The reader is reminded again that Peter's words have power. It was while Peter spoke that Ananias and Sapphira fell at his feet.[47] But this time his words have brought life: Cornelius has been commanded to rise and now receives the gift of the Holy Spirit. It becomes clear, then, why Luke has been recalling the beginning of Acts. Cornelius's house experiences—it might be said—a mini-Pentecost. When the Holy Spirit is poured out (ἐκκέχυται), they begin speaking in other tongues and magnifying God (λαλούντων γλώσσαις καὶ μεγαλυνόντων τὸν θεόν) and by-standers are amazed (ἐξέστησαν, 10:45–46). This is exactly what happened on Pentecost.[48]

Cornelius, his household, and his friends are then given permission to be baptized because they have "received the Holy Spirit just as we did" (10:47). There can now be no doubt about what has taken place. If Peter knew not what he said when he commanded Cornelius to rise it is no matter, for he has now seen the effect of his words: Cornelius is now part of the community who will be vindicated on the last day. As the scene closes, Luke once again recalls the Tabitha episode. Just as Peter remained (μεῖναι, 9:43) with Simon the tanner, so now Cornelius asks him to "remain" (ἐπιμεῖναι) with him (10:48). Cornelius is hospitable.

Luke thus appears to justify the initial foray of the Christian announcement into the Gentile world through eschatology and ethics. By setting the scene in a series of resurrection-like miracles, the event suggests an eschatological outlook. This, coupled with Peter's sermon jumping immediately from Jesus' resurrection to the day of judgment, suggests again that these are the last days. Those who are raised now will be raised and vindicated on the last day. The reason Cornelius can be resurrected is because he, like Tabitha, is godly. And the most concrete way Luke can demonstrate this is by pointing to the sharing of possessions. Cornelius, like Tabitha, is charitable, and the story concludes with Cornelius inviting Peter to remain in his own home. He can do this because he and Peter are part of the same people

46. As Parsons, *Acts*, notes, Cornelius has at this point faded from prominence in the story, thus giving way to the corporate experience of the Spirit by all the Gentiles present, 155.

47. Horton, *Death and Resurrection*, suggests that Luke may be deliberately recalling the Ananias and Sapphira episode with mention of Peter's feet, 75.

48. The verb ἐκχέω appears in Acts 2:17–18, 33. Luke twice notes the amazement of the crowds on Pentecost: λαλούντων αὐτῶν ταῖς ἡμετέραις γλώσσαις τὰ μεγαλεῖα τοῦ θεοῦ, 2:11; ἐξίσταντο δὲ καὶ ἐθαύμαζον, 2:7.

now. He is no longer "common" or "unclean" because—evidently—he, Peter, and the risen Lord all share at the same table.

Philippi: Acts 16:1–40

Introduction

Paul and Silas's mission in Philippi comes at a pivotal moment in the narrative. The Jerusalem council has just decided that Gentiles are to be included in the restoration of the "tent of David" (15:16) and Paul now begins his second missionary journey. Judeans are noticeably absent from the time spent in Philippi, which is atypical for Paul's evangelistic visits. Paul usually visits the local synagogue before doing anything else.[49] Instead, what is found in Philippi is the conversion of two Gentiles amidst Philippian rejection. The two Gentiles who convert immediately invite Paul into their homes. Those who accept Paul's message, in other words, also hospitably accept him. The city's rejection is demonstrated when they lead him out of the city limits and ask him to leave. The absence of Judeans in the midst of Gentile acceptance and rejection suggests that Gentile inclusion into the restored tent of David (cf. 15:16) takes place not by their entry into the synagogue, but by the entry of Christians into their homes.

Structure

Paul's second missionary journey, like the first, forms a literary unit and is told as a there-and-back-again story: the journey begins and ends in Antioch (15:30, 18:22).[50] In addition to geographical markers, Luke indicates that the second journey is a literary unit by beginning and ending the sequence on the same motifs. The sequence begins with a story that demonstrates that, despite the Jerusalem council's decree, the question of Judean Law's place in Christianity will still be a matter of dialogue. Paul circumcises Timothy "because of the Judeans," even though he has proclaimed and will continue to proclaim the council's verdict (16:3–4). Paul then hears the Macedonian call. Through a vision in the night, he is given instructions on where to preach (16:9–10). At the end of the sequence,

---

49. The following episode in Thessalonika and Berea is typical (17:1–15).

50. The first missionary journey (13:1—14:28) is a little more explicitly a there-and-back-again: Luke is careful to mention by name the towns that Paul returns to Antioch through, which are all the towns he visited already in his mission in reverse (14:19–28).

Paul is in Corinth where, after telling the Judeans that he will now turn to the Gentiles (18:6), he again has a vision in the night in which he is told to remain in Corinth and preach (18:9). Thereafter, Luke again raises the question of the Judean Law. The Judeans in Corinth claim to Gallio that Paul is telling people to worship God "apart from the law" (παρὰ τὸν νόμον, 18:13). The sequence then closes with Paul performing another outward sign of obedience: taking a vow, he cuts his hair (18:18). The sequence of missionary encounters is therefore bracketed on either side with the question of the law and evidence of divine guidance.

The individual missionary visits are also all rhetorically related. Luke, for example, deliberately mentions in each new town that both men and women are part of the burgeoning movement.[51] Each story is one of mixed success: whether Judean or Gentile, some accept and some reject. Luke also rotates the stories between Gentile and Judean: in Philippi and Athens, Paul interacts almost exclusively with Gentiles; in Thessalonika and Berea[52] and in Corinth, Paul interacts almost exclusively with Judeans.[53] While each scene builds on previous ones, the two Judean scenes and the two Gentile scenes are characterized similarly. In Judean contexts, Paul argues from the Scriptures in synagogues about where he tries to persuade them that Jesus is the Christ (17:3; 18:5). Among the Gentiles, Paul gets irritated by false religion and disambiguates theistic titles to make them signify the God Paul proclaims. In Philippi, there is a mantic girl who says that Paul is the proclaimer of the ambiguously-named "most high God" (τοῦ θεοῦ τοῦ ὑψίστου, 16:17).[54] Becoming irritated (διαπονηθείς, 16:18), Paul casts the girl's demon out. In Athens, Paul is provoked (παρωξύνετο) by the idols in the city (17:16, cf. v. 23) and unveils for them the "unknown god" (ἀγνώστῳ θεῷ, 17:23).

All of this is to say, again, that the mission in Philippi comes as a key moment in the narrative. The Jerusalem council has declared that Gentiles can be a part of the rebuilding of the tent of David without needing to be circumcised. But that does not mean the place of the Law in Christian expansion will not continue to be a matter of controversy. Beginning and ending the literary sequence with Paul observing a bodily aspect of the Law frees Paul from any accusation that he is forsaking the Law. But Gentile

51. In Philippi, it is Lydia and the jailer (16:11–15, 25–34); in Thessalonika and Berea Luke mentions that both women and men were converts (17:4, 12); in Athens, Luke mentions Dionysius the Areopagite and Damaris (17:33); and in Corinth, it is Priscilla and Aquila (18:2).

52. It appears Luke wishes to count Thessalonika and Berea as one scene since the Thessalonians come to Berea in order to defame Paul (17:13).

53. Luke mentions the Gentiles in both of these scenes (17:4, 18:6).

54. On the meaning of this phrase in the story, see p. 158 below.

circumcision is not what validates the Gentile mission. Divine guidance through visions in the night does that.[55] The Gentiles who do convert observe another sort of law—the law of hospitality.

Lydia

After Paul's vision of the Macedonian man beckoning him to come preach the Gospel, Luke says that they[56] went to Philippi. Philippi is not only named after one of the more memorable Macedonian figures of history,[57] but it is also now a κολωνία of Rome (16:12). They have come, in other words, to a very Gentile place. This information prepares for the anti-Roman charge laid against them in the next scene.

One Sabbath day Paul and his companions hear that there is a place of prayer outside the city by the river.[58] There they find some women gathered (16:13), among whom they meet a woman named Lydia. Luke's

55. The second vision is in Corinth (18:6–8). It is significant that right before Paul has this vision, he tells the local Judeans that he is turning to Gentiles. This also mirrors Paul's first vision, for that vision directed him to the Gentile mission in Philippi.

56. This is the first of the "we" passages in Acts. If there is significance to Luke's use of the first person plural, it escapes me. See also 20:5—21:18 and 27:1—28:16. A recent comprehensive study on the topic is William Campbell's *We Passages in the Acts of the Apostles* (Atlanta: Society of Biblical Literature, 2007). He argues that the "we" character replaces Barnabas as the one who legitimizes Paul and his ministry at key points in the narrative. This is why the first "we" passage comes immediately after Paul and Barnabas disagree about John Mark (15:36–41). Pervo, *Acts*, suggests this as a possibility as well, 396. But I am not sure Paul needs to be legitimized by anyone (or anything) at this point in the narrative. Fitzmyer, *Acts*, thinks the best explanation is that the first person plural "we" was "already in a source used by the author and that source was a diary or travel notes that the author himself (Luke) would have kept and incorporated into Acts when he later came to compose it," 103; cf. 98–102. Barrett, *Acts*, says of Acts 16, "there is no reason to doubt the *prima facie* meaning of the text. A person whose words are reported, whether himself or an editor, was with Paul in Troas, 2:766. Cf. Eckey's discussion, *Die Apostelgeschichte*, 2:351–52. But if Luke was using a source who was present at the events described, it is still puzzling what effect he intended keeping the first person plural to have on his audience. He has already claimed that eyewitnesses are his sources (Luke 1:2). Including a first person account hardly bolsters that claim. For an overview of scholarship on the "we" passages, see Wehnert, *Die Wir-Passagen*.

57. Indeed, the city was founded by Philip of Macedonia in 356 BCE, Fitzmyer, 584.

58. A "place of prayer" (προσευχὴν) could refer to a synagogue, but in this instance there does not appear to have been a structure since Luke normally says there was a synagogue if a structure was present (Acts 13:5; 17:1, 10, 17; 18:19). See Parsons, *Acts*, 229. Bock, *Acts*, however, thinks the opposite is true: precisely because Paul always goes to a synagogue, the place of prayer must have been one, 533. Whether there was a synagogue or not is really of no consequence for the present argument.

characterization of her is limited: she is a seller of purple from Thyatira and a worshipper of God (16:14). The most that can be said, in other words, is that she is a Judean-friendly woman of some means.[59] She may not be the richest woman in Philippi, but she at least has the means to entertain guests.[60]

Luke characterizes her conversion in familiar terms. He says that it is through hearing of Paul's words that she believes (ἤκουεν ... προσέχειν τοῖς λαλουμένοις ὑπὸ τοῦ Παύλου, 16:14). Cornelius, we will recall, also converted upon hearing the word (10:44). Luke also mentions that "the Lord opened her heart," which recalls Peter's words about Gentile converts at the Jerusalem council. Peter had contended that God is the "knower of hearts" (ὁ καρδιογνώστης) and has "cleansed the hearts" of Gentiles (καθαρίσας τὰς καρδίας αὐτῶν, 15:8–9). Finally, Lydia and her whole house are baptized (16:15), which recalls every convert in the narrative up until this point.

After her baptism, Luke says that Lydia "urged" (παρεκάλεσεν) them to "remain" (μένετε) in her house, and they are persuaded. Again, this is familiar: a Gentile convert immediately offers hospitality to Paul and his companions. Like Cornelius, she receives message and messenger. Indeed, her hospitality appears to be evidence of her conversion.[61] She says, "if you have judged me to be faithful to the Lord (εἰ κεκρίκατέ με πιστὴν τῷ κυρίῳ εἶναι), come into my house and remain" (16:15). This is not to say that Lydia would not have offered hospitality to others either before or after her conversion. But neither would her conversion be convincing had she not invited them into her home. Paul and his traveling companions' acceptance of her invitation moreover validates her desire to demonstrate her faithfulness through hospitality. Philippi, so far, is a site of success among the Gentiles.

The Jailer

The success with Lydia, however, quickly gives way to conflict. Paul and his companions' acceptance of Lydia's hospitality is followed by, "and it was while we were going to prayer ... " (ἐγένετο δὲ πορευομένων ἡμῶν εἰς τὴν προσευχὴν, 16:16). The transition is a little awkward. The reader is left

---

59. Up until this point in the narrative, the substantive participle of σέβω has referred only to those who are associated with Judeans (see 13:43, 50; cf. Fitzmyer, *Acts*, 586; Spencer, *Acts*, 164; Eckey, *Die Apostelgeschichte*, 2:362; de Boer, "God-Fearers in Luke–Acts".

60. On Lydia's means, see Pervo, *Acts*, 403–4; Fitzmyer, *Acts*, 585–86; Barrett, *Acts*, 2:782–83; Reimer, *Women*, 71–150.

61. Cf. C. Hays, *Ethics*, "under Luke's pen, hospitality verifies the genuineness of the conversion of new believers." As a general rule, Hays's verdict seems correct. But, as I argue below, Malta appears to be an exception to that rule. See p. 172.

wondering what happened to their acceptance of Lydia's hospitality. But the point seems to be that Paul and his companions' meeting of Lydia happened in the midst of the following scenes.[62] Indeed, the scene that follows did not happen all at once, but over the course of "many days" (16:18).

"While going to prayer," Luke says they were met by a slave girl who had a "spirit of divination" (πνεῦμα πύθωνα).[63] The girl's talents provided a source of income to her "lords" (τοῖς κυρίοις, 16:16).[64] The girl follows Paul and his companions crying out, "these men are servants of the most high God (τοῦ θεοῦ τοῦ ὑψίστου εἰσίν)" and that they "proclaim the way of salvation" (καταγγέλλουσιν ὑμῖν ὁδὸν σωτηρίας, 16:17). The reader will instantly recognize the slave girl's words as true. Not only is ὁδός one of the proper names for the Christian movement (9:2), but the words also recall Paul's last encounter with a diviner at the beginning of his first missionary journey. Paul had questioned the "son of the devil," Elymas the magician, why he perverted the straight ways of the Lord (διαστρέφων τὰς ὁδοὺς τοῦ κυρίου τὰς εὐθείας, 13:10).[65] The reader will also recognize the words as those that have come in Lukan eschatological proclamations.[66] The words "way of salvation" in particular recall John the Baptist's exhortation to flee the soon-coming wrath. Peter's sermon on Pentecost, as well, spoke of salvation from the present crooked generation (2:40) in the last days (2:17).

But the reader at the same time senses that something is amiss with the mantic girl's words. She is possessed by a πνεῦμα, which signals that she, like

62. Pervo, *Acts*, says that Luke is not clear here and thus makes the transition unintelligible, 404. Cf. Barrett, *Acts*, who says this is "not one of Luke's best sentences," 2:784. But this is an unnecessary conclusion if one takes into account that Paul and Silas went to prayer on more than one day and that the slave girl annoyed them on more than one of those days. It appears that Luke puts the story this way because he wants to introduce Paul's sojourn in Philippi with a story of hospitality—that is why Lydia comes first and not in the midst of the several days in which they went to pray and were annoyed by the mantic girl.

63. "Python" (πύθωνα) refers "to the soothsaying divinity, originally conceived of as a snake or dragon that inhabited Delphi, which was originally known as Pythia," Bock, *Acts*, 535; cf. Barrett, *Acts*, 2:785; Eckey, *Die Apostelgeschichte*, 2:364; BDAG, 896–97.

64. Both Pervo, *Acts* (404), and Spencer, *Acts* (163–64), suggest that Luke contrast the two females in the story (cf. Smith, *Literary Construction*, who thinks there is both a comparison and contrast between Lydia and the slave girl, 39–40). But, as I argue below, it appears more likely that Luke contrasts Lydia with the leaders of the city. Lydia is hospitable; the leaders of the city are not.

65. The attentive reader will recognize language that recalls John the Baptist's preaching here as well: ἑτοιμάσατε τὴν ὁδὸν κυρίου, εὐθείας ποιεῖτε τὰς τρίβους αὐτοῦ . . . καὶ ἔσται τὰ σκολιὰ εἰς εὐθείαν καὶ αἱ τραχεῖαι εἰς ὁδοὺς λείας (see Luke 3:4–6).

66. It is worth noting that in the other Gentile encounter on this missionary journey at the Areopagus, Paul speaks of the about-to-be judgment (μέλλει κρίνειν), 17:31.

Elymas, is trying to twist the straight ὁδός of the Lord.[67] Her words thus cut both ways: on the one hand the reader will recognize the words as true; on the other, the reader is left to wonder what the Gentile passerby thought of these words. Θεὸς ὕψιστος was used in Gentile contexts, and it did not refer in those contexts to the Judean God.[68]

The confusion is quickly dissipated when Paul commands (παραγγέλλω) the πνεῦμα to come out. The name of Jesus identifies who the θεὸς ὕψιστος is and through whom the salvation that Paul announces comes (16:18). But this leads to conflict. The aforementioned κύριοι see what has happened and are upset that their income will now be stunted (16:19). The reader can now remark that the Christian announcement does not evidently result only in shared possessions among the saved; it also upsets existing forms of economic exchange. As will be the case in Ephesus a few chapters later (19:23–40), the threat to economic exchange posed by the Christian announcement is, in part, a threat to the locals' way of life—indeed, as the Philippians say momentarily, it is anti-Roman.[69]

The κύριοι (16:19) drag Paul and his companions into the ἀγορά and tell the magistrates that these Judeans (16:20) are stirring up the city and that they are "proclaiming a custom which it is not right for us to receive or to do as Romans" (καταγγέλλουσιν ἔθη ἃ οὐκ ἔξεστιν ἡμῖν παραδέχεσθαι οὐδὲ ποιεῖν Ῥωμαίοις οὖσιν, 16:21).[70] The magistrates have them beaten and then command (παραγγείλαντες) that they be put into prison (16:23). Luke says that "receiving this command" (παραγγελίαν τοιαύτην λαβὼν), the prison keep throws them into the innermost part of the prison and puts them in wooden stocks (16:24). The language of "commanding" recalls Paul's own words to the possessed girl: he had commanded (παραγγέλλω) the spirit to leave the girl. Now Paul is ironically, with a command, imprisoned for it.

67. For more on the role of magic in Luke–Acts, see Reimer, *Miracle and Magic*; and Twelftree, *Name of Jesus*, 129–56.

68. On the ambiguity of the title θεὸς ὕψιστος in this passage, see Rowe, *World Upside Down*, 24–25. Cf. Barrett, *Acts*, who suggests that "a resident in Philippi, with no first-hand knowledge of Judaism, might well identify the one Jewish God with the highest god in his own pantheon," (cf. Eckey, *Die Apostelgeschichte*, 2:365). Barrett adds that it is a Pauline word and is therefore appropriate to the context. But precisely because a Philippian could identify the one Judean God with the highest god in his own pantheon Paul must disambiguate the term for his Philippian audience. Bock, *Acts*, does not think that title is ironically true (536), but it appears to me that irony is exactly what Luke is attempting here since the slave girl also says that Paul and Silas announce the ὁδὸν σωτηρίας.

69. In Ephesus, Artemis will come into disrepute, in response to which the crowds begin chanting, "great is Artemis of the Ephesians!" (μεγάλη ἡ Ἄρτεμις Ἐφεσίων, 19:28).

70. At this point, the slave girl disappears from the narrative. On this issue, see Reimer, *Women*, 151–94.

With nothing else to do, Paul and Silas do what they have been doing throughout their time in Philippi—they pray (16:25). As they do this, the foundations of the prison shake, the doors open, and their chains fall off. The obedient jailer is awakened by the commotion, and seeing all of the doors open, pulls out his sword to kill himself. He undoubtedly goes to this extreme because he would be killed anyway if he did not kill himself.[71] But Paul prevents him by yelling out that he and the rest of the prisoners are still present (16:28).[72]

Prison escapes by divine intervention have almost become commonplace at this point in the narrative. Peter has twice escaped the grip of those who wanted to kill him in a midnight prison flight (5:17–26; 12:6–17). But this scene is different from Peter's in that it is not exactly an escape: Paul and Silas do not leave; rather, it is the jailer who must lead them out (προαγαγὼν αὐτοὺς ἔξω, 16:30). This is odd, but it accounts for what would otherwise be a peculiar response from the jailer: "Sirs, what must I do to be saved?" (κύριοι, τί με δεῖ ποιεῖν ἵνα σωθῶ; 16:30). Paul and Silas have already saved his life by remaining in their cell, and by doing so the prison keep apparently sees Paul and Silas for who they are—they are κύριοι. The vocative on the lips of the jailer means only "sirs," but one can also see that Luke is toying with the vocabulary in this episode. Paul delivers the slave girl from her possession, making her κύριοι (16:16, 19) no longer such. The magistrates of the city at the insistence of these former κύριοι bind Paul and Silas in prison. With the prison doors subsequently opened by Paul and Silas's prayers, the jailer unwittingly confirms with his address that Paul and Silas are the ones who can command binding and freeing—not the magistrates, and not the owners of the girl.

Salvation is what the jailer inquires about, and so Paul tells him what he must do to be saved (σωθήσῃ, 16:31). The jailer's words would seem to confirm the Christian signification of the slave girl's provocative proclamation and as such also recall former eschatological proclamations in Luke's

---

71. As Gaventa, *Acts of the Apostles*, points out, Herod killed the jailers who missed Peter's midnight escape (12:19), 240.

72. It is a little odd that the other prisoners do not flee when the chains fall off and the door opens. Pervo, *Acts*, suggests rather sarcastically that it was "the strength of [Paul's] charismatic character" that kept all the prisoners from leaving, 409. But Luke seems to imply that there was some sort of rapport between Paul and Silas and the other prisoners—they listen to Paul and Silas sing (16:25). When the gates open the reader can therefore imagine that the other prisoners realize that it is on account of Paul and Silas that freedom is an option. This, in turn, makes it imaginable that they remained in the prison to see what Paul and Silas would do next. There were also not necessarily very many prisoners in the prison. Only two prisoners apart from Paul and Silas are needed to get the plural οἱ δέσμιοι.

works. Again, at this point in the narrative, to be saved is to be saved in the last days from a crooked generation. So the jailer is saved, and what follows is a demonstration of hospitality on his part. "Receiving them in that hour of the night" (παραλαβὼν αὐτοὺς ἐν ἐκείνῃ τῇ ὥρᾳ τῆς νυκτὸς), he washes their wounds and then sets a table before them at which they eat and rejoice together (16:34).[73] All of this recalls the other convert in Philippi. Like Lydia, it is his whole house that believes and is baptized (16:31, 34). And like Lydia, the jailer's first deed is to invite Paul and Silas into his abode.

The following morning, word comes that Paul and Silas are permitted to leave in peace. But they still refuse. Paul is indignant: "beating us who are Roman men in public uncondemned, they cast us into prison, and now in secret they cast us out?" (δείραντες ἡμᾶς δημοσίᾳ ἀκατακρίτους, ἀνθρώπους Ῥωμαίους ὑπάρχοντας, ἔβαλαν εἰς φυλακήν, καὶ νῦν λάθρᾳ ἡμᾶς ἐκβάλλουσιν;). He insists that the magistrates themselves should come and lead them out (ἐξαγαγέτωσαν, 16:37). Paul's words are both an indictment and a challenge. The magistrates' mistake is egregious: Paul and Silas are Roman citizens.[74] If anyone should have received a chance to defend themselves and not be beaten and thrown in prison (especially over an anti-Roman charge), then it should have been them.[75] Paul's challenge for the magistrates to come and lead them out (ἐξαγαγέτωσαν, 16:37) moreover recalls the jailer's actions. The first time Paul and Silas refused to leave jail, the jailer led them out (προαγαγὼν αὐτοὺς ἔξω, 16:30) and brought them into his own home, setting a table before them. What will the magistrates do when they lead Paul and Silas out?

Despite being given a second chance, the magistrates do not take it. They do indeed come themselves to lead them out, but they come only out

---

73. Pervo, *Acts*, suggests that the joy (ἠγαλλιάσατο, 16:34) with which the jailer and Paul and Silas eat might be intended to recall the joy (ἀγαλλιάσει, 2:46) of the Jerusalem community. Cf. Johnson, *Acts*, 301.

74. Scholars have often noted that it is odd that Paul and Silas wait until the next day to make this information known. See e.g., Pervo, *Acts*, 413–14; Bock, *Acts*, 539, 543–44; Parson, *Acts*, 235. But it is possible to imagine that there was no opportunity to mention citizenship. One needs only to consider the closing scene of the current missionary journey where in Corinth Paul is "about to open his mouth in defense" but is prevented from doing so—he must defer to the proconsul (18:14). In the riotous anger of the people of Philippi, it is easy to imagine that Paul was not able say anything. A separate issue is how Paul would have been able to demonstrate his citizenship (Barrett, *Acts*, 2:801–2), but Luke evidently assumes that he was able to do so.

75. Paul is saved from getting whipped after his arrest in Jerusalem by appealing to his citizenship (22:22–28). But this situation is different from Philippi in that the centurion has taken Paul into the barracks before commanding him to be beaten. The less chaotic atmosphere makes it more believable that Paul could communicate his citizenship before receiving his lashes.

of fear after hearing that Paul and Silas are Roman citizens (10:38). Luke says that after they came, "they apologized to them, and leading them out, they asked them to leave the city" (παρεκάλεσαν αὐτοὺς καὶ ἐξαγαγόντες ἠρώτων ἀπελθεῖν ἀπὸ τῆς πόλεως, 10:39). From there, Luke says Paul and Silas go to Lydia, and after encouraging the believers, they leave the city. The mention of Lydia in the last moment of the episode at Philippi functions as an *inclusio*. But it is not just that. The mention of Lydia recalls her hospitality, since it is to her home where Paul and Silas go after being let out of jail. Placing her at the end of the story puts the rejection of the city's leaders into sharper contrast. Whereas they ask Paul and Silas to leave, Lydia had urged them to remain in her home (cf. 16:15).

Like the subsequent scenes in Paul's second missionary journey, the episode at Philippi is one of mixed success. There are two significant converts: a woman and a man, both with their entire households, are added to the Way. They both receive the message and then immediately receive Paul and his companions into their homes. The city, by contrast, rejects. The masters of the slave girl contend that Paul and Silas announce an ἔθος that is not permitted for Romans to "receive" (παραδέχεσθαι, 16:21). In rejecting the ὁδός that Paul announces, they reject Paul. They beat and imprison him, and when he is acquitted, they ask him and his companions to leave the city. What Paul announces cannot be received, so neither can he. All of this shows again that Luke ties the acceptance or rejection of salvation with hospitality. Those who invite Paul and his companions into their homes demonstrate that they have found a home in the tent of David (cf. 15:16).

Shipwreck in Malta: Acts 27:1—28:31

Introduction

Paul's shipwreck in Malta is the culmination of the mission to the Gentiles. As with other Gentiles in the narrative, the Maltans demonstrate their readiness to receive the Christian announcement by extending hospitality to Paul. Their reception comes on the cusp of a sea voyage that appears to point to eschatological fulfillment.[76] At the close of Luke's second vol-

---

76. Pervo, *Acts*, also suggests that the sea voyage is intended to have a symbolic meaning, but says that the sea voyage (drawing on parallels with Jonah) is meant to signify the (again symbolic) death and resurrection of Paul. This parallels Paul with Jesus in Luke's Gospel. I am unconvinced that Luke is trying to recall Jonah in this narrative (the common language between Acts 27:18–19 and Jonah 1:5 does not seem strong enough to me). It seems more likely that Luke wants the reader to see the connections with Greaco-Roman stories (which Pervo also argues). Pervo also notes the

ume, in other words, Luke again appears to bring eschatology and ethics together.[77]

The shipwreck narrative also culminates an issue that has been growing since the beginning of the narrative. The eschatological hope that is proclaimed in Acts is emphatically Israel's hope. That is why, again, Peter addresses Ἰουδαῖοι on the day of Pentecost (2:5), and that is why a council must convene in Jerusalem to discuss Gentile inclusion (Ch. 15). After three missionary journeys to Judean and Gentile alike, Paul himself returns to Jerusalem where he proclaims Israel's hope (26:7).[78] The issue, however, is that Paul is rejected in Jerusalem. Paul's rejection, while expected,[79] is nonetheless perplexing. Why has Jerusalem rejected Israel's hope? This question is left open even at the end of the narrative, where, though some accept, most of the Judeans in Rome reject Paul's proclamation of hope. But though it appears that hope may be lost for Israel as a whole to see the light, eschatological hope itself is not lost. In between rejection in Jerusalem and Rome, Luke narrates a shipwreck. The genre of shipwreck puts Israel's hope into

---

significance of light/darkness as I do, but thinks that they are metaphors for life/death. While this is true, Pervo misses the connections this story has with Paul's concluding speech before Festus and Agrippa and therefore misses the fact that it symbolizes eschatological hope, 644–67. Horton, *Death and Resurrection*, also suggests that Paul's shipwreck might be read as Paul experiencing a symbolic death and resurrection. He admits, however, that it is not as clear in this instance as in others in the book of Acts. Horton moreover notices the role light and darkness plays in the narrative, but, like Pervo, does not notice how these tropes recall Paul's final defense before Festus and Agrippa, 56–59. Jipp, *Hospitality*, pointing to Paul's foretelling of the disaster, suggests that Luke attempts to characterize Paul as a prophet like Jesus in the shipwreck narrative, 31–33. This is undoubtedly true on some level. The eucharistic overtones of Paul's early morning meal alone are strongly suggestive in this direction. But is characterizing Paul as a prophet like Jesus of primary interest in the narrative?

77. Talbert, *Reading Luke–Acts*, does not see eschatology playing a role in the shipwreck and Malta episodes. He instead sees the shipwreck on the shores of Malta as Luke's attempt to say that Paul's deliverance "was due to the divine plan, not Paul's own human prowess." The snakebite moreover demonstrates Paul is not a guilty man. Talbert concludes by asserting that these conclusions "fit nicely into the larger Lukan literary and theological landscape," 195. But perhaps they fit a little too nicely. Luke has already demonstrated the Paul's comings and goings are due to the divine plan (see e.g., 16:6–10). And to whom does Luke need to demonstrate that Paul is innocent? The reader has known that Paul is innocent since his arrest in Jerusalem. Talbert fails to account for why Luke needs to reiterate what he has already clearly demonstrated throughout the narrative.

78. Cf. 28:20.

79. Paul's suffering in Jerusalem is predicted in Acts 20:22–23 and 21:10–14.

Graeco-Roman idiom,[80] and the Maltans' reception of Paul suggests that eschatological hope has found a home among the Gentiles.[81]

Structure

The shipwreck narrative comes in between Paul's appearances in Jerusalem and Rome. After the conclusion of his third missionary journey, Paul and his traveling companions make their way to Jerusalem. There, despite his and the church's best efforts, Paul is put on trial. After the shipwreck in Malta, Paul and his traveling companions finally arrive in Rome. There, Paul—still in chains—is again required to make a defense for himself before Judean investigators. The trial scenes associated with Jerusalem and Rome parallel each other in the content of Paul's defense. Paul says in all three trials after his Jerusalem arrest that he is on trail for "hope" ($\dot{\epsilon}\lambda\pi\dot{\iota}\varsigma$, 23:6; 24:15; 26:6–7). In Rome, Paul says that he is in chains on account of "the hope of Israel" ($\tau\tilde{\eta}\varsigma$ $\dot{\epsilon}\lambda\pi\dot{\iota}\delta o\varsigma$ $\tau o\tilde{\upsilon}$ $\dot{I}\sigma\rho\alpha\dot{\eta}\lambda$, 28:20). Paul's rhetoric of hope is notable because the term is used only three other times in the narrative. Two are isolated instances earlier in Acts (2:26; 16:19). The third appears in the shipwreck narrative (27:20). The term's appearance in the shipwreck narrative suggests that Luke intends the term to unite thematically the scenes stretching from Jerusalem to Rome.

Apart from the way in which the term hope appears to tie the narrative together, the shipwreck narrative is tied in other respects both to the scenes in and around Jerusalem and the concluding scene in Rome. In his third and final defense after his Jerusalem arrest, Paul announces that "a light is about to be proclaimed to the people and to the nations" ($\phi\tilde{\omega}\varsigma$ $\mu\dot{\epsilon}\lambda\lambda\epsilon\iota$ $\kappa\alpha\tau\alpha\gamma\gamma\dot{\epsilon}\lambda\lambda\epsilon\iota\nu$ $\tau\tilde{\omega}$ $\tau\epsilon$ $\lambda\alpha\tilde{\omega}$ $\kappa\alpha\dot{\iota}$ $\tau o\tilde{\iota}\varsigma$ $\dot{\epsilon}\theta\nu\epsilon\sigma\iota\nu$, 26:23). Light also appears to be a key trope in the shipwreck narrative: in darkness hope is lost (27:20), but with the dawning of day, the ship's crew is saved (27:39). As we have seen, light is an important trope in Luke's double work. Simeon proclaimed that a

---

80. As Alexander, *Acts,* suggests, "the narrator is implicitly laying claim to a cultural territory which many readers, both Greek and Judeo-Christian, would perceive as inherently 'Greek,'" 85; cf. Jipp, *Hospitality,* 28–30; Marguerat, *Historian,* 231–56; Parsons, *Acts,* 352–53; Spencer, *Acts,* 229–30.

81. Neither Paul nor Luke, however, has apparently given up on Israel. Paul still proclaims Israel's hope in Rome (28:20). Israel has not *in toto* rejected, for a few cannot do that on behalf of the whole (Bauckham, "Restoration" in Scott, *Restoration,* 486–87). Indeed, even in Rome, some Judeans believe. The issue appears simply that rejection from Judeans pushes the Gospel into the Gentile world, making Christianity an emphatically Judean *and* Gentile movement.

light would be given to the nations through Jesus (Luke 2:32), and Paul said that he and his traveling companions are that light (Act 13:47).

The connection between the shipwreck narrative and the concluding scene in Rome is one of contrast. Whereas the Maltans hospitably receive Paul and his traveling companions, the Judeans at Rome are ambivalent in their reception of Paul. While some accept Paul's message, many do not (28:20). Whereas Paul is said to have healed the residents of Malta, healing remains out of the reach of the Judeans at Rome. Paul concludes his words to the Roman Judeans by say that if they would but turn, God would heal them (ἰάσομαι αὐτούς, 28:27).

Paul in Jerusalem

The shipwreck narrative, as was pointed out above, comes in a series of events in which Paul announces the hope of Israel. It is this theme of hope that sets the stage for the sea voyage that immediately follows. Paul, despite repeated warnings about what awaits him there, heads to Jerusalem. Upon arrival, he is advised by the leaders of the Christian movement to take a vow with some other men in the community to demonstrate his commitment to the Judean ἔθοι (21:21–24). But despite their best efforts, Paul still finds himself in trouble. Some Asian Judeans say that they saw Paul bring Greeks into the temple, so they drag him outside of the temple in order to kill him (21:31). But a centurion catches wind of the ruckus taking place, goes into the crowd, and arrests him. From here on, Paul will be a prisoner. In the following scenes, Paul is tried before three tribunals: the Judean council, Felix, and Festus and Herod Agrippa II.[82] In each of his trials, Paul puts before his judges what he claims is the reason for his chains: hope.

Before the Sanhedrin, Luke says that Paul notices that the group is made up of both Sadducees and Pharisees. Seeing this, he announces that it is on account of "hope and the resurrection of the dead" (ἐλπίδος καὶ ἀναστάσεως νεκρῶν ἐγὼ κρίνομαι, 23:6) that he is on trial. Again, the word ἐλπίς has not yet been used in Acts to refer to what Christians proclaim. In Paul's second and third trials, he two more times says he announces hope. Before Felix, Paul says that his fellow Judeans can have no complaint against him because he, like the Judeans who are there (αὐτοὶ οὗτοι, 24:15), worships the God of their fathers, believing all that is in the Law and the Prophets (λατρεύω τῷ πατρῴῳ θεῷ πιστεύων πᾶσι τοῖς κατὰ τὸν νόμον καὶ τοῖς ἐν τοῖς προφήταις γεγραμμένοις, 24:14). And it is based on his belief in the Law and the Prophets that he says that he has hope (ἐλπίδα), which he and his fellow

---

82. 22:30—23:11; 24:1–27; 26:1–32, respectively.

Judeans are waiting for (ἣν καὶ αὐτοὶ οὗτοι προσδέχονται, 24:15). This hope is the "resurrection of the righteous and the unrighteous, which is about to be" (ἀνάστασιν μέλλειν ἔσεσθαι δικαίων τε καὶ ἀδίκων, 24:15).[83]

Similarly, before Festus and Agrippa, Paul says that it is because of the hope that was promised by God to his fathers that he is on trial (νῦν ἐπ' ἐλπίδι τῆς εἰς τοὺς πατέρας ἡμῶν ἐπαγγελίας γενομένης ὑπὸ τοῦ θεοῦ ἔστηκα κρινόμενος, 26:6).[84] This is the hope, he says, for which the twelve tribes have been worshipping with zeal night and day to attain (εἰς ἣν τὸ δωδεκάφυλον ἡμῶν ἐν ἐκτενείᾳ νύκτα καὶ ἡμέραν λατρεῦον ἐλπίζει καταντῆσαι, 26:7). These three trial scenes together make Paul's claim to be announcing hope very clear. But his claim is also suggestive of something further. Luke seems to suggest that if Paul is on trial because he announces the hope of Israel— the hope of resurrection—then it appears that to put Paul on trial is to put hope itself on trial.

Paul culminates his defense of hope with an account of his Damascus road experience. After Paul summarizes his former hatred for those who confessed the name of Jesus (26:9–11), he describes to Festus and Agrippa how when he was "on the way" (κατὰ τὴν ὁδὸν) to Damascus he saw "a light from heaven brighter than the sun shining around" him (οὐρανόθεν ὑπὲρ τὴν λαμπρότητα τοῦ ἡλίου περιλάμψαν με φῶς, 26:13). As he has before,[85] Paul describes how Jesus asks him why he is persecuting him, but in this final account of the exchange, Paul includes more of their dialogue. Jesus, Paul says, told him,

> For this reason I have appeared to you, to appoint you as a ser-
> vant and as a witness of the things which you have seen and of
> the things which I will show you, choosing you out of the people

83. Mason, "Speech-Making II," suggests that Paul plays a rhetorical game with Felix when he reduces the reason for his arrest to the belief in the resurrection of the dead, when, in reality, it is the particular issue of Jesus' resurrection that is at stake, 162–63. Paul, however, has not been charged by his Judean compatriots (at least on the official record) for proclaiming Jesus as raised from the dead, but for supposedly teaching against the Law and the temple and for bringing Greeks into the temple (21:28; cf. 23:29 24:5–6, 18–19). It therefore makes perfect sense for Paul's defense to be that he believes everything in the Law and the Prophets and that the hope he professes is the emphatically Israel's hope. Paul does conclude his apology to Felix by saying that he cried out in the council that he was on trial for the resurrection of the dead, but he makes no claim that this is what he is in fact on trial for before Felix. Cf. Soards, *Speeches in Acts*, 118–89. For more on Paul's post-arrest apologetic speeches, see Porter, *Paul of Acts*, 151–71; and Soards, *Speeches in Acts*, 111–26.

84. Here Paul does claim that he is on trial for the hope of Israel, but he immediately qualifies that claim by making clear that the hope of Israel he proclaims is through Jesus of Nazareth (26:9–11).

85. See 22:3–21; cf. 9:1–9 and 9:26–30.

and out of the nations into which I send you to open their eyes, and to turn them from darkness to light and from the power of Satan to God . . . "

εἰς τοῦτο γὰρ ὤφθην σοι, προχειρίσασθαί σε ὑπηρέτην καὶ μάρτυρα ὧν τε εἶδές με ὧν τε ὀφθήσομαί σοι, ἐξαιρούμενός σε ἐκ τοῦ λαοῦ καὶ ἐκ τῶν ἐθνῶν εἰς οὓς ἐγὼ ἀποστέλλω σε ἀνοῖξαι ὀφθαλμοὺς αὐτῶν, τοῦ ἐπιστρέψαι ἀπὸ σκότους εἰς φῶς καὶ τῆς ἐξουσίας τοῦ σατανᾶ ἐπὶ τὸν θεόν Acts 26:16–18

Paul then tells his judges that he did not hesitate to fulfill his heavenly commission (26:19–20).

In the final account of his conversion, Paul makes his own encounter with Christ the paradigm for what must happen for everyone. Just as a light (φῶς) shone on him to lead him out of darkness into light, so will it shine on others to do the same. Just as Paul was taken "out of the people and out of the nations," so also will this light shine on Israel and Gentiles alike (26:23). And, finally, the blindness that results from his heavenly vision is interpreted symbolically: just as his eyes were opened by Ananias, so now Paul will "open the eyes" (ἀνοῖξαι ὀφθαλμοὺς) of those to whom he is sent (16:18). Paul then says that this which he proclaims is only that which "the Prophets and Moses said would take place, that the Christ must suffer, that he is the first of the resurrection of the dead—he is about to proclaim light to the people and to the nations" (ὧν τε οἱ προφῆται ἐλάλησαν μελλόντων γίνεσθαι καὶ Μωϋσῆς, εἰ παθητὸς ὁ χριστός, εἰ πρῶτος ἐξ ἀναστάσεως νεκρῶν φῶς μέλλει καταγγέλλειν τῷ τε λαῷ καὶ τοῖς ἔθνεσιν, 26:22–23). A light shone on him, and it will shine on all through him. The reader will recall at this point Paul's words in his first sermon on his first missionary journey in Antioch of Pisidia. The Lord, Paul said, spoke to him with the words of Isa 49:6, "I have made you a light to the nations that you may bring salvation to the ends of the earth" (τέθεικά σε εἰς φῶς ἐθνῶν τοῦ εἶναί σε εἰς σωτηρίαν ἕως ἐσχάτου τῆς γῆς, 13:47). But most importantly, the reader will note here that the light Paul is and proclaims is the light of eschatological salvation. Indeed, Jesus is only the first (πρῶτος) to be raised from the dead.

Paul's trials thus conclude by setting the eyes of the reader to the eschatological future. Israel's hope of resurrection is Paul's announcement, and he proclaims at the culminating trial that the light of God's salvation is about to dawn over the horizon. One would almost expect this to be the climax of the Luke's narrative, for the narrative has now come full circle, beginning and ending in Jerusalem with the announcement of God's salvation through the resurrection of Jesus of Nazareth. But it is, of course, not the end of the story. Indeed, there is a sense of failure on Paul's part. After the third of his spirited defenses of the hope of resurrection, Festus is not moved. It is quite the opposite: he thinks Paul is crazy (26:24). But it is not only that Paul has failed to convince his tribunals. There is a more glaring tragedy in the fact that Paul, the announcer of Israel's hope, has been rejected by Jerusalem. They have rejected the light of God's salvation by rejecting the light-bearer.[86] This identification of the message with the messenger raises the question of what will become of the announcement of God's eschatological salvation. There is a sense that eschatological hope itself is distant and out of reach, not imminent, as Paul is quietly nudged off to Rome. It is to the destiny of message and messenger that Paul's maritime journey is devoted.

Storm and Shipwreck

There are several factors that suggest from the outset that Luke intends the story of Paul's shipwreck to point symbolically beyond itself. The first is the sheer length of the narrative.[87] Length indicates that it is important to Luke's overall rhetorical purposes. The second is related to the first, and has already been suggested earlier: this story comes both as the conclusion of Paul's missionary endeavors and at the conclusion of Luke's whole narrative. The story's placement makes it a likely venue to revisit themes that have been important to his narrative as a whole. Finally—and most importantly—there is the matter of its genre. As scholars have repeatedly noted about this passage, Luke is using a common type-scene in Graeco-Roman literature.[88] An early Christian reader's ability to recognize this should not be underestimated.[89] That Luke is using the Greaco-Roman type-scene of a shipwreck as Paul's final encounter with Gentiles should not escape attention.[90]

86. Cf. again Acts 13:49.

87. Pervo, *Acts*, 644; Spencer, *Acts*, 229.

88. The sea is also used symbolically in Judean literature. Jonah's shipwreck is pregnant with meaning. Isaiah speaks of the Leviathan and Behemoth residing in the sea (Isa 27:1; 51:9–10). The author of the Apocalypse speaks of the sea being "no more" when he sees the new heaven and new earth (Rev 21:1). Judean precedent does not mean that Luke must be doing something similar, but it does make the suggestion that he is more plausible.

89. Talbert, *Reading Luke–Acts*, provides a catalogue of shipwreck stories in Greek and Roman literature. He finds seventeen Greek and twelve Roman authors who include the type-scene of storm and shipwreck in their writings (some authors have multiple instances). He moreover notes common tropes that frequently appear in these stories, including a warning not to sail, sailing in a bad season, and darkness—all of which appear in Luke's story, 177–79. Cf. Alexander, *Context*, 84–86; cf. Parsons, *Acts*, 352–53; Spencer, *Acts*, 229–30.

90. Marguerat, *Historian*, notes that travel narratives in general and sea voyages

Luke introduces the shipwreck story with Paul being put aboard a ship with a friendly centurion who during their travels allows Paul to be cared for by friends (27:3). This characterization, as will be seen, sets the condition for the crew's ultimate salvation at the time of the wreck. It is in Fair Havens where they eventually land that the conditions for the ensuing disaster are set. They spend a longer time than they should at the port, thus making it the time of the year ("after the fast") in which it is dangerous to continue sailing (27:9). Winter is coming. Paul advises those in charge that he has been made privy to information that they should know: he has seen that, should they sail, there will be much loss to their cargo, ship, and their lives (27:10). But the centurion and ship owner choose not to listen precisely because of the coming winter. Fair Havens is not so fair in the winter, so they want to attempt a last minute dash to Phoenix, which is a favorable place to spend the cold months given its geographical position (27:12).[91]

Things go smoothly at first: they have a south wind (νότου) that carries them on their intended route (27:13). But things quickly take a turn for the worst. A "northeastern temptuous wind" (ἄνεμος τυφωνικὸς ὁ καλούμενος εὐρακύλων) comes upon them and begins to drive them mercilessly along (27:15). Chaos ensues: they first almost lose the ship's boat, their only means of escape (27:16–17; cf. v. 30). They then realize they might be in danger of running aground in the north of Africa, so they let down "the sea anchor" (τὸ σκεῦος)[92] in an apparent attempt to slow the pace of their drift. Luke says at this point that they were "greatly storm-tossed" (σφοδρῶς δὲ χειμαζομένων, 27:18). The participle χειμαζομένων with the same root as "wintering" (παραχειμάζω, 27:12) confirms that Paul's prediction has become true. The crew begin desperately to throw the ship's tackle overboard.

It is at this point of despair that Luke gives his first indication of how the seagoing journey points beyond itself: "with the sun and stars not appearing for many days, and the bad whether insisting not a little, all hope of our being saved was finally abandoned" (μήτε δὲ ἡλίου μήτε ἄστρων ἐπιφαινόντων ἐπὶ πλείονας ἡμέρας, χειμῶνός τε οὐκ ὀλίγου ἐπικειμένου, λοιπὸν περιῃρεῖτο ἐλπὶς πᾶσα τοῦ σῴζεσθαι ἡμᾶς, 27:20). Luke uses of the

---

were often times used by Graeco-Roman authors symbolically to point to, among other things, a character's path of initiation or road to virtue, 239–46. It is therefore not unlikely that Luke also intended his sea voyage to be more than just a good story. Cf. Robbins, "By Land by Sea," who suggests that the sea voyage genre was used by ancient authors "to interpret many situations in life," 54; cf. 47–81.

91. Luke says it faces both southwest and northwest (27:12).

92. Following the NRSV, cf. Pervo, *Acts*, who in addition to understanding the phrase to mean "letting down the anchor," also considers "letting down the sails," 659; cf. BDAG, 927–28.

noun ἐλπίς, the term Paul has just repeatedly used speaking about the hope of Israel, the hope of resurrection, in his trials. Luke couples this contextually charged word with the infinitive τοῦ σῴζεσθαι, a verb that has been used in Luke's narrative solely to refer to eschatological salvation (cf. e.g., 2:40; 16:30–31).[93] And the loss of hope of salvation comes in complete and persistent darkness—neither the sun nor the stars have been seen for days. The loss of hope in the darkness contrasts with Paul's defense before Festus and Agrippa. Not only was he resolute that the hope (ἐλπίς) of salvation in the resurrection will come, but he also concluded his defense in Jerusalem on the promise of light. Jesus, he said, is "about to proclaim light (φῶς)" to Israel and to the Gentiles (26:23).

This contrast creates a tension in the narrative. Is there still hope? Paul proclaimed Israel's hope of resurrection in his Jerusalem arrest trials. Yet, despite proclaiming Israel's hope, Jerusalem rejects him. Indeed, they attempted to kill him. Paul, the one shown the light, the one who is the proclaimer of light, the one who is the light himself is now lost at sea in darkness. If now Paul himself has no hope for being saved, then what can be said of eschatological hope, the hope of resurrection, the "hope to be saved" (ἐλπὶς . . . τοῦ σῴζεσθαι)?[94] The outlook is grim.

But hope is evidently not lost. Just as a series of events signified the ship members' spiral into hopelessness, so now a series of events signifies their coming salvation. Paul tells those on the ship that they will survive because of him. This is the case not only because he foresaw this disaster (27:21), but also because an angel of God appeared to him in the night informing him that he must stand before Caesar and that all those of on the ship have been granted (κεχάρισταί) to him (27:24). Paul says that they will run aground on an island (27:26), and sure enough, the sailors immediately find evidence that they are coming upon land (27:27–29). Paul thus guarantees salvation. But he then also claims to be the means of salvation: some of the sailors scheme to take the ship's boat in an attempt to save themselves, but Paul informs them that they are "not able to be saved" (σωθῆναι οὐ δύνασθε) unless they remain in the ship (27:31).

93. The only time it is used not to refer explicitly to being "saved" as a Christian is in 4:9, where Luke, as he does here, capitalizes on the word's ability to have multiple signification. In 4:9 it refers both to the cripple's healing and to the Christian salvation that is offered to all. Here in 27:20, it refers primarily to being saved from the storm, but also points symbolically to the same eschatological salvation Luke has used the verb so consistently to refer to. Cf. Jipp, *Hospitality*, 33–34.

94. Paul will of course eventually die after he arrives in Rome (though this is not in Luke's narrative). But the point here is that Paul cannot die yet: he must make it to Rome. The condition of the narrative that Paul must make it to his final destination enables the shipwreck scene to point to eschatological events.

Expectation of salvation builds with the promise of daylight. Luke says that "when day was about to be" (ἄχρι δὲ οὗ ἡμέρα ἤμελλεν γίνεσθαι), Paul counseled everyone to receive food, for they had now gone fourteen days without eating and they needed their strength. The meal they eat, like the promise of light, appears to point beyond itself. Commentators have not missed the obvious correspondences between this meal and Jesus' meals with his disciples. Paul hosts the meal: "taking the bread he gave thanks and after breaking it they began to eat" (λαβὼν ἄρτον εὐχαρίστησεν τῷ θεῷ ἐνώπιον πάντων καὶ κλάσας ἤρξατο ἐσθίειν, 27:35). The mention of "giving thanks" and "breaking" in particular recall previous symbolic meals in Lukan writings.[95] Even more significantly, Paul tells them to eat because "this is for your σωτηρίας" (27:34).[96] Paul's words appear at once to confirm and extend the symbolism of the meal and the shipwreck narrative as a whole. Those who eat food with Paul are guaranteed the same salvation he is, because that is evidently what food can do in Lukan thought. The risen Jesus ate with the disciples; Peter ate with Cornelius; now Paul eats with those who have been granted (κεχάρισταί, 27:24) to him.

Salvation comes with light. Luke says that it was "when day broke" (ὅτε δὲ ἡμέρα ἐγένετο) that they see land (27:39). As they run the ship aground, the soldiers scheme to kill the prisoners so that they will not escape. But the kindly centurion once again comes to Paul's aid. Luke says that the centurion, "wishing to save Paul" (βουλόμενος διασῶσαι τὸν Παῦλον, 27:43), prevented them from carrying out their plans. Luke concludes the shipwreck story saying that "it was in this way that all were saved upon the land" (οὕτως ἐγένετο πάντας διασωθῆναι ἐπὶ τὴν γῆν, 2744). All are saved because Paul is saved.

Luke thus overlays his story of Paul's shipwreck with eschatological symbolism through the reuse of words and imagery he has just used in his narrative to refer to the soon to be resurrection of the dead. In the darkness, hope of salvation is lost. But because Paul is the bearer of hope, hope comes through him. The mutual destiny of Paul and passengers is symbolized in the partaking of a meal together. Immediately after the meal, the light of day shines, at once making the ship passengers' rescue visible and a reality. The symbolism of the journey suggests that if hope is not lost for those on the ship, then it appears the hope of salvation, the hope of resurrection is

95. See Luke 22:7–38 (the last supper) and Luke 24:13–34 (the road to Emmaus). Cf. Jipp, *Hospitality*, 35–36; Pervo, *Acts*, 664; Bock, *Acts*, 740; Barrett, *Acts*, 2:1208–10; Eckey, *Die Apostelgeschichte*, 2:570–71.

96. The NRSV translates it "for it will help you survive," which not only obscures what is actually there in the Greek, but also completely hides the symbolic nature of the words. Cf. Soards's discussion of the term, *Speeches in Acts*, 130.

not lost either. Luke, in other words, has not let Paul's closing remarks to Agrippa and Festus recede into the background of the narrative. A light really is about to shine.

But one matter is still left unresolved. If there is still hope, then who is there who will hope? Again, Paul's proclamation of Israel's hope was rejected by Jerusalem. To be sure, some Judeans and some Gentiles have been baptized along the way in Acts, but there is still a sense that something is amiss at this point in the narrative. Paul is a shipwrecked prisoner in an unrecognizable land, and he has ultimately ended up there because of the rejection he experienced in Jerusalem. If there is hope, then there must be some who will receive that hope. And to receive that hope, they must receive Paul. A clue has already been given in the genre of the narrative about where Luke thinks the hope of resurrection will find a home. Luke has just used the Graeco-Roman type-scene of a shipwreck. This alone suggests that hope will find a home among the nations. This suspicion is confirmed in the following scene.

Hospitable Maltans

Once their salvation is secured on dry land, Luke says that they recognize the place as the island of Malta (διασωθέντες τότε ἐπέγνωμεν ὅτι Μελίτη ἡ νῆσος καλεῖται, 28:1). What follows are two scenes of reception by the residents of the island—first by those who (apparently) happen to be in the area, and second by a man named Publius, a "leading man of the island" (τῷ πρώτῳ τῆς νήσου, 28:7).[97] What is notable about these two demonstrations of hospitality is that they come in reverse. Whereas in Caesarea and in Philippi hospitality follows proclamation and miracle, here it precedes it.

The first reception Paul and those with him receive comes not from just any group of Gentiles. They are βάρβαροι, non-Greek Gentiles. Like Cornelius, and like the colony of Philippi, Luke again characterizes Paul's encounter with people that epitomize Gentileness. These barbarians show Paul and his companions "untypical kindness" (οὐ τὴν τυχοῦσαν φιλανθρωπίαν). They light a fire and "receive" (προσελάβοντο) them because it has again begun to rain and it is cold (28:2). But then misfortune strikes: Paul is helping to gather sticks for the fire when a serpent emerges and fastens itself to Paul's hand (28:3). The barbarians think this must be justice striking down a murder (28:4–5), but Paul is unfazed. Upon seeing Paul's continued health, the barbarians change their minds. Not only is he not a murderer, he must

---

97. Cf. C. Hays, *Ethics*, who notes that hospitality is the major theme of these scenes, 252–53; and Jipp, *Hospitality*, 1–58.

be a god (ἔλεγον αὐτὸν εἶναι θεόν, 28:6). The barbarians' verdict may not be orthodox,[98] but that does not necessarily mean Luke does not think it a perceptive conclusion on their part.[99] Paul has indeed been the source of salvation—guaranteeing it, and providing it in an early morning meal. Paul does not simply proclaim salvation, he gives it.

The scene then switches to Paul's second hospitable reception. Publius, an evidently rich and powerful man of the island, like the resident barbarians, "receives" (ἀναδεξάμενος) them and "kindly entertains them as guest" (φιλοφρόνως ἐξένισεν, 28:7). After three days of this, word comes to Paul that Publius' father is ill with fever and dysentery. Paul lays hands on him and heals him (ἐπιθεὶς τὰς χεῖρας αὐτῷ ἰάσατο αὐτόν, 28:8). This results in Paul's beginning an island-wide healing ministry: "all those who had illnesses were brought and healed" (28:9). The scene then closes with a reiteration of the kindness they receive. They honored them with many honors (πολλαῖς τιμαῖς ἐτίμησαν), even giving them supplies when they embark on their next maritime journey to Rome (28:10).

The fact that the barbarians are hospitable first, and then only afterward recognize Paul as a divinely ordained healer, puts into stark relief the enthusiasm with which Paul and those with him are received. As such, the reception Paul receives among the barbarians is the antithesis of his experience in Jerusalem. Among his own, his own rejected him. A shipwrecked prisoner among barbarians, however, and he is shown hospitality, honor, and recognized as a bearer of divinity. Their reception of Paul moreover completes the narrative of hope. Hope is not lost because there is hope for the Gentiles. In the Greaco-Roman epic of a shipwreck, Luke has suggested that eschatological hope remains. In the reception by the Maltan barbarians, Luke has suggested that the hope of resurrection has found a home away from home.[100]

98. Scholars have pointed out that the last time Paul was called a god (in Lystra), he was horrified (Act 14:8–18). See Fitzmyer, *Acts*, 783; Barrett, *Acts*, 2:1224; Bock, *Acts*, 744; Parsons, *Acts*, 361; Jipp, *Hospitality*, 45. But there is no indication in the Maltan episode that Luke wants the reader to see the Maltans exclamation in the same light. Cf. Keener's discussion of "'Divine' Humans," *Acts*, 2:1782–86. On the Lystra episode, see Rowe, *World Upside Down*, 18–23.

99. Jipp, *Hospitality*, similarly suggests that the islanders' conclusion, while unorthodox, is perceptive, 45–46. Bock, *Acts*, suggests that their conclusion indicates that they recognize Paul as one who is "in close contact with God," 744.

100. Jipp, *Hospitality*, wonders why Gentile salvation is depicted symbolically instead of directly through conversions or Christological proclamation, 37. It appears that Luke has done this because there are still many more Gentiles who need to hear the Christian proclamation. By depicting it symbolically, Luke does not limit the story to a localized instance of proclamation and conversion, but promises that the proclamation will go "to the ends of the earth" (1:8).

Rome

Luke closes his second volume the same way he opened it: on the question of the kingdom and Israel (cf. 1:6). Paul meets Judeans in Rome to whom he proclaims the kingdom of God (τὴν βασιλείαν τοῦ θεοῦ, 28:23). Luke links this final scene of his narrative with what has come immediately before, building again on the themes of eschatological hope and hospitable reception.

The Judeans Paul meets in Rome, Luke says, are the "leading Judeans" (τοὺς ὄντας τῶν Ἰουδαίων πρώτους, 28:17). The label πρῶτος recalls Publius, for he had the same title (28:7). Paul claims to the Judeans that he has been wrongly arrested and that it is only because of the persistent accusations of the Jerusalem Judeans that he has appealed to Caesar. Paul then urges them to hear what he has to say, for, he says, "it is on account of the hope of Israel" (τῆς ἐλπίδος τοῦ Ἰσραὴλ) that he is in chains (28:20). Here Luke speaks one last time of hope in his narrative. Its use here at once links this scene with what has come before and at the same time suggests again that Luke intended the term to be understood symbolically in the shipwreck narrative. Hope is the concluding note of Luke's second volume.

A day is set for Paul to make his case, upon which, Luke says, Paul receives them into his dwelling. Paul attempts to persuade them from morning until evening from the Law of Moses and the Prophets concerning the kingdom (28:23). Some accept (28:24–25), but the encounter ends on a grim note. Just as at the beginning of Acts, Luke indicates that many in Israel have neither eyes to see nor ears to hear. At the beginning of his narrative he demonstrated this through the miracles of Pentecost and of the healed a cripple, but now he states it starkly through the words of Isaiah: "Go to this people and say, 'hear with hearing and do not understand, and seeing, see and do not see" (28:26–27; cf. Isa 6:9).[101] For one last time Luke identifies the acceptance of Paul himself with the acceptance of his announcement. The quotation of Isaiah begins with an imperative, πορεύθητι (28:26), but it is unclear who the command is given to. Yet Luke appears to suggest that it is Paul who has been commanded to "go" because that is what he has done. He is the sent prophet, the bearer of the prophetic message.[102]

Paul's concluding words recall one last time the shipwreck and Malta scenes, thereby, again, leveling a critique at the Judeans. The Isaiah quotation ends on the promise of healing (καὶ ἰάσομαι αὐτούς) which recalls

---

101. πορεύθητι πρὸς τὸν λαὸν τοῦτον καὶ εἰπόν· ἀκοῇ ἀκούσετε καὶ οὐ μὴ συνῆτε καὶ βλέποντες βλέψετε καὶ οὐ μὴ ἴδητε·

102. We should recall that Luke has already identified an unnamed figure in Isaiah with Paul (13:47).

Paul's healing of the Gentiles on Malta. Gentiles have seen and heard and been healed, but will Judeans?[103] Paul then concludes, "let this be known to you that this salvation of God has been sent to the Gentiles" (γνωστὸν οὖν ἔστω ὑμῖν ὅτι τοῖς ἔθνεσιν ἀπεστάλη τοῦτο τὸ σωτήριον τοῦ θεουν, 28:28). The aorist passive ἀπεστάλη, "has been sent," along with the mention of "salvation" (τὸ σωτήριον) again suggests that the shipwreck in Malta is what is in view. Paul has received the Judeans into his home, but they do not reciprocate by receiving the message of salvation. He had to do nothing to be received by barbarians.

Conclusion

The Gentiles have been included. The logic of their inclusion follows the same philosophy of ministry that was found in Luke's Gospel. When Jesus sent out the Seventy he told them to go into whatever homes and cities would receive them. In those places, they were to announce, "the kingdom of God has drawn near" (Luke 10:9, 11). Those who received the Seventy with hospitality, Jesus said, received him and the one who sent him (Luke 10:16). To hospitably accept the divine messengers, in other words, was also to receive the Divinity himself. Similarly in Acts, Cornelius, the converts in Philippi, and the Maltans all symbolize their acceptance of the Christian announcement by hospitably receiving those sent by God.

The message announced by Jesus' envoys in Luke 10 is that "the kingdom of God has drawn near," (Luke 10:9, 11). The message announced by Jesus' messengers in Acts is not identical, but it is similar. Peter performs resurrection-like miracles, which point to eschatological fulfillment. After he raises Cornelius, he tells him of the coming judgment of the living and the dead (10:42), and the Spirit is poured out in a mini-Pentecost. As Peter made clear on the day of Pentecost, the Spirit poured out means it is the last days (2:17). In Philippi, salvation is also proclaimed. Luke needs to say nothing more than "way of salvation" (ὁδὸν σωτηρίας, 16:17) to recall the eschatological announcement that has been proclaimed since the beginning of Acts—and, indeed, since John the Baptist. Finally, eschatological hope is Luke's concluding note. The light that is about to shine on the world is symbolized in the light of day that brings salvation to a sinking ship.

As we have seen in Luke's Gospel and at the beginning of Acts, the formation of a people appears to be at least part of the reason why Luke brings

103. Jipp, *Hospitality*, says "Paul's final encounter with Jewish leaders in 28:17–31 stands in sharp contrast to the Sea Voyage (27:1–44) and the Malta episode (28:1–10)," 271.

eschatology and ethics together. Again, salvation is a social event. This is put into stark relief at the very least by the repeated references to the hope of Israel at the end of Acts. But we have also seen it in the emphasis on hospitality. To receive the message is to receive the messenger. And to receive is to share one's possessions. Shared food symbolizes the messenger's and the receiver's joint identity and therefore joint eschatological destiny.

While the ending of Acts has and may continue to be a point of discussion among scholars,[104] the one thing that cannot be denied is that it is a fitting end when one considers the emphasis on eschatology and ethics throughout Luke's double work. John the Baptist's eschatological announcement and ethical exhortation are mirrored in Paul's concluding—and on-going—actions. Luke says that Paul remained in his own quarters for two whole years where he received (ἀπεδέχετο) all those who came to him (28:30). And to those he received, he proclaimed the kingdom of God (τὴν βασιλείαν τοῦ θεου, 28:31). If Paul's imprisonment would appear to be a hindrance to doing what Christians ought, Luke makes clear that it is not. It is in fact quite the opposite: "unhindered" (ἀκωλύτως), he says, Paul shares his possessions in the last days (28:30–31).

104. For a recent study and a summary of previous analyses, see Troftgruben, *A Conclusion Unhindered.*

6

Conclusion

Introduction

This study began with two aims. The first and primary aim was to demonstrate a relationship between eschatology and ethics in Luke's two volumes. The second was to ask why Luke thinks an ethic of shared possessions is necessary in the last days. Both objectives have been met.

Summary of Findings

Eschatology and Ethics

The second chapter of this study began the exegetical task by considering the opening proclamations of both John the Baptist and Jesus. John the Baptist's opening proclamation is markedly eschatological: he warns the crowds that the ax is already laid at the root of the tree. His eschatological proclamation is then followed by ethical exhortations concerned particularly with possessions. Those who have food and clothing ought to give to those who have none. Luke's infancy narrative sets the stage for John the Baptist's eschatological and ethical preaching. John the Baptist is characterized as the eschatological Elijah foretold by Malachi whose task it is to prepare a people for the Lord's coming. John the Baptist's preaching moreover then sets the stage for Jesus' opening proclamation. Jesus announces good news for the poor and the acceptable year of the Lord. Jesus' opening proclamation, like John the Baptist's, is both eschatological and ethical.

Having established that Jesus' ministry begins with an emphasis on eschatology and ethics, the third chapter of this study set out to explore whether these two related themes continue to appear in Jesus' ministry. Not only do these two themes continue to appear in Jesus' public ministry, we also found when they do so, Luke also reuses language from John the Baptist's opening proclamation. Jesus sends the Seventy into a harvest where they are supposed to announce "the kingdom of God has drawn near" (Luke 10:9, 11). The Seventy are moreover characterized as John the Baptist: they go out "before his face" to prepare for him (Luke 10:1; cf. 9:53, 7:27). Those who accept Jesus and his eschatological announcement are those who hospitably accept his messengers.

In Luke 16, Jesus again announces that the kingdom of God is proclaimed. In this context, he invokes John the Baptist by name as a sign of the kingdom's announcement: "the Law and the Prophets were until John, since then the kingdom of God is proclaimed" (Luke 16:16). Jesus' announcement moreover comes in the context of two parables (the Unjust Steward, and the Rich Man and Lazarus) about the importance of using possessions to secure an eternal dwelling.

Jesus' entry into Jerusalem also links ethics with eschatology. Immediately before entering Jerusalem, Jesus tells a parable of a king going into a far-off land to receive his kingdom. According to that parable, those who do not accept the king's rule will be slaughtered before him. On his approach to Jerusalem, Jesus is entertained by a tax collector who is declared a child of Abraham, both for giving back to those he cheated and for giving half of his possessions to the poor. Zacchaeus's actions and title as a child of Abraham recall John the Baptist's preaching (cf. Luke 3:8, 10–11). By contrast, Jesus is met in the temple by people who have turned his house into a den of thieves by making it a marketplace.

The fourth chapter of this study considered the continued relationship between eschatology and ethics at the beginning of Acts. The miracle of Pentecost occasions Peter's announcement that "these are the last days" (Acts 2:17). He tells the crowd that the outpouring of the Holy Spirit is happening because of Jesus' resurrection from the dead. His listeners must now save themselves from "this crooked generation" (Acts 2:40). Language of "crooked generation" in the context of eschatological proclamation again recalls John the Baptist's preaching. The crowds moreover ask Peter "what shall we do?" (Acts 2:37), just as the crowds asked John the Baptist (cf. Luke 3:10). Luke then describes the common life of the Jerusalem community. At the center of the summary statement, Luke says they had "all things common" (2:44). Ethics again follows eschatological proclamation.

In Acts 3–4, a second miracle occasions a second sermon from Peter. A cripple is healed and Peter announces that Jesus is the one who healed him. Peter then explains that Jesus has been raised from the dead and that his hearers must repent so that "times of refreshing" might come (Acts 3:20). After being arrested and tried, Peter and John are released. Luke then describes for a second time the life of the Jerusalem community: they had all things common and there were no poor among them. The centrality of possessions to the Jerusalem community and its eschatological proclamation is put into stark relief by the example of Ananias and Sapphira.

Finally, the fifth chapter of this study considered the continued relationship between eschatology and ethics in the Gentile mission. Luke appears to characterize the three scenes that comprise the Cornelius episode as resurrection-like miracles. Aeneas, Tabitha, and Cornelius are all commanded by Peter to "rise." Characterizing Cornelius's conversion in this way suggests that Luke overlays the triplet of episodes with eschatological imagery. Cornelius is known for his charity, which recalls the believing community's actions earlier in the narrative. He is moreover hospitable to Peter and Peter's circumcised compatriots. Having received the Christian announcement, he receives those who announced it to him.

Paul's experience in Philippi is similar to Peter's in Caesarea. Paul and his traveling companions are hospitably received by Lydia after they share the Christian announcement with her. After Paul exorcises the evil spirit of a slave girl who says that Paul and Silas announce "the way of salvation" (Acts 16:17), Paul and Silas are arrested. "Way of salvation" is again language that recalls John the Baptist's preaching. A midnight earthquake gives Paul and Silas the opportunity to share the Christian announcement with their jailer. He, like Lydia, immediately receives them into his home. The authorities of the city, by contrast, do not show the same hospitality to Paul and Silas. Despite finding out that Paul is a Roman citizen, they ask him to leave the city.

In Paul's culminating encounter with the Gentiles, Luke again blends eschatology with ethics. Paul announces the hope of Israel three times after his Jerusalem arrest, but the hope of salvation appears lost in the darkness of a sea storm. Luke reuses language and imagery at the climax of the storm that Paul had just used in his post-arrest defenses to speak of coming eschatological events. The sea voyage thus suggestively points to eschatological events. Salvation comes with light, and the Barbarians of Malta meet Paul and his traveling companions with unusual hospitality. Paul's reception suggests that eschatological hope has found a home among the Gentiles. After arriving in Rome, Paul continues to do what, according to Luke, Christian ought to do: he hospitably receives people into his abode as he continues to proclaim the kingdom of God.

Why Eschatology and Ethics?

This study has resisted an attempt to identify a singular, reductive reason why Luke thinks it is necessary to share possessions in the last days. Again, Luke wrote a narrative, and narratives as a genre generally resist tidy summarization. We have, however, identified what appears to be at least part of the connective tissue between eschatology and ethics.

At every point in Luke's narrative where he speaks of sharing possessions in the last days, the identification and formation of the people of God are in view. John the Baptist was "to prepare a people for the Lord" (Luke 1:17, 76–77). When he begins preaching, he tells his crowds that in order to be the children of Abraham—i.e., the people of the Lord—they must share their possessions. Jesus instructs his hearers to make friends with their money, which suggests that in order to attain entry into an "eternal dwelling" (Luke 16:9), one must be associated with the people of God through one's use of possessions. When those who have received the Holy Spirit on the day of Pentecost form a community, they do so around common possessions. And when the Gentiles receive the Spirit just as the Judeans did, part of the logic of their inclusion in the people of God is the hospitality they demonstrate.

Consequences

The first and most important consequence of this study is that the scholars we surveyed in the first chapter of this study who acknowledged—however parenthetically in some instances—that there appears to be a relationship between eschatology and ethics in Luke–Acts were correct.[1] Scholars will continue to ask questions about and study the scope and consistency both of Luke's eschatology and his ethics. But no matter what question scholars pose to Luke on these two matters in the future, this study has demonstrated the need to acknowledge that there is a relationship between eschatology and ethics in Luke's two volumes. This is moreover not an incidental observation, but appears fundamental, given the centrality of both themes in Luke's work.

As we saw in the survey of scholarship in the first chapter of this study, many scholars of Lukan eschatology who acknowledged that Luke's ethics were related to his eschatology suggest that it was eschatological delay that informed both his ethics and his work as a whole.[2] While this study has

---

1. See p. 5 above.
2. See p. 6 above.

by no means disproved the claim that Luke was writing in response to or propagating a theology of eschatological delay, it has at the very least demonstrated that this claim is problematic. John the Baptist announces that the wrath is "about-to-be" (Luke 3:7). Peter says on the day of Pentecost that "these are the last days" (Acts 2:17). And Paul informs Festus and Agrippa that "a light is about to shine" on Israel and the nations (Acts 26:23). Further study might show that Luke's eschatological expectations are not so different from other NT authors who expected an imminent eschaton.

This study also has consequences for future studies on the particular question of Lukan ethics. The majority of Lukan scholars who have studied Luke's ethics of possessions have framed their studies on the question of consistency: what does Luke actually require of Christians, given that in some instances people give away everything and in others give away only part?[3] Apart from the way in which this study challenges any attempt to find a singular, systematic claim that lies behind the diversity of Luke's narrative, this study also challenges the focus many other studies of Luke's ethics have put on the individual. To be clear, there is often a focus on the individual in Luke's two volumes. Jesus instructs individuals to make friends for themselves with their money (Luke 16:9). But this study has put into focus that Luke is just as concerned with the role possessions play in the identification and formation of the people of God. Future studies need to put equal weight on the function shared possessions have both for the individual and for the corporate people of God in Luke's works.

Further Studies

Apart from the ways in which this study might fuel further studies in Lukan eschatology and ethics, the foregoing exegesis might also encourage further study in several other areas.

First, it might prove fruitful to explore the ways in which Luke knits his narrative together both at the level of individual pericopae with their surrounding contexts and to his narrative as a whole. This study has attempted to place each pericope within Luke's literary structure(s). Luke contrasts Jesus' reception in Jericho and his reception in Jerusalem by correlating the various scenes in each city via the reuse of themes and lexemes. Luke knits the series of scenes from Paul's arrest in Jerusalem to his arrival in Rome with the tropes of hope and light. Future studies in Luke–Acts would do well to resist the assumption that Luke has haphazardly pasted one story after another from his sources without much thought for why one

---

3. See p. 11 above.

story should come after another. The advent of literary studies in the field has already encouraged much work in this direction, but there is still more to be done. Scholars might in addition investigate the ways Luke unites his work as a whole. The tropes of light, sight, and hearing appeared in just about every passage considered in this study. Luke even bookends his two works on these tropes: Simeon sees the light of salvation in the infant Jesus; Paul tells the Judeans in Rome that they neither have the eyes to see nor the ears to hear what God is doing. More study of these rhetorical techniques would surely be fruitful.

Second, this study has suggested in two instances that Luke was a very capable user of the OT Scriptures. In both the quotation of Isa 61:1–2 in Luke 4:18–19 and the quotation of Joel 3:1–5 in Acts 2:17–21 we observed that Luke manipulates his quotations of scripture for his own purposes. Part of his manipulations include inserting phrases into the quoted scripture from another passage. Isa 58:6 is included in his quotation of Isa 61:1–2, and Isa 2:2 is included in Joel 3:1–5. It appears very likely that the reason Luke thought these were fitting insertions was because they appeared in thematically parallel contexts. These two instances by no means indicate that Luke knew the contexts of every scripture he quoted. But it at the very least suggests that further study would be worthwhile to investigate the forms of Luke's scriptural quotations. Such an investigation might not only shed light on Luke's purposes, but might also indicate what text forms of the OT Luke was using as his sources.

Finally, as we have already suggested, it might be worthwhile to revisit the relationship between Luke–Acts and other NT writings on the question of eschatology and ethics. Paul says that because it is the last days the unmarried should remain as they are (1 Corinthians 7). Luke says that because it is the last days one ought to share one's possessions. The ethical issues at stake are very different. But what appears to be clear—at least in these two instances—is that both Paul and Luke think that eschatological expectation ought to determine present action.

Bibliography

Abbott, H. Porter. *The Cambridge Introduction to Narrative*. Cambridge: Cambridge University Press, 2002.

Ådna, Jostein, and Hans Kvalbein, eds. *The Mission of the Early Church to Jews and Gentiles*. WUNT 127. Tübingen: Mohr/Siebeck, 2000.

Alexander, Loveday. *Acts in Its Ancient Literary Context: A Classicist Looks at the Acts of the Apostles*. LSNT 289. London: T. & T. Clark, 2006.

———. *The Preface to Luke's Gospel: Literary Convention and Social Context in Luke 1.1–4 and Acts 1.1*. SNTSMS 78. Cambridge: Cambridge University Press, 1993.

Allen, Garrick V., and John Anthony Dunne. *Ancient Readers and Their Scriptures: Engaging the Hebrew Bible in Early Judaism and Christianity*. Leiden: Brill, forthcoming.

Alter, Robert. *The Art of Biblical Narrative*. New York: Basic Books, 1981.

Anderson, Kevin L. *"But God Raised Him from the Dead": The Theology of Jesus' Resurrection in Luke–Acts*. Eugene, OR: Wipf & Stock, 2007.

Auerbach, Erich. *Mimesis: The Representation of Reality in Western Literature*. Translated by Willard R. Trask. Princeton: Princeton University Press, 1968.

Baker, Coleman A. *Identity, Memory, and Narrative in Early Christianity: Peter, Paul, and Recategorization in the Book of Acts*. Eugene, OR: Pickwick Publications, 2011.

Bal, Mieke. *Narratology: Introduction to the Theory of Narrative*. 2nd ed. Toronto: University of Toronto Press, 1997.

Bammel, Ernest. "The Baptist in Early Christian Tradition." *NTS* 18 (1971) 95–128.

Bar-Efrat, Shimeon. *Narrative Art in the Bible*. Translated by Dorothea Shefer-Vanson. Bible and Literature Series 17. Sheffield: Almond, 1989.

Barrett, C. K. *A Critical and Exegetical Commentary on the Acts of the Apostles*. 2 vols. International Critical Commentary. Edinburgh: T. & T. Clark, 1994–1998.

Bartholomew, Craig G., Joel B. Green, and Anthony C. Thiselton, eds. *Reading Luke : Interpretation, Reflection, Formation*. Grand Rapids: Zondervan, 2005.

Bauckham, Richard. "The Restoration of Israel in Luke–Acts." In *Restoration: Old Testament, Jewish, and Christian Perspectives*, edited by James M. Scott, 435–88. Journal for the Study of Judaism Supplements 72. Leiden: Brill, 2001.

———. "The Rich Man and Lazarus: The Parable and the Parallels." *NTS* 37 (1991) 225–46.

————. *The Book of Acts in Its Palestinian Setting*. Grand Rapids: Eerdmans, 1995.

Blenkinsopp, Joseph. *Isaiah 40–55*. Anchor Bible 19A. New York: Doubleday, 2002.

Bock, Darrell L. *Acts*. Baker Exegetical Commentary on the New Testament 5. Grand Rapids: Baker Academic, 2007.

————. *God's Promise Program, Realized for All Nations: A Theology of Luke and Acts*. Grand Rapids: Zondervan, 2012.

————. *Luke*. 2 vols. Baker Exegetical Commentary on the New Testament 3. Grand Rapids: Baker, 1994.

Böhlemann, Peter. *Jesus und der Täufer: Schlussel zur Theologie und Ethik des Lukas*. SNTSMS 99. Cambridge: Cambridge University Press, 1997.

Bovon, François. *Luke 1: A Commentary on the Gospel of Luke 1:1—9:50*. Translated by Christine M. Thomas. Hermeneia. Minneapolis: Fortress Press, 2002.

————. *Luke 2: A Commentary on the Gospel of Luke 9:51—19:27*. Translated by Donald S. Deer. Hermeneia. Minneapolis: Fortress Press, 2013.

————. *Luke the Theologian: Fifty-Five Years of Research (1950–2005)*. 2nd rev. ed. Waco: Baylor University Press, 2006.

Brawley, Robert L. *Centering on God: Method and Message in Luke–Acts*. Literary Currents in Biblical Interpretation. Louisville: Westminster John Knox, 1990.

————. *Luke–Acts and the Jews: Conflict, Apology, and Conciliation*. Society of Biblical Literature Monograph Series 33. Atlanta: Scholars, 1987.

————. *Text to Text Pours Forth Speech: Voices of Scripture in Luke–Acts*. Indiana Studies in Biblical Literature. Bloomington: Indiana University Press, 1995.

Brooke, George J. "Luke–Acts and the Qumran Scrolls: The Case of MMT." In *Luke's Literary Achievement: Collected Essays*, edited by C. M. Tuckett, 72–90. JSNTSup 116. Sheffield: Sheffield Academic, 1995.

Brown, Raymond E. *The Birth of the Messiah: A Commentary on the Infancy Narratives in Matthew and Luke*. 2nd ed. Anchor Bible Reference Library. Garden City, NY: Doubleday, 1993.

Burridge, Richard A. *Imitating Jesus: An Inclusive Approach to New Testament Ethics*. Grand Rapids: Eerdmans, 2007.

Byrne, Brendan J. *The Hospitality of God: A Reading of Luke's Gospel*. Collegeville, MN: Liturgical, 2000.

Cadbury, Henry J. Review of *The Theology of St. Luke* by Hans Conzelmann. *JBL* 80 (1961) 304–5.

————. *The Making of Luke–Acts*. London: Macmillan, 1927.

Campbell, William Sanger. *The "We" Passages in the Acts of the Apostles: The Narrator as Narrative Character*. Studies in Biblical Literature 14. Atlanta: Society of Biblical Literature, 2007.

Carroll, John T. *Response to the End of History: Eschatology and Situation in Luke–Acts*. SBLDS 92. Atlanta: Scholars, 1988.

Chester, Andrew. *Messiah and Exaltation: Jewish Messianic and Visionary Traditions and New Testament Christology*. WUNT 207. Tübingen: Mohr/Siebeck, 2007.

Collins, Adela Yarbro, and John J. Collins. *King and Messiah as Son of God: Divine, Human, and Angelic Messianic Figures in Biblical and Related Literature*. Grand Rapids: Eerdmans, 2008.

Conzelmann, Hans. *Acts of the Apostles: A Commentary on the Acts of the Apostles*. Translated by James Limburg et al. Philadelphia: Fortress, 1987.

————. *The Theology of St. Luke*. Translated by Geoffrey Buswell. London: Faber & Faber, 1960.

Cooper, Lane. *The Poetics of Aristotle: Its Meaning and Influence*. Ithaca, NY: Cornell University Press, 1923.

Darr, John A. *On Character Building: The Reader and the Rhetoric of Characterization in Luke–Acts*. Literary Currents in Biblical Interpretation. Louisville: Westminster John Knox, 1992.

de Boer, Martinus C. "God-Fearers in Luke–Acts." In *Luke's Literary Achievement: Collected Essays*, edited by C. M. Tuckett, 50–71. JSNTSup 116. Sheffield: Sheffield Academic, 1995.

De Long, Kindalee Pfremmer. *Surprised by God: Praise Responses in the Narrative of Luke–Acts*. BZNW 166. Berlin: de Gruyter, 2009.

Degenhardt, Hans Joachim. *Lukas, Evangelist der Armen: Besitz und Besitzverzicht in den lukanischen Schriften. Eine traditions- und redaktionsgeschichtliche Untersuching*. Stuttgart: Katholisches Bibelwerk, 1965.

Denova, Rebecca I. *The Things Accomplished among Us: Prophetic Tradition in the Structural Pattern of Luke–Acts*. JSNTSup 141. Sheffield: Sheffield Academic, 1997.

DeSilva, David A. *Honor, Patronage, Kinship and Purity: Unlocking New Testament Culture*. Downers Grove, IL: InterVarsity, 2000.

Dinkler, Michal Beth. *Silent Statements: Narrative Representations of Speech and Silence in the Gospel of Luke*. BZNW 191. Berlin: de Gruyter, 2013.

Dupont, Jacques. *Les Beatitudes*. Etudes bibliques. Paris: Gabalda, 1969.

————. *Salvation of the Gentiles: Essays on the Acts of the Apostles*. Mahwah, NJ: Paulist, 1979.

Eckey, Wilfried. *Die Apostelgeschichte: der Weg des Evangeliums von Jerusalem nach Rom*. Neukirchen-Vluyn: Neukirchener, 2000.

Eco, Umberto. *The Role of the Reader: Explorations in the Semiotics of Texts*. Advances in Semiotics. Bloomington: Indiana University Press, 1979.

Eilers, Claude. *Roman Patrons of Greek Cities*. Oxford Classical Monographs. Oxford: Oxford University Press, 2002.

Ellis, E. Earle. *Eschatology in Luke*. Philadelphia: Fortress, 1972.

Evans, Craig A. and James A. Sanders. *Luke and Scripture: The Function of Sacred Tradition in Luke–Acts*. 1993. Reprint, Eugene, OR: Wipf & Stock, 2001.

Ferda, Tucker S. "John the Baptist, Isaiah 40, and the Ingathering of the Exiles." *Journal for the Study of the Historical Jesus* 10 (2012) 154–88.

Fitzmyer, Joseph A. *The Acts of the Apostles*. AB 31. New York: Doubleday, 1998.

————. *The Gospel according to Luke: Introduction, Translation, and Notes*. 2 vols. AB 28, 28A. Garden City, NY: Doubleday, 1981–1985.

Flessen, Bonnie J. *An Exemplary Man: Cornelius and Characterization in Acts 10*. Eugene, OR: Pickwick Publications, 2011.

Freedman, David Noel, ed. *The Anchor Bible Dictionary*. 6 Vols. New York: Doubleday, 1992.

Fuller, Michael E. *The Restoration of Israel: Israel's Re-Gathering and the Fate of the Nations in Early Jewish Literature and Luke–Acts*. BZNW 138. Berlin: Walter de Gruyter, 2006.

Gaventa, Beverly Roberts. *The Acts of the Apostles*. Abingdon New Testament Commentaries. Nashville: Abingdon, 2003.

Genette, Gérard. *Narrative Discourse Revisited*. Translated by Jane E. Lewin. Ithaca, NY: Cornell University Press, 1988.

Goodacre, Mark S. *Goulder and the Gospels: An Examination of a New Paradigm.* JSNTSup 133. Sheffield: Sheffield Academic, 1996.

Goodrich, John K. "Voluntary Debt Remission and the Parable of the Unjust Steward." *JBL* 131 (2012) 547–66.

Goulder, Michael D. *Luke: A New Paradigm.* 2 vols. JSNTSup 20. Sheffield: JSOT Press, 1989.

Green, Joel B. *The Gospel of Luke.* New International Commentary on the New Testament. Grand Rapids: Eerdmans, 1997.

Gregory, Andrew F. and C. Kavin Rowe. *Rethinking the Unity and Reception of Luke and Acts.* Columbia: University of South Carolina Press, 2010.

Gregory, Andrew F. *The Reception of Luke and Acts in the Period before Irenaeus: Looking for Luke in the Second Century.* WUNT 2/169. Tübingen: Mohr Siebeck, 2003.

Gregory, Bradley C. "The Postexilic Exile in Third Isaiah: Isaiah 61:1–3 in Light of Second Temple Hermeneutics." *JBL* 126 (2007) 475–96.

Haacker, Klaus B. "Der Geist Und Das Reich Im Lukanischen Werk: Konkurrenz Oder Konvergenz Zwischen Pneumatologie Und Eschatologie?" *NTS* 59 (2013) 325–45.

Haenchen, Ernst. *The Acts of the Apostles: A Commentary.* Translated by Bernard Noble and Gerald Shinn. Oxford: Blackwell, 1971.

Halliwell, Stephen. *The Poetics of Aristotle: Translation and Commentary.* London: Duckworth, 1987.

Harrill, J. Albert. "Divine Judgement Against Ananias and Sapphira (Acts 5:1–11): A Stock Scene of Perjury and Death." *JBL* 130 (2011) 351–69.

Hauerwas, Stanley. *Vision and Virtue: Essays in Christian Ethical Reflection.* Notre Dame, IN: University of Notre Dame Press, 1974.

Haya-Prats, Gonzalo. *Empowered Believers: The Holy Spirit in the Book of Acts*, edited by Paul Elbert. Translated by Scott A. Ellington. Eugene, OR: Cascade Books, 2011.

Hays, Christopher M. *Luke's Wealth Ethics: A Study in Their Coherence and Character.* WUNT 2/275. Tübingen: Mohr/Siebeck, 2010.

Hays, Richard B. *The Moral Vision of the New Testament: Community, Cross, New Creation: A Contemporary Introduction to New Testament Ethics.* San Francisco: HarperSanFrancisco, 1996.

Herman, David. "Introduction." In *The Cambridge Companion to Narrative*, edited by David Herman, 3–21. Cambridge Companions to Literature. Cambridge: Cambridge University Press, 2007.

Hiers, Richard H. "The Problem of the Delay of the Parousia in Luke–Acts." *NTS* 20 (1974) 145–55.

Horsley, Richard A. *The Liberation of Christmas: The Infancy Narratives in Social Context.* New York: Crossroad, 1989.

Horton, Dennis J. *Death and Resurrection: The Shape and Function of a Literary Motif in the Book of Acts.* Eugene, OR: Pickwick Publications, 2009.

Ireland, Dennis J. *Stewardship and the Kingdom of God: An Historical, Exegetical, and Contextual Study of the Parable of the Unjust Steward in Luke 16:1–13.* NovTSup 70. Leiden: Brill, 1992.

Jervell, Jacob. *Luke and the People of God: A New Look at Luke–Acts.* Minneapolis: Augsburg, 1972.

———. *The Theology of the Acts of the Apostles*. New Testament Theology. Cambridge: Cambridge University Press, 1996.

Jipp, Joshua W. *Divine Visitations and Hospitality to Strangers in Luke–Acts: An Interpretation of the Malta Episode in Acts 28:1–10*. NovTSup 153. Leiden: Brill, 2013.

Johnson, Luke Timothy. "The Lukan Kingship Parable (Lk. 19:11–27)." *NovT* 24 (1982) 139–59.

———. *The Acts of the Apostles*. Sacra Pagina. Collegeville, MN: Liturgical, 1992.

———. *The Gospel of Luke*. Sacra Pagina. Collegeville, MN: Liturgical, 1991.

———. *The Literary Function of Possessions in Luke–Acts*. SBLDS 39. Missoula, MT: Scholars, 1977.

Jong, Irene J. F. de, René Nünlist, and Angus M. Bowie, eds. *Narrators, Narratees, and Narratives in Ancient Greek Literature Studies in Ancient Greek Narrative*. Mnemosyne 257. Leiden: Brill, 2004.

Kaestli, Jean-Daniel. *L'Eschatologie dans l'oeuvre de Luc : Ses Caracteristiques et Sa Place dans le Developpement du Christianisme Primitif*. Nouvelle série théologique 22. Geneve: Labor et fides, 1969.

Karris, Robert J. "Poor and Rich: The Lukan Sitz Im Leben." In *Perspectives on Luke–Acts*, edited by Charles H. Talbert. Perspectives in Religious Studies: Special Studies Series 5. Edinburgh: T. & T. Clark, 1978.

Käsemann, Ernst. *Essays on New Testament Themes*. Trans. by W. J. Montague. London: SCM, 1964.

Keck, Leander E., and James L. Martyn. *Studies in Luke–Acts: Essays Presented in Honor of Paul Schubert*. Nashville: Abingdon, 1966.

Keener, Craig S. *Acts: An Exegetical Commentary*. Vol. 1. Grand Rapids: Baker Academic, 2012.

Kim, Kyoung-Jin. *Stewardship and Almsgiving in Luke's Theology*. JSNTSup 155. Sheffield: Sheffield Academic, 1998.

Kimball, Charles A. *Jesus' Exposition of the Old Testament in Luke's Gospel*. JSNTSup 94. Sheffield: JSOT Press, 1994.

Koet, B. J. *Five Studies on Interpretation of Scripture in Luke–Acts*. Studiorum Novi Testamenti auxilia 14. Leuven: Leuven University Press, 1989.

Landry, David, and Ben May. "Honor Restored: New Light on the Parable of the Prudent Steward (Luke 16:1–8a)." *JBL* 119 (2000) 287–94.

Laurentin, Rene. *Structure et Theologie de Luc I–II*. Etudes bibliques. Paris: Gabalda, 1964.

Lehtipuu, Outi. *The Afterlife Imagery in Luke's Story of the Rich Man and Lazarus*. NovTSup 123. Leiden: Brill, 2007.

Longenecker, Bruce W. *Hearing the Silence: Jesus on the Edge and God in the Gap: Luke 4 in Narrative Perspective*. Eugene, OR: Cascade Books, 2012.

Lust, J. *A Greek-English Lexicon of the Septuagint*. Stuttgart: Deutsche Bibelgesellschaft, 1992.

Lyons, Michael. "Paul and the Servant(s): Isaiah 49,6 in Acts 13,47." *Ephemerides Theologicae Lovanienses* 89 (2013) 345–59.

Maddox, Robert. *The Purpose of Luke–Acts*. Forschungen zur Religion und Literatur des Alten und Neuen Testaments 126. Gottingen: Vandenhoeck & Ruprecht, 1982.

Mallen, Peter. *The Reading and Transformation of Isaiah in Luke–Acts*. Library of New Testament Studies 367. London: T. & T. Clark, 2008.

‥rat, Daniel. *The First Christian Historian: Writing the "Acts of the Apostles."* SNTSMS 121. Cambridge: Cambridge University Press, 2002.

Marshall, I. Howard. *Luke: Historian and Theologian.* 3rd ed. Exeter: Paternoster, 1988.

———. *The Gospel of Luke: A Commentary on the Greek Text.* Exeter: Paternoster, 1978.

Marshall, Jonathan. *Jesus, Patrons, and Benefactors: Roman Palestine and the Gospel of Luke.* WUNT 2/259. Tübingen: Mohr/Siebeck, 2009.

Mason, Steve. "Speech-Making in Ancient Rhetoric, Josephus, and Acts: Messages and Playfulness, Part II." *Early Christianity* 3 (2012) 445–67.

Mason, Steve. "Why Did Judaeans Go to War with Rome in 66–67 CE? Realist-Regional Perspectives." In *Jews and Christians in the First and Second Centuries: How to Write Their History,* edited by Peter J. Tomson and Joshua Schwartz, 126–206. Compendia rerum Iudaicarum ad Novum Testamentum 13. Leiden: Brill, 2014.

Matera, Frank J. *New Testament Ethics: The Legacies of Jesus and Paul.* Louisville: Westminster John Knox, 1996.

McCabe, David R. *How to Kill Things with Words: Ananias and Sapphira under the Prophetic Speech-Act of Divine Judgment.* Bloomsbury T. & T. Clark, 2013.

McComiskey, Douglas S. *Lukan Theology in the Light of the Gospel's Literary Structure.* Eugene, OR: Wipf & Stock, 2007.

McWhirter, Jocelyn. *Rejected Prophets: Jesus and His Witnesses in Luke–Acts.* Minneapolis: Fortress, 2014.

Mealand, David L. "Community of Goods and Utopian Allusions in Acts II–IV." *Journal of Theological Studies* 28 (1977) 96–99.

———. *Poverty and Expectation in the Gospels.* London: SPCK, 1980.

Merenlahti, Petri. *Poetics for the Gospels?: Rethinking Narrative Criticism.* London: T & T Clark, 2002.

Metzger, Bruce M. "Seventy or Seventy-Two Disciples?" *NTS* 5 (1959 1958) 299–306.

———. *A Textual Commentary on the Greek New Testament.* 2nd ed. Stuttgart: Deutsche Biblegesellschaft, 1994.

Metzger, James A. *Consumption and Wealth in Luke's Travel Narrative.* Biblical Interpretation Series 88. Leiden: Brill, 2007.

Meynet, Roland. *L'Évangile de Luc.* Rhétorique sémitique 1. Paris: Lethielleux, 2005.

———. *Rhetorical Analysis: An Introduction to Biblical Rhetoric.* JSOTSup 256. Sheffield: Sheffield Academic, 1998.

———. *Treatise on Biblical Rhetoric.* Translated by Leo Arnold. International Studies in the History of Rhetoric 3. Leiden: Brill, 2012.

Moessner, David P. *Lord of the Banquet: The Literary and Theological Significance of the Lukan Travel Narrative.* Minneapolis: Fortress, 1989.

Moore, Stephen D. *Literary Criticism and the Gospels: The Theoretical Challenge.* New Haven: Yale University Press, 1989.

Mount, Christopher N. *Pauline Christianity: Luke–Acts and The Legacy of Paul.* NovTSup 104. Leiden: Brill, 2002.

Moxnes, Halvor. *The Economy of the Kingdom: Social Conflict and Economic Relations in Luke's Gospel.* Overtures to Biblical Theology. Philadelphia: Fortress, 1988.

Neyrey, Jerome H. "God, Benefactor and Patron: The Major Cultural Model for Interpreting the Deity in Greco-Roman Antiquity." *Journal for the Study of the New Testament* 27 (2005) 465–92.

Nickelsburg, George W. E. "Riches, the Rich, and God's Judgment in 1 Enoch 92–105 and the Gospel according to Luke." *NTS* 25 (1979) 324–44.

Nielsen, Anders E. *Until It Is Fulfilled: Lukan Eschatology according to Luke 22 and Acts 20.* WUNT 2/126. Tübingen: Mohr/Siebeck, 2000.

Nielsen, Jasper Tang, and Mogens Müller. *Luke's Literary Creativity*. Library of New Testament Sudies 550. London: Bloomsbury T. & T. Clark, 2016.

Nineham, D. E. *Studies in the Gospels: Essays in the Memory of R. H. Lightfoot*. Oxford: Blackwell, 1957.

Nolland, John. *Luke 1—9:20*. Word Biblical Commentary 35A. Dallas: Word, 1989.

———. *Luke 9:21—18:34*. Word Biblical Commentary 35B. Dallas: Word, 1993.

Pao, David W. *Acts and the Isaianic New Exodus*. WUNT 2/130. Tübingen: Mohr/ Siebeck, 2000.

Parsons, Mikeal C. *Acts*. Paideia. Grand Rapids: Baker Academic, 2008.

———. *Body and Character in Luke and Acts: The Subversion of Physiognomy in Early Christianity*. Waco: Baylor University Press, 2011.

Parsons, Mikeal C., and Richard I. Pervo. *Rethinking the Unity of Luke and Acts*. Minneapolis: Fortress, 1993.

Pervo, Richard I. *Acts*. Hermeneia. Minneapolis: Fortress, 2009.

Phillips, Thomas E. "Reading Recent Readings of Issues of Wealth and Poverty in Luke and Acts." *Currents in Biblical Research* 1/2 (2003) 231–69.

———. *Acts Within Diverse Frames of Reference*. Macon, GA: Mercer University Press, 2009.

Porter, Stanley E., ed. *The Messiah in the Old and New Testaments*. Grand Rapids: Eerdmans, 2007.

———. *The Paul of Acts: Essays in Literary Criticism, Rhetoric, and Theology*. WUNT 115. Tübingen: Mohr/Siebeck, 1999.

Rahlfs, Alfred. *Psalmi cum Odis*. 2nd ed. Septuaginta: Vetus Testamentum graecum 10. Göttingen: Vandenhoeck & Ruprecht, 1967.

Reimer, Andy. *Miracle and Magic: A Study in the Acts of the Apostles and the Life of Apollonius of Tyana*. JSNTSup 235. London: Sheffield Academic, 2002.

Reimer, Ivoni Richter. *Women in the Acts of the Apostles: A Feminist Liberation Perspective*. Translated by Linda M. Maloney. Minneapolis: Fortress, 1995.

Rindge, Matthew S. *Jesus' Parable of the Rich Fool: Luke 12:13–34 among Ancient Conversations on Death and Possessions*. Society of Biblical Literature Early Christianity and Its Literature 6. Atlanta: Society of Biblical Literature, 2011.

Rindoš, Jaroslav. *He of Whom It Is Written: John the Baptist and Elijah in Luke*. Österreichische biblische Studien 38. Frankfurt: Lang, 2010.

Robbins, Vernon K. "By Land by Sea: The We-Passages and Ancient Sea-Voyages." In *Sea Voyages and Beyond: Emerging Strategies in Socio-Rhetorical Interpretation*, edited by Vernon K. Robbins. Emory Studies in Early Christianity 14. Blandford Forum, UK: Deo, 2010.

Roth, S. John. *The Blind, the Lame, and the Poor: Character Types in Luke–Acts*. JSNTSup 144. Sheffield: Sheffield Academic, 1997.

Rothschild, Clare K. *Baptist Traditions and Q*. WUNT 190. Tübingen: Mohr/Siebeck, 2005.

———. *Luke–Acts and the Rhetoric of History: An Investigation of Early Christian Historiography*. WUNT 2/175. Tübingen: Mohr/Siebeck, 2004.

Rowe, C. Kavin. *Early Narrative Christology: The Lord in the Gospel of Luke*. Grand Rapids: Baker Academic, 2009.

———. *World Upside Down: Reading Acts in the Graeco-Roman Age*. Oxford: Oxford University Press, 2009.

Ryan, Marie-Laure. "Toward a Definition of Narrative." In *The Cambridge Companion to Narrative*, edited by David Herman. Cambridge Companions to Literature. Cambridge: Cambridge University Press, 2007.

.cr, Michael A. *Restoring the Kingdom: The Role of God as the "Ordainer of Times and Seasons" in the Acts of the Apostles*. Eugene, OR: Pickwick Publications, 2011.

Sanders, Jack T. *The Jews in Luke–Acts*. London: SCM, 1987.

———. *Ethics in the New Testament: Change and Development*. London: SCM, 1975.

Schmidt, Thomas E. *Hostility to Wealth in the Synoptic Gospels*. JSNTSup 15. Sheffield: JSOT Press, 1987.

Schmithals, Walter. "Lukas-—Evangelist Der Armen." *Theologia Viatorum* 12 (1974–1973) 153–67.

Schnelle, Udo. *Theology of the New Testament*. Translated by M. Eugene Boring. Grand Rapids: Baker Academic, 2009.

Schottroff, Luise, and Wolfgang Stegemann. *Jesus and the Hope of the Poor*. Translated by Matthew J. O'Connell. 1986. Reprint, Eugene, OR: Wipf & Stock, 2009.

Schrage, Wolfgang. *The Ethics of the New Testament*. Edinburgh: T. & T. Clark, 1988.

Schultz, Brian. "Jesus as Archelaus in the Parable of the Pounds (Lk. 19:11–27)." *NovT* 49 (2007) 105–27.

Schurer, Emil. *The History of the Jewish People in the Age of Jesus Christ (175 B.C.–A.D. 135)*, edited by Géza Vermès and Fergus Millar. Rev. ed. Edinburgh: T. & T. Clark, 1973.

Seccombe, David Peter. *Possessions and the Poor in Luke–Acts*. Studien zum Neuen Testament und seiner Umwelt B/6. Linz: Studien zum Neuen Testament und seiner Umwelt, 1982.

Sleeman, Matthew. *Geography and the Ascension Narrative in Acts*. SNTSMS 146. Cambridge: Cambridge University Press, 2009.

Smith, Mitzi J. *Literary Construction of the Other in the Acts of the Apostles: Charismatics, the Jews, and Women*. Princeton Theological Monograph Series 154. Eugene, OR: Pickwick Publications, 2012.

Soards, Marion L. *The Speeches in Acts: Their Content, Context, and Concerns*. Louisville: Westminister John Knox Press, 1994.

Spencer, F. Scott. *Acts*. Readings: A New Biblical Commentary. Sheffield: Sheffield Academic, 1997.

Squires, John T. *The Plan of God in Luke–Acts*. SNTSMS 76. Cambridge: Cambridge University Press, 1993.

Sterling, Gregory E. "'Athletes of Virtue': An Analysis of the Summaries in Acts (2:41–47; 4:32–35; 5:12–16)." *JBL* 113 (1994) 679–96.

———. *Historiography and Self-Definition: Josephos, Luke–Acts, and Apologetic Historiography*. NovTSup 64. Leiden: Brill, 1992.

Sternberg, Meir. *The Poetics of Biblical Narrative: Ideological Literature and the Drama of Reading*. Indiana Literary Biblical Series. Bloomington: Indiana University Press, 1985.

Strauss, Mark L. *The Davidic Messiah in Luke–Acts: The Promise and Its Fulfillment in Lukan Christology*. JSNTSup 110. Sheffield: Sheffield Academic, 1995.

Strazicich, John. *Joel's Use of Scripture and the Scripture's Use of Joel: Appropriation and Resignification in Second Temple Judaism and Early Christianity*. Biblical Interpretation Series 82. Leiden: Brill, 2007.

Talbert, Charles H. *Reading Luke–Acts in Its Mediterranean Milieu*. NovTSup 107. Leiden: Brill Academic, 2003.

———. *Reading Luke: A Literary and Theological Commentary on the Third Gospel*. NY: Crossroad, 1982.

Tannehill, Robert C. "The Magnificat as Poem." *JBL* 93 (1974) 263–75.

———. "Israel in Luke–Acts: A Tragic Story." *JBL* 104 (1985) 69–85.

Bibliography

————. *The Narrative Unity of Luke–Acts: A Literary Interpretation*. 2 vols. Foundations and Facets. Philadelphia: Fortress, 1986.

Theissen, Gerd. "Wanderradikalismus: Literatursoziologische Aspekte Der Überlieferung von Worten Jesu Im Urchristentum." *Zeitschrift für Theologie und Kirche* 70 (1973) 245–71.

————. *Social Setting of Pauline Christianity: Essays on Corinth*. Translated and edited by John Schütz. Philadelphia: Fortress, 1982.

————. *Studien zur Soziologie des Urchristentums*. WUNT 19. Tübingen: Mohr/Siebeck, 1979.

Tiede, David Lenz. *Prophecy and History in Luke–Acts*. Philadelphia: Fortress, 1980.

Troftgruben, Troy M. *A Conclusion Unhindered: A Study of the Ending of Acts within Its Literary Environment*. WUNT 2/ 280. Tübingen: Mohr/Siebeck, 2010.

Twelftree, Graham. *In the Name of Jesus: Exorcism among Early Christians*. Grand Rapids: Baker Academic, 2007.

Tyson, Joseph B. *Luke–Acts and the Jewish People: Eight Critical Perspectives*. Minneapolis: Augsburg, 1988.

Udoh, Fabian E. "The Tale of an Unrighteous Slave (Luke 16:1–8 [13])." *JBL* 128 (2009) 311–35.

Verhey, Allen. *The Great Reversal: Ethics and the New Testament*. Grand Rapids: Eerdmans, 1984.

Wehnert, Jürgen. *Die Wir-Passagen der Apostelgeschichte: Ein lukanisches Stilmittel aus jüdischer Tradition*. Göttinger theologische Arbeiten 40. Göttingen: Vandenhoeck & Ruprecht, 1989.

Wendel, Susan J. *Scriptural Interpretation and Community Self-Definition in Luke–Acts and the Writings of Justin Martyr*. NovTSup 139. Leiden: Brill, 2011.

Wenk, Matthias. *Community-Forming Power: The Socio-Ethical Role of the Spirit in Luke–Acts*. Sheffield: Sheffield Academic, 2000.

Wheatley, Alan B. *Patronage in Early Christianity: Its Use and Transformation from Jesus to Paul of Samosata*. Princeton Theological Monograph Series 160. Eugene, OR: Pickwick Publications, 2011.

Whitmarsh, Tim, and Shadi Bartsch. "Narrative." In *The Cambridge Companion to the Greek and Roman Novel*, edited by Tim Whitmarsh. Cambridge: Cambridge University Press, 2008.

Wilder, Amos Niven. *Eschatology and Ethics in the Teaching of Jesus*. Rev. ed. 1978. Reprint, Eugene, OR: Wipf & Stock, 2014.

Wilson, Stephen G. *The Gentiles and the Gentile Mission in Luke–Acts*. SNTSMS 23. Cambridge: Cambridge University Press, 1973.

Wink, Walter. *John the Baptist in the Gospel Tradition*. 1968. Reprint, Eugene, OR: Wipf & Stock, 2000.

Wolter, Michael. *Das Lukasevangelium*. Handbuch zum Neuen Testament 5. Tübingen: Mohr/Siebeck, 2008.

York, John O. *The Last Shall Be First: The Rhetoric of Reversal in Luke*. JSNTSup 46. Sheffield: JSOT Press, 1991.

Zehnle, Richard F. *Peter's Pentecost Discourse: Tradition and Lukan Reinterpretation in Peter's Speeches of Acts 2 and 3*. Nashville: Abingdon, 1971.

Ziegler, Joseph. *Duodecim Prophetae*. 2nd ed. Septuaginta 13. Göttingen: Vandenhoeck & Ruprecht, 1967.

————. *Isaias*. 2nd ed. Septuaginta 14. Göttingen: Vandenhoeck & Ruprecht, 1967.